YALE HISTORICAL PUBLICATIONS | MISCELLANY, 103

WARRIOR GOVERNMENT IN EARLY MEDIEVAL JAPAN

A STUDY OF THE KAMAKURA BAKUFU, SHUGO, AND JITŌ

JEFFREY P. MASS

NEW HAVEN AND LONDON, YALE UNIVERSITY PRESS, 1974

Published with assistance from the foundation
established in memory of Philip Hamilton McMillan
of the Class of 1894, Yale College.

Designed by Sally Sullivan
and set in Times Roman type.
Printed in the United States of America by
The Murray Printing Co., Forge Village, Mass.

Published in Great Britain, Europe, and Africa by
Yale University Press, Ltd., London.
Distributed in Latin America by Kaiman & Polon,
Inc., New York City; in Australasia and Southeast
Asia by John Wiley & Sons Australasia Pty. Ltd.,
Sydney; in India by UBS Publishers' Distributors Pvt.,
Ltd., Delhi; in Japan by John Weatherhill, Inc., Tokyo.

TO KAZUKO

CONTENTS

PREFACE

The 1180s appearance of the Kamakura military government
(*bakufu*) marked an important stage in the maturation of the
provincial warrior aristocracy in Japan. The bakufu's emergence
meant a shift in the center of gravity away from the court and
absentee estate-holding to a warrior class now seeking to wield
authority in its own right. How this military regime came into being,
and how it exercised power through its officers in the field (*shugo*
and *jitō*), will serve as the major concerns of the present study.

Any scholarly undertaking naturally profits from the encourage-
ment and assistance of friends and teachers. In my case, Professor
John Whitney Hall of Yale, under whose direction I completed the
Ph.D., deserves first mention. Tirelessly he went through my
early drafts, always trying to keep author and subject in some
reasonable tandem. He has been a wise and sympathetic mentor,
and my debt to him is without limit. In Japan, my greatest thanks
go to Professor Seno Seiichirō of Tokyo University. Every week for
almost two years I studied old documents with him, and my concern
with sources derives largely from his influence. Professor Seno is a
true scholar and friend.

My medievalist colleagues in this country deserve recognition,
especially Paul Varley, Neil Kiley, G. C. Hurst, and Prescott Winter-
steen. I have profited greatly from their wide knowledge. Others who
must be mentioned are Edwin Lee, who introduced me to Japanese
history; Toyoda Takeshi, scholar-in-residence during the 1972 Yale
Seminar on Medieval Japan; Tom Swann, friend and confidant from
my earliest days as a graduate student; and Ron de Paolo, historian
at large who read and commented on several of my drafts. My
manuscript editor at Yale Press, Judy Metro, has done what I

thought might not be possible—helped turn a manuscript into a book. Finally, I wish to thank the Fulbright Commission in Japan for supporting my research during 1969–71 and the East Asian Prize Fellowship committee at Yale for continuing that subsidy until 1973. To members of the latter group I am especially grateful.

THE PROVINCES OF MEDIEVAL JAPAN

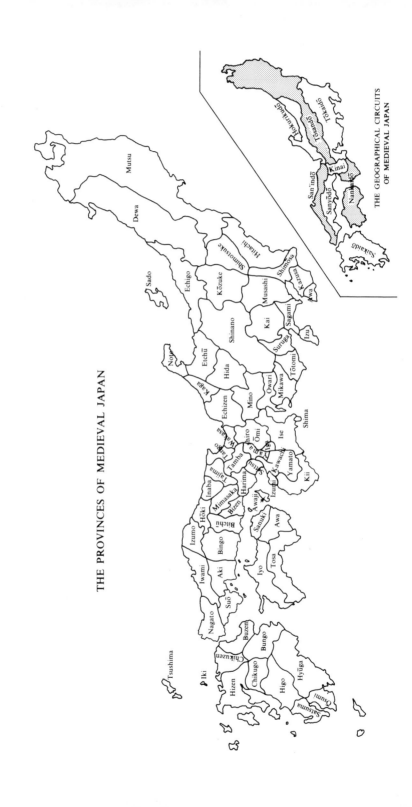

Mutsu

Dewa

Sado

Echigo

Shimotsuke

Hitachi

Kōzuke

Shimōsa

Shinano

Musashi

Kazusa

Kai

Awa

Etchū

Noto

Hida

Sagami

Suruga

Izu

Kaga

Echizen

Mino

Owari

Mikawa

Tōtōmi

Echizen

Wakasa

Shiro

Ōmi

Ise

Shima

Tango

Tajima

Tanba

Settsu

Kawachi

Izumi

Yamato

Inaba

Mimasaka

Harima

Awaji

Kii

Hōki

Bizen

Izumo

Bitchū

Sanuki

Awa

Bingo

Iwami

Aki

Iyo

Tosa

Suō

Tsushima

Nagato

Iki

Buzen

Chikuzen

Bungo

Hizen

Chikugo

Higo

Hyūga

Satsuma

Ōsumi

THE GEOGRAPHICAL CIRCUITS
OF MEDIEVAL JAPAN

Hokurikudō

Tōsandō

Tōkaidō

San'indō

Kinai

Sanyōdō

Nankaidō

Saikaidō

INTRODUCTION

In mid-twelfth-century Japan the highest authority of state and its complement, the proprietary authority over land, were jointly held by a civil aristocracy consisting of the imperial house, noble families with ancient genealogies, and Buddhist and Shintō religious institutions. This dominant political and economic power was exercised through a system of government with public and private dimensions. A statist conception of authority had originated in the seventh and eighth centuries when the top rank of society, seeking to escape the weakness of a family-based polity, adopted new institutions of land control and central and local administration, mirroring the Chinese system of imperial government.[1] The country was divided into provinces (*kuni*), districts (*gun* or *kōri*), and villages (*gō*), each with an administrative chief holding authority as an imperial official. Cultivated paddy land, now "nationalized," was parceled and assigned as sustenance shares to the general population; conversely, a uniform scale of public taxes was levied and the receipts became the new economic basis of the state. What gave the system its coherence were coordinate rank and title hierarchies embracing all officialdom and centering in the new imperial capital of Nara (710–84). The islands of Japan had now been welded for the first time into a single entity.

The succeeding Heian period (794–1185) experienced a gradual unraveling of this elaborately conceived bureaucratic scheme. Strictly speaking this marked decay, but another emphasis may be more accurate.[2] The basic hierarchy of interests, defined at the

1. Easily the best account in English is John W. Hall, *Government and Local Power in Japan, 500–1700* (Princeton, N.J., 1966), chaps. 2 and 3.
2. Recent historiographical trends regarding the Tokugawa period (1600–1868) are brought to mind. The stress is no longer on "dynastic decline" but rather on maturation and change. Both the Heian and Tokugawa polities were remarkably successful.

1

beginning of the age, continued intact for almost 400 years. Hence the capital city of Kyoto (Heian-kyō), far from seeing its power largely eroded, remained in 1150 the country's single source of all legally cognizable authority and legitimacy. As we shall see, this meant that ultimate leverage remained in central hands until the founding of the Kamakura *bakufu*.

The key to this remarkable survival lies in the changes that took place within—not in opposition to—the old system. These changes occurred on several levels. At the top, the public aspects of the earlier bureaucratic monolith were worn away by a parceling out of privatized authority among the great noble–official families of Kyoto. This led, according to a familiar story, to the Fujiwara family's eventually coming to outstrip the imperial house in both political influence and private wealth. From the late ninth century, the regent's branch of the Fujiwara was normally able to dictate the imperial succession and dominate within the high noble council. What is significant in this is that such maneuverings among the ruling elite involved no serious dislocation to the polity as a whole. A carefully defined concensus of conduct continued to restrict permissible activities according to position within the social hierarchy. It is for this reason that a competition for ultimate state authority could develop among a narrow caste of aristocrats, with little threat of intruders penetrating from the outside. On the one hand, then, capital nobles were colleagues meeting in council to decide affairs of state; on the other, they became heads of extensive patronage systems designed to further private interests.[3] In both instances, common interests and a common background precluded breakdown and diffusion of authority.

Courtier privatization of the imperial state directly affected the provinces. As the search for wealth and aristocratic life style intensified, there was a tendency for provincial governors to eschew residing in the hinterland areas to which they had been appointed. This led in time to a loosening of the command lines between capital and provinces, a reflection of the growing desire for income and

3. For clientage and the security of the high nobility in Heian Japan see the essays by G. Cameron Hurst and Cornelius J. Kiley in John W. Hall and Jeffrey P. Mass, eds., *Medieval Japan: Essays in Institutional History* (New Haven, 1974), chaps. 2 and 5.

jurisdiction rather than everyday governance. Such new elasticity permitted the rise of "absentee provincial offices" (*rusudokoro*) administered by resident officials (*zaichōkanjin*) of more or less permanent tenure. The latter were given considerable leeway in converting to private gain their duly authorized public powers. But simultaneously they continued to depend on capital aristocrats, who were their patrons, for patents of investiture and settlement of disputes. In this way both sectors of government—central and local—were able to prosper. A sharing of responsibilities and profits—not final authority—became the hallmark of Heian government.

Gradual reduction of the public domain was another expression of the general trend toward privatization. From the start, there had been exceptions to the land-allotment system permitting certain types of land to be registered as the permanent and often tax-free holdings of the central nobility. In addition, reallotments gradually fell into disuse and were replaced by tax-yielding local tenures held in perpetuity and by reclamation projects leading to much the same thing. A concept of private land in the sense of permanent occupancy was born, which helped promote one of the period's major developments. The great families and temples of Kyoto began to press for creation of personally held blocs of private estate lands. By assuming control over the major reclamation projects, and later by soliciting local commendations under promise of protection against provincial tax collectors, the central elite managed to gain possession of domains called *shōen*, for which they acquired legal authority and tax exemption. Economic historians denominate the period from mid-Heian through Kamakura as the age of shōen.

It is important to recognize the degree to which public authority over land was now being transformed. In effect, two categories of land and land administration had emerged by 1100: the shōen, which were fashioned into income-producing units under the explicit proprietorship of the court nobility, and public land (*kokugaryō*, literally "provincial domains"), which came to be administered as the private sphere of governors.[4] A final stage in this process was the assign-

4. The degree of "privateness" was much more secure for shōen, however. These latter were under the permanent proprietorship of central holders, while kokugaryō were merely lands to be exploited economically during the often brief tenure of a governorship.

ment of whole provinces as veritable proprietorships (*chigyōkoku*). Distribution was controlled by the ultimate policy-making council within the court elite, and resulting configurations represented, in a sense, the balance of power within the high nobility. Recipient individuals and institutions acquired the right to nominate (in effect, to appoint) provincial governors from among lesser central families numbered as allies and private clients. In this way public taxes came to be openly channeled into private coffers. Yet it was the shōen pattern that ultimately became dominant.[5] This was because the incorporation of private estates best fit the needs of all parties to the transaction. In return for the commendation of small public-sector units, central aristocrats would expedite removal of such areas from provincial purview and, in many cases, allow donors to assume (or maintain) control over dues collection, policing, and other aspects of local administration. The shōen was now registered as the private holding of the central commendee, and the latter could expect to draw revenues from that land. But the proprietor was an absentee figure who expanded his shōen portfolio by compromise. In time, this resulted in a condition of tiers of authority forming within estates.[6] It is this phenomenon that has come to be known as the *shiki* system—a hierarchy of titles connoting privileges and income shares deriving from a unitary piece of land.[7]

At the top of the system were the two shōen titles of *honke* (patron or protector) and *ryōke* (proprietor), both of which could be aspired to only by those of the highest court ranks. The upper proprietary class was thus a closed caste since Kyoto was its own arbiter in the matter of assigning high status. Traditional noble families of the capital city, along with Buddhist and Shintō religious institutions, constituted the shōen-owning stratum of Heian Japan.

5. Not everywhere, however. In frontier regions, and occasionally nearer the center (e.g., Wakasa and Bizen provinces), shōen volume never exceeded the acreage of public sector. See chaps. 2 and 3 in the present study and Hall, *Government and Local Power*, chap. 6.

6. Marc Bloch's apt description for early feudal Europe is brought to mind: "How many persons there are who can say, each with as much justification as the other, 'That is my field' " (*Feudal Society* [Chicago, 1964], 1:116).

7. Reference here is only to the hierarchy of interests within shōen. Public-sector territorial units and administrative offices continued to use the old imperial nomenclature but were now privatized and similarly conceived as shiki.

At the middle level was a managerial class, and it was the condition of representatives of this group that determined the extent of a central owner's actual control. Location of the estate, the background and nature of its incorporation, and the vitality of the proprietor concerned were only three of the many factors producing great diversity on this point. At bottom, however, the basic issue was actually quite simple: did agents sent out by the proprietor manage (or seek to manage) an estate, or was it administered without proprietary interference by persons local in origin? The character of the ranking managerial post of *azukari dokoro* (literally, "custodial office") expresses this duality. Although numerous examples exist in which the bearer of that title was himself a shōen's major or exclusive commender, other cases are known in which similarly prominent donors were designated merely as *gesu* ("lower officer"). When the latter condition prevailed, the way would be open for dispatch from the center of another kind of azukari dokoro—a proprietary deputy. The extent of such an intruder's actual local involvement would generally determine whether a shōen enjoyed harmony or tension between central and local interests. On a slightly lower level, other administrative titles, among them *sōtsuibushi, kumon*, and *tadokoro*, came to be assigned to resident families of reputation.

Closest to the soil was a class of families whose house holdings are generically traceable to the allotment and reclamation lands of the eighth century. After the lapse of reallotment, and after the family collective had become the functioning unit of taxation for fields held in perpetuity, the *myōshu*, as head of this collective, emerged as the basic common denominator of Heian local administration. With the passage of time, some myōshu developed into a bottom fringe of the new fighting class called *bushi*, but in most parts of the country they remained essentially farmers. The actual workers of the fields and other dependent groups were under their supervision.

An important parallel to this hierarchical system of landholding was a leadership arrangement in the provinces that favored men higher on the imperial scale rather than lower. In other words, families with strong central connections and genealogies linking them to the capital had a tremendous advantage over houses that were strictly local. The former held all the major titles in the absentee governor's office and were in the best position to gain extensive land managerships. To this political and economic dominance was then added military supremacy. As control from the center became more indirect during the tenth century, there developed a noticeable increase in lawlessness and local instability. Armed units began to form as a means of securing life and land, and men came together in relationships that would soon resemble the vassalage of Europe. This comparison cannot be pushed too far, however, since the greatest of Japan's warrior combinations were led by men whose prestige derived from a still highly functional central government. The fighting class in Japan was not building its power either in opposition to Kyoto or atop the ruins of an already defunct state. Instead, the country's leading warriors received peacekeeping deputations and provincial and estate constabulary titles as the basis for their local police powers. To retain this status, and to profit from it, they continued to support the old polity.

It is clear then that the hierarchical nature of the shiki system and Kyoto's exclusive ownership of shōen imposed ultimate limits on warrior development. Provincial figures, no matter how powerful, acquired, possessed, or lost rights in land by dint of superior documentation. This meant that when warriors engaged in warfare all gains achieved would have to be legitimized by—that is, shared with —someone in the capital. In the absence of any perception of an alternative arrangement, the provincial elite simply forfeited all chance to become a landholding class in its own right. The leading houses in the provinces moved no farther during Heian times than a privatization of local rights under a system of authority that remained essentially Kyoto-capped.[8]

While warrior bands of various sizes and degrees of cohesion appeared during the eleventh and twelfth centuries, two loosely organized associations embracing most of these ultimately became dominant. These were the Taira (Heishi or Heike) and the Minamoto (Genji), both of whose scions traced their genealogies back to the

8. This is not to deny that local warriors failed quite often to hold back taxes and make trouble generally for proprietors. But any prolongation of such activities would have led to a failure to renew documents or an outright withdrawal of central legitimation. This would have made the holder vulnerable to legal challenges from ambitious clansmen, neighbors, or others, Details in chap. 2.

imperial line. Unlike other warriors who sank roots in specific local areas, the Taira and Minamoto leaders were regional or even national figures. Their land rights and their vassals were located in many parts of the country. Moreover, both chieftains were simultaneously court nobles: they were members of competing patronage blocs, serving as provincial governors and specially deputized commanders. The full natures of these two clans will be examined in Part 1. The court's increasing reliance on Taira and Minamoto to enforce central decisions was eventually climaxed in the 1150s. A series of disputes in the capital allowed the Taira to become full-fledged members of the ruling oligarchy. During the succeeding generation the Taira leader, Kiyomori, proceeded to tighten his hold over Kyoto until by 1179 he became all-powerful. A period of extended Heishi rulership seemed about to begin. However at this point, something totally unexpected occurred. In 1180 the Gempei (Genji versus Heishi) War broke out, and it was this struggle that carried Japan into a new age. On the surface, the fighting involved a confrontation between the two great warrior leagues, one in power, and the other challenging from without. But in fact the warfare was far more complex. The Minamoto leadership had raised the possibility of entirely new goals—a warrior regime with the authority to guarantee local land rights, and a basic reordering of the relationship between capital and provinces.

From his base area in the Kantō, the Genji chieftain, Yoritomo, began this quest by asserting governance over the east and by offering patents of confirmation in return for pledges of vassalage. The region's greatest warriors quickly became his provincial lieutenants. This was followed by the establishment of a permanent headquarters in Kamakura and a program designed to outfit a new regime with institutions. What Yoritomo had not anticipated was the impact his successes would have on fighting men elsewhere. Beginning in 1181, warriors in other parts of the country started calling themselves Genji, and using this as a cover to attack absentee land rights. A regional movement was now being transformed into a national civil war.

From this point, Yoritomo began to look beyond the east. His opportunity came in 1183, when the Taira were forced to flee Kyoto and he himself was called in as new imperial protector. But the

Genji chief did not personally go to the capital: he assumed his protectorate through the instrumentality of his regime. Deploying trusted easterners in the west, Yoritomo sought to recruit vassals countrywide while trying at the same time to restore peace. This involved a somewhat contradictory policy since the men joining his band did so in hopes of gaining support for their newly intensified claims over land. These latter were the very cause of most local disruption. How to resolve this dilemma became the major concern of the day. Early in 1185 the Taira were defeated, but, as feared, local disturbances did not cease. The Genji chieftain was thus impelled to take another critical step. To increase his leverage over all fighting men he extracted from the court an open-ended peacekeeping authorization. The war was now over, but Yoritomo continued to assert national powers. His regime, soon to be known as the bakufu, had established itself as the new police arm of state. This responsibility, however, proved unexpectedly onerous, and before long an effort was underway to carve out a more workable but permanent jurisdiction. The Genji leadership ultimately settled on two tracks of authority. The two were *shugo* and *jitō*.

The most striking fact about the *shugo* (provincial constable) is that the post was a pristine invention of the bakufu, with legally defined duties thoroughly distinguishing it from enforcement officers of the later Heian period. The title was thus free from any association with traditional court-centered hierarchies. Almost everything— appointments, dismissals, responsibilities, loyalties—was controlled and determined by Kamakura, the bakufu capital. At the same time, the office as it was later defined in law was not a product of the years of wartime expansion. It was not in fact until the 1190s, a consolidation phase of bakufu development, that a figure recognizable as the "Kamakura shugo" finally emerged. This would indicate that the usual view positing an 1185 creation of shugo by Kamakura's forcing the court to authorize them may be in error. A network of bakufu-controlled provincial constables developed mainly from the need to streamline—not to aggrandize—Kamakura's authority.[9]

9. The Kamakura regime did appoint a handful of shugo-denominated figures during the war, but these bear little relationship to their later namesakes. See chap. 4.

If the shugo was an original creation born during a period of post-war stabilization, the *jitō* (estate manager) was a figure molded by the Gempei fighting and then adopted by the new regime. During a brief five-year period of conflict a relatively unimportant title underwent a massive growth in usage and reshaping of its basic character. By the end of 1185 the jitō appeared as a new combination of military figure, Kamakura vassal, and management-level shōen official.

Technically jitō were established as local representatives of the bakufu, charged with carrying out Kamakura's expressed willingness to stabilize the country and to maintain the new status quo. However, from early on many of these jitō revealed a restlessness and dis-satisfaction with the status quo, moving instead to enhance their local authorities over land. Utilizing a unique condition of their office whereby they could be dismissed or disciplined only by their private military lord in Kamakura, jitō took it upon themselves to exceed their inherited administrative and police duties. The result was that by early in the thirteenth century the class of jitō had gained recognition as a distinct warrior elite. This status was not the same as that previously held by the resident public officers (zaichōkanjin) of late Heian times. The latter, as we have noted, remained in varying degrees part of the Kyoto-controlled polity. By contrast, the jitō, with their immunity, were entirely without precedent; they were beyond direct proprietary superintendence and came to be cast as essentially "anti-Kyoto." Whereas there exist large numbers of petitions to Kamakura requesting jitō dismissals or exemptions, there are literally no central owner appeals for jitō appointments.

Naturally, what made this post unwanted on the one side was what made it attractive for local warriors on the other. Assignments were of two general types: to lands already held under a traditional shōen or public-land title, and to areas confiscated and distributed as bequests for loyal service. It was by means of the latter technique that Kamakura gained a direct influence in western Japan; recipients of external jitō awards were exclusively men from the Kantō. New postings took place especially in the wake of important political or military incidents. For instance, at the conclusion of the 1221 Jōkyū War, Kamakura vastly augmented its corps of jitō appointees in the western provinces. But the real significance of jitō is not to be measured numerically; individual holders of this post were slowly beginning to close ground with the traditional estate-owning class of Kyoto. By the end of the thirteenth century there were jitō on the verge of becoming proprietors in their own right. A major promise of the Gempei War was about to be fulfilled. The role of the bakufu in all this is most enlightening. Kamakura was caught in a dilemma due principally to its seizure in the 1180s of sole authority for jitō appointments and dismissals. Whereas the bakufu leadership wished to deploy jitō across the entire face of Japan, it was subsequently forced to reduce the rate of new postings as a step toward restabilizing the countryside. Similarly, while Kamakura recognized the desirability of promoting legitimate jitō interests, it could ill afford the extremes of condoning free license on the land or moving too harshly against too many of its own men. The result was a warrior regime, which, in order to perpetuate itself, sought out a safe middle path. It was this that induced the so-called good government of Kamakura times.[10] The bakufu came to function as a peacemaker between the traditional proprietary interests of the capital aristocracy and the newer power interests—principally jitō—directly on the land.[11]

Such a view of Japan's first warrior government derives essentially from a more complete understanding of the nature of shugo and jitō. Up to now these local appointees have been seen as expressions on the provincial and estate levels of an 1185 Yoritomo master plan to achieve a countrywide hegemony. This interpretation is only partially correct. The following study will suggest a view of the shugo as an 1190s Yoritomo invention essentially to aid the bakufu in keeping the latter's own vassals in check; and a view of the jitō as war-period outlaws with whom Yoritomo, as emergency police chief, became unavoidably identified.

10. Traditional histories have credited the Kamakura regime with maintaining order essentially out of loyalty to the imperial house. But baser and sounder motives were clearly at work. See chap. 5.

11. Our concern in this study is limited to the period generally before 1275. Thus the effects of the Mongol invasions (1274 and 1281), the character of Hōjō rule, and other aspects of the late Kamakura polity are not treated. Disaffected warriors overthrew the Kamakura regime in 1333 and replaced it with another bakufu under the house of Ashikaga.

The story of the bakufu's role in Japan's national life is, in any event, inextricably bound up with the story of shugo and jitō. All three deserve our close attention.

PART 1:
JAPAN BEFORE 1180

1 ASCENDANCY OF THE TAIRA

Warrior hegemony in Japan was anticipated by a brief period in which the Taira, rivals of the Minamoto, established themselves as military–nobles at court. In many surveys hegemony by these two great clans is depicted as largely sequential. One group of warrior overlords was simply superseded by another. In fact, the Taira and Minamoto represented wholly different approaches to power. To understand the gulf between them is to appreciate the historical significance of their age.

The story of the Taira's rise begins in the late eleventh century when, after more than two hundred years of Fujiwara hegemony, the imperial family undertook to revive itself. This involved an updating of the *In-no-chō*, a private chancellery from which a retired emperor might hope to conduct imperial house affairs without interference from the Fujiwara. The move was an historic one because it signaled final acceptance by emperors of the new conditions of privatized authority. The imperial line would reassert itself, even if this meant abandoning much of the imperial state. The lead in this endeavor was taken by the retired emperor (*In*) Shirakawa, who pressed a search for the new accouterments of power. These included a portfolio of privately owned estates and a patronage system that would extend into the provinces. It was from this need for province-level clients that the In and a branch of the Taira eventually joined forces.

The specific Taira lineage that entered service with Shirakawa had settled in the region of Ise-Iga early in the eleventh century. In that area, however, the great Nara temple of Tōdaiji possessed numerous shōen along with its own patronage organization. The Ise Taira, as they were called, were thus temporarily set back in their efforts to gain a more secure foothold.[1] This circumstance continued basically without change until the In's office experienced its revitalization later in the century. An opportunity for alliance and mutual benefit now presented itself. In the episode that apparently sealed the relationship, Taira Masamori in 1097 commended to Rokujō-In (one of several chapels set up by the ex-emperor to receive new proprietorships) a number of land parcels hitherto controlled by Tōdaiji.[2] It was a pattern that would be repeated many times during the next several generations.

A major element in the In–Heishi alliance was the retired emperor's power to disburse a share of the country's governorships. As the In's leading protégé, Masamori received successive appointments to at least nine provinces.[3] This had two important effects: it permitted the Taira leader to expand his range of contacts far beyond Ise-Iga, and it provided the ex-emperor with an opportunity to increase his family's proprietorships in many parts of the country. A highly discriminatory policy was adopted by the In to advance the latter cause. Taira governors were to protect and promote domainial holdings of In-sponsored chapels and to obstruct the shōen (or shōen plans) of competitors. In return, Masamori and his successors were invested with numerous estate managerships.[4] Both sides to the alliance prospered from this arrangement. During the

1. Taira Korehira became governor of Ise in 1006. Uwayokote Masataka, "Jōkyū no ran rekishiteki hyōka," *Shirin* 39.1 (1956): 25. The Taira's relationship with this region during the eleventh century is discussed in Takeuchi Rizō, "Heishi seiken seiritsu no shojōken," *Nihon rekishi* 163 (1962): 6-7. (Hereafter cited as Takeuchi, "Heishi shojōken.")

2. The register of commended parcels is reproduced in Takeuchi, "Heishi shojōken," p. 9. The full story of Masamori's alliance with the In and the commendations to Rokujō-In appears in Ryō Susumu, "Rokujō-In ryō to Taira Masamori," *Heian jidai* (Tokyo, 1962): 120 ff.

3. Iida Hisao, "Heishi to Kyūshū," in Takeuchi Rizō hakushi kanreki kinenkai, comp., *Shōensei to buke shakai* (Tokyo, 1969), p. 50.

4. For examples of this alliance see: a document of 1132 showing Echizen governor Tadamori (Masamori's son) working to promote the interests of a shōen (Ushigahara) founded in 1090 by the In (*Daigo Zōjiki*, 1132/9/23 kan senshi, in Takeuchi Rizō, ed., *Heian ibun* (Tokyo, 1963-68), 5: 1909, doc. 2241); and an 1133 excerpt from the *Chōshūki* detailing a management post held by Taira Tadamori in Kyushu's Kanzaki Estate (Seno Seiichirō, ed., *Hizen-no-kuni Kanazaki-no-shō shiryō*, Kyūshū shōen shiryō sōsho 2 [Fukuoka, 1963], doc. 9, p. 8). *Heian ibun* hereafter cited as *HI*.

first half of the twelfth century the imperial patronage combination became the wealthiest and most successful in the land.[5]

The In–Heishi alliance continued largely without interruption into the 1150s.[6] At this point a dispute over the imperial succession and other issues led, according to a familiar story, to various Genji and Heishi warrior factions' being called into the capital in 1156. The resulting skirmish, called Hōgen-no-ran, was followed in 1159–60 by another series of minor battles (Heiji-no-ran) among the survivors of the earlier encounter. At its conclusion in 1160 Taira Kiyomori emerged as the dominant military power in Kyoto. It was Kiyomori who was to lead his family to political mastery over the capital and the brief hegemony bearing his family's name.

It is most significant, however, that such mastery developed only slowly. Contrary to the picture usually drawn, Kiyomori did not immediately become ruler within Kyoto. In varying degrees, he was obliged to share authority with the In until a coup d'etat in 1179 finally eliminated imperial opposition.[7] This concept of shared power is central to any treatment of the Taira's rise and precipitate decline a generation later, and it requires close attention.

Of immediate note is that Hōgen and Heiji, while serving to eliminate the Taira's Minamoto rivals, were fought principally to enhance the position of Go-Shirakawa, the new In.[8] In 1160, therefore, the Taira leader remained essentially a provincial aristocrat awaiting rewards from his family's traditional sponsor. The settlements after the two military encounters clearly reveal this. In the wake of the Hōgen affair, Kiyomori, hitherto governor of Aki, was made governor of Harima and deputy imperial officer for Kyushu;

5. For details, see G. Cameron Hurst, "Insei: Abdicated Sovereigns in the Politics of Late Heian Japan" (Ph.D. diss. Columbia University, 1972).

6. Like his father, Taira Tadamori received at least nine governor posts under In sponsorship, while his own son, Kiyomori, received three. Iida, "Heishi to Kyūshū," p. 50.

7. Ishimoda Shō was the first to amplify this view. See "Heishi seiken to sono botsuraku" and "Heishi seiken ni tsuite," *Kodai makki seiji shi josetsu* (Tokyo, 1964), pp. 384–402, 470–87. Not all scholars accept this approach, e.g., Matsumoto Shimpachirō, "Rokuhara jidai," *Chūsei shakai no kenkyū* (Tokyo, 1967), pp. 231–50, which emphasizes a conquest from the provinces. But the facts hardly support this.

8. Go-Shirakawa became emperor in 1155 and ex-emperor in 1158.

he received no land rights.[9] In fact, the Heishi clan actually *lost*
privileges in land—and to the In's treasury. Those dispossessed had
been caught on the wrong side in the war. The imperial family thus
emerged from the Hōgen Disturbance with an enhanced portfolio of
interests—from local rights, which it was now free to distribute, to
full proprietorships seized from defeated Kyoto aristocrats.[10]

The Heiji Disturbance was much more advantageous for Kiyomori, but here too the division of the spoils was of greater benefit
to the In than to the Heishi. Shōen that became managerships of
the Taira simultaneously became proprietary holdings of Go-
Shirakawa. Our conclusion is that Kiyomori's twin victories did
not end—or even dramatically change—a patron–client relationship now into its third generation.[11] The course that the Taira
leader's promotions would take was largely discretionary with the
In.

Within months of the end of Heiji, Kiyomori was given several
new appointments. These had the effect of elevating him to membership within the high nobility, a distinction no Taira or Minamoto
had ever achieved.[12] It is for this reason that observers, quite properly, have cited an unprecedented development: a warrior's
entrance into the ruling elite. But the titles he received point equally
in another direction. Kiyomori's promotion to adviser (*sangi*) to
the imperial state council (*dajōkan*), captain of the outer palace
guards, and (a year later) chief of the central police office, were all
of clear value to the In. Go-Shirakawa was at this time locked in
a political struggle with the nominal emperor Nijō, around whom a
faction had formed. Thus the In determined to utilize Kiyomori,

9. Takeuchi Rizō, "Heishi seiken to insei," *Iwanami Kōza, Nihon rekishi 5,
chūsei 1* (Tokyo, 1962), p. 72.

10. A register of lands confiscated from three persons—Left Minister Fujiwara
Yorinaga, Taira Masahiro, and Taira Tadasada—reveals the discrepancies in
rank and land tenure between the high nobility and members of the Taira clan.
This register, along with other source excerpts relating to the Hōgen land settle-
ment, appear in Ōmori Kingorō, *Buke jidai no kenkyū* (Tokyo, 1927), 1:289–99.
(Hereafter cited as Ōmori, *Buke.*)

11. E.g., a document of 1161 shows Kiyomori as a member of the In's chancellery, a natural setting for a client. *Myōhōin Monjo*, 1161/1 Go-Shirakawa Hōō
In-no-chō kishinjō an, in *HI*, 7:2516–17, doc. 3123.

12. That is, no scion of the warrior lineages of the Taira and Minamoto. Both
clans had central branches that belonged to the estate-owning nobility, but such
lines, despite a common surname, functioned virtually as independent families.

the military chieftain, in a conspicuous display of power. Not only was the Taira leader given charge of the palace guards and made police commissioner over the capital, but he was intruded into the dajōkan, the highest organ of state. None of this was the result simply of demands laid down by the victor in battle.[13]

Precisely when the Taira leader began to sense the possibilities of advancing his private interests at the *expense* of the In is difficult to determine. But Kiyomori was obviously ambitious, and he proved very adroit at exploiting the fissures within Kyoto society. In a well-known power move, for example, he arranged a strategic marriage between his daughter and Fujiwara Motozane, soon to become imperial regent (*sesshō*). The latter conveniently died the following year (1166), and Kiyomori moved to have his inheritance (a bloc of shōen owned by the regent's line) fall to his own daughter. Shortly thereafter, Kiyomori achieved one of his most spectacular successes—appointment as prime minister (*dajōdaijin*), a post considered so exalted it was usually kept vacant.[14] Following the regular practice, the Taira leader resigned from this office, but this in no way compromised his rapidly expanding influence. By becoming a "retired prime minister," Kiyomori undermined Go-Shirakawa's position as Kyoto's preeminent elder statesman.

Actually, considerable evidence exists to show that even now the two men were able to cooperate (or share responsibility) on some issues; the Taira's traditional dependence on the In proved easier to continue than to break off. For example, Kiyomori did not appropriate for himself a central protectorship over the countryside. Much as before, documents from the In's office maintained their supremacy in the areas of guaranteeing provincial land rights and prohibiting local outrages.[15] Indeed, even in the matter of confirm-

13. Takeuchi, "Heishi seiken to insei," pp. 68–69. In the early 1160s, however, Kiyomori was also close to Nijō. Perhaps he was already looking ahead. Actual governmental decisions were made by the council of high nobles, which, while separate from the dajōkan, had a roughly parallel membership.

14. The marriage strategy is described in Fujiwara Jien, *Gukanshō*, Kokushi taikei 14 (Tokyo, 1901), p. 512. Kiyomori's court promotions are itemized in *Kugyō bunin* 1, Kokushi taikei 9 (Tokyo, 1899), pp. 459–70.

15. E.g., a blanket order affecting all estates owned by the prestigious Iwashimizu Hachiman Shrine. Public officials throughout the country (*shokoku no zaichōkanjin*) were to defend those shōen from local violence. This was in 1176. *Iwashimizu Monjo*, 1176/6/10 Go-Shirakawa In-no-chō kudashibumi, in *HI*, 7:2901–02, doc. 3765.

ing the holdings of Kiyomori's kinsmen and followers, it was the In's office, not the Taira leader's, that apparently issued the documents. As we shall see presently, this was because the clientage relationship was still basically intact. The In, not Kiyomori, was the chief executive over lands jointly held by both.

By the mid-1170s, however, conditions were clearly changing. As one indication, the rivalries that had led to Hōgen, Heiji, and aftermath and that solidified the Kiyomori–Go-Shirakawa alliance had now been replaced by an entirely new set of relationships. Perhaps more than the In himself, his entourage vigorously opposed the Heishi, who for their part had forged a political and military tie with the Enryakuji, a powerful temple adjacent to Kyoto. In 1177, one of the In's closest advisers was denied a certain military title, which was then assigned instead to Kiyomori's heir, Shigemori. This was followed by Go-Shirakawa's forcing the priest Meiun, Kiyomori's link with Enryakuji, to renounce his vows and turn over to the In's treasury some thirty-nine parcels of land. Barely a week later came the Shishigatani affair, involving the Taira leader's exposé of a full-scale plot against his family. Kiyomori reacted quickly by executing or ordering the exile of the conspirators. During the following year a factional dispute erupted within Enryakuji, which caused a reduction of that temple's reliability as a buttress for the Heishi. These several developments fueled a decision by the In to move even more aggressively.[16]

The anti-Taira conspiracy was given impetus by two personal misfortunes that befell Kiyomori in 1179. In the sixth month of that year, the daughter of Kiyomori, who in 1166 had been so instrumental in her father's acquisition of the Fujiwara lands, suddenly died. The In used her death as a pretext for seizure of the "Fujiwara inheritance." Two months later Kiyomori's heir, Shigemori, also died; Echizen Province, which earlier had passed to Shigemori's son as a provincial proprietorship, was now confiscated by the In. The vulnerability of the Taira's grip on events thus stood exposed, causing Kiyomori to make a fateful choice. He gathered troops in the eleventh month and proceeded to order the dismissal

16. Yasuda Genkyū (formerly Motohisa), *Nihon zenshi 4, chūsei 1* (Tokyo, 1958), pp. 19–24. (Hereafter cited as Yasuda, *Chūsei.*) Enryakuji soon came to oppose the Heishi.

or demotion of all who had opposed him. Go-Shirakawa was placed under house arrest, and the newly vacated government posts were freely distributed to his own kinsmen.[17] The Heishi leader now became master of Kyoto.

The ease with which Kiyomori accomplished this feat is somewhat deceptive, however. On the debit side was the revulsion in Kyoto with an act of violence, the sole aim of which was aggrandizement of the Taira house. Hōgen, and by extension, Heiji, had been military episodes on behalf of "imperial authority." The net effect, by contrast, of the 1179 seizure was a massive enlargement in Kiyomori's personal control, but at the expense of established procedure and the economic and political interests of major Kyoto institutions. Having broken the rules by forcefully upsetting the basic collegiality of central governance, the Taira leader would find it that much harder to reweld the capital in the face of the 1180 Genji threat. On that occasion—despite the Taira's overwhelming strength on paper—Kiyomori had little more to sustain his dominance than the resources of his own house. Just what these were, and why in substance they were so meager, is logically our next topic.

A well-known passage from the thirteenth-century work *Gukan-shō* states that more than 500 landed holdings were confiscated from the Tai a at the time of their flight from Kyoto in 1183. This impressive total, however, cannot be corroborated by contemporary evidence, and Japanese scholars have been able to enumerate and name barely more than one-fifth of that number.[18] This may well indicate that the Taira never did possess private lands in such volume. But even more significant is the doubt recently cast by historians regarding the degree to which Kiyomori was able to exploit the public and private domains he did hold.

Heishi relationships with land fall into three general categories—

17. Ibid., p. 25. The coup and its aftermath are described in Fujiwara Kane-zane, *Gyokuyō* (Tokyo, 1967), entries for 1179/11/14–29, 2:306–18. Also in *Hyakurenshō*, Kokushi taikei 14, entries for 1179/11/15–28, pp. 130–31.

18. *Gukanshō*, p. 536. Yasuda Genkyū, "Heike mokkanryō ni tsuite," in Yasuda Genkyū, ed., *Shoki hōkensei no kenkyū* (Tokyo, 1964), p. 316. (Hereafter cited as Yasuda, "Mokkanryō.") Only partial lists of the Heike-confiscated lands survive, e.g., *Koga Monjo*, 1184/4/5 and 1184/4/6 Minamoto Yoritomo kudashi-bumi an, in *HI*, 8:3126–27, docs. 4151–52.

proprietary, managerial, and *gesu* or the even lower-level rights possessed by Heishi retainers. Regarding the first group, it would appear to have been the proprietor's (*ryōke*) title that was held by the Taira. For most of these, the guarantor's (*honke*) privilege belonged to the In.[19] Normally, this would have given to the Heishi the actual executive authority. Professor Yasuda, however, interprets this particular division in quite the reverse way, a pattern fully in keeping with the patron–client nature of that relationship in other areas.[20] The implication is that resistance by Go-Shirakawa to Taira territorial autonomy was a large factor in Kiyomori's relative failure to recruit vassals from within domains he possessed but did not effectively control.[21]

What little we know of the second category—*azukari dokoro* management posts—tends to corroborate a deference to In superiority. We can cite, for example, the 1166 case of Taira Shigehira and the newly formed Ōta Estate in Bingo Province. Barely a year before Kiyomori's accession to the prime minister's title, his son, Shigehira, was invested by the ex-sovereign in a mere domain managership.[22] Equally revealing (if more complex) was the *shiki* breakdown for Munakata Shrine in northern Kyushu. At the highest level (honke) was the imperial house, followed by Taira Yorimori (a half brother of Kiyomori) as proprietor (ryōke), and Taira Moritoshi (a leading retainer) as manager. Unfortunately, we do not know when or how the latter two appointments were made, but if the usual pattern prevailed, the In's office probably made the investitures.[23] As late as 1178, we find an edict of this type concern-

19. E.g., the case of Shiraku Estate in Tamba Province. This shōen is listed as the holding (*ryō*) of Hōshōgon-In, another of the imperial family's chapels. Kiyomori's name appears below the name of the domain. *Tōji Hyakugō Monjo*, 1159/int.5 Hōshōgon-In ryō shōen no chūmon, in *HI*, 6:2454–55, doc. 2986.

20. Yasuda, "Mokkanryō," pp. 324–25, 336. For a somewhat different view of the division, see Uwayokote Masataka, "Juei ni jūgatsu senshi to Heike mokkanryō," *Nihon rekishi* 228 (1967), pp. 22–23.

21. One expression of this is the remarkable *absence* of Kiyomori documents relating to shōen. This immediately sets the Taira apart from other Kyoto estate-owners. See my "Emergence of the Kamakura Bakufu," *Medieval Japan*, chap. 6.

22. *Nibu Jinja Monjo*, 1166/1/10 Go-Shirakawa In-no-chō kudashibumi an, in *HI*, 7:2664–65, doc. 3375.

23. The basic information regarding shiki levels over Munakata comes from two documents: (1) the honke authority of the imperial house and the post-1185

ing the azukari dokoro post of Hizen Province's Matsuura Domain.[24]

The third category, sub-azukari dokoro land rights, takes us down to the level of rank-and-file Heishi. Several distinctions are necessary here. First, there is an enormous difference between men who fought during the Gempei War under the Taira label and the much smaller group who were originally Kiyomori's retainers. The gesu-type land rights confiscated by the bakufu came mostly from families whose Heishi credentials were recent, amorphous, or even counterfeit (see chapter 5). Second, houses possessing links with the Taira from other generations were not necessarily Taira members after 1160; all regions of Japan possessed myriad families with Heishi ties long since defunct. And third, even the Taira surname was no certain indicator of active Heishi affiliation: few among the prominent Heishi offshoots in local areas were true Kiyomori vassals.

Who, then, *were* the Taira leader's followers? Kiyomori's band in 1160 numbered only 300 men and consisted principally of warriors who had united with the Taira during the course of Kiyomori's (or his father's) successive governorships.[25] As such, they were lower-ranking members of the In's patronage system and received many of their rewards accordingly. It was men like Taira Moritoshi, Taira Iesada, and Saeki Kagehiro who carried most of the burden for inflating the Heishi band. Moritoshi, for instance, was active in both northern and southern Kyushu, while Iesada was

---

bakufu dispossession of the now deceased Moritoshi are recalled in *Munakata Jinja Monjo*, 1256/1 Daigūin-no-chō kudashibumi, in Itō Shirō, ed., *Munakata gunshi* (1932), 2: 167–68; (2) the identification of Yorimori with Munakata appears in *Koga Monjo*, 1184/4/6 Minamoto Yoritomo kudashibumi, in *HI*, 8:3129, doc. 4152. See also Munakata Jinja fukkō kiseikai, comp., *Munakata Jinja shi* (Tokyo, 1966), 3:692–93. Yorimori, it should be pointed out, achieved sufficient court status to serve as ryōke over shōen only after Kiyomori's death in 1181. But a reference in the 1256 record (above) suggests Moritoshi's involvement in Munakata during the time of Kiyomori. Perhaps the Taira chief was ryōke before Yorimori.

24. *Tōji Hyakugō Monjo*, 1178/6/20 Go-Shirakawa In-no-chō kudashibumi, in *HI* 8:2948–50, doc. 3836. See also Saga kenshi hensan iinaki, comp., *Saga kenshi* (Saga, 1968), 1:408, 424.

25. Yasuda, *Chūsei*, p. 14. This was the number, at any rate, that fought under him at Heiji. Families from Ise-Iga were also represented, e.g., Taira Iesada. Iida, "Heishi to Kyūshū," pp. 52–53.

Kiyomori's main deputy over that island.[26] Saeki Kagehiro was the
Taira's leading vassal in Aki Province. Through the latter's efforts
(and a ten-year Kiyomori governorship, 1146–56), Aki emerged
as the main Heishi stronghold in western Japan. But such examples
are clearly exceptional. Kiyomori developed no regular rewards
program to induce men to join his band, and he failed even to issue
personal confirmations of local land rights.[27] The Taira leader paid
scant attention to his local base, allowing those who wished to
become Heishi to attach themselves loosely to his own agents.

The basic reasons Kiyomori paid so little heed to the construction
of a vassal system center on the absence of both need and precedent. The Minamoto were in powerless exile, and there was no
way to predict the future uses of local organization. In the circumstances of the 1160s, Kiyomori's entrance into the ruling elite was
revolutionary enough; his goals and perceptions lay entirely in the
capital. Once ensconced there, however, the Heishi leader encountered difficulties, most deriving from his Ise Taira ancestry. His
promotions, as we have seen, were rapid and numerous, yet even
after reaching the top of the court structure he failed to overcome
certain key deficiencies. As a provincial client fewer than ten years
removed, the Taira leader had neither escaped the sway of the ex-
emperor nor created an independent central organization.[28] It was

26. For Moritoshi, see n. 23 and *Iriki-In Monjo*, 1183/8/8 Shimazu-no-shō
bettō Tomo Nobuaki ge, in *HI*, 8:3100, doc. 4101. Also Asakawa Kan'ichi,
The Documents of Iriki (Tokyo, 1955), p. 95. Iesada was a vassal carryover from
Kiyomori's father, Tadamori. From 1180, Iesada's son became active in Kyūshū.
Iida, "Heishi to Kyūshū," pp. 52–53.

27. A policy of Heishi jitō appointments into the holdings of others is alleged
by many scholars but not based on any contemporary evidence. Only in Aki
Province, and then into limited land units, does documentation survive for
Heishi-promoted jitō. See chapter 4 for details. Moreover, only *one* Kiyomori
document survives of a type that other central owners issued in great abundance:
a decree confirming a local management title (gesu shiki). See *Itsukushima Jinja
Monjo*, 1164/6 gon-chunagon (Taira Kiyomori) ke mandokoro kudashibumi, in
HI 7:2609, doc. 3285. On another point, the Taira family's well-known com-
mercial interests, especially its involvement in the Inland Sea and continental
trade, undoubtedly provided reward opportunities for some Heishi vassals. But
here too the question of extent is the important one: we do not know whether the
Taira ever sought to integrate growing numbers of local persons into its trade
network.

28. E.g., the Taira's *mandokoro*, or house chancellery, was never very large or
active.

one thing to seek the same shōen managerships for his clansmen that he himself had recently aspired to; it was altogether another to rule vast blocs of shōen as a central proprietor in the capital.[29] His major concerns, at any rate, were clearly removed from local organization.

There is an important converse side to this. As Kiyomori ascended the imperial ladder in Kyoto, perceptions of the Taira began to change in the provinces. The more the Taira sought to model themselves as central aristocrats, the more they apparently engendered local hostility and distrust (p. 26). We see in this a fundamental Heishi weakness. The Taira had abandoned much of their provincial legacy but were finding it difficult to achieve parity with the long-established institutions of the capital. Their attention had been deflected from the provinces, but their development as central nobles was painful and slow. This anomalous condition would ultimately contribute to the Taira demise.

A final illustration of the limitations of Heishi power concerns the public land sector, with reference to governorships and provincial proprietorships. Based on a traditional source, it was believed until recently that the Taira possessed thirty or more proprietary provinces and that vassal recruitment and overall military strength were correspondingly advanced.[30] Specifically, it was asserted by scholars that Kiyomori's conversion to vassal status of the warrior units (rōtō) attached to provincial offices (kokuga) was the main Taira means of gaining a foothold in central and western Japan.[31] Since the mid-1950s, however, an opposite view has been gaining general acceptance. The Heishi, asserts this newer school, met with nothing but resistance from indigenous officials (zaichōkanjin) of the various provincial offices. Far from the promotion of their houseman (ke'nin) system, the Taira—who were guilty of distributing governorships within a very select circle—were singularly

29. A prime example is the Fujiwara regent's bloc of shōen whose inheritance Kiyomori had steered to his daughter in 1166 (p. 19). Except for Taira Moritoshi's activities in Shimazu Estate in 1183, we have no information at all as to what was done with these lands. See n. 26.

30. The fictional war tale Gempei Seisuiki gives this figure of "more than thirty chigyōkoku." Reproduced in Watanabe Tamotsu, Genji to Heishi (Tokyo, 1967), p. 139.

31. See, e.g., Satō Shin'ichi's claim that Taira military strength was organized through kokuga: "Shoki hōken shakai no keisei," in Toyoda Takeshi, ed., Shin Nihon shi taikei, chūsei shakai (Tokyo, 1954), 3:7.

unsuccessful in establishing control over men whose localized concerns simply outweighed all other obligations. The agents (*mokudai*) dispatched to represent centrally based Heishi masters were looked on as unwanted intruders from the capital.[32]

The proof for these speculations is found in the following data. As demonstrated by Professor Kikuchi, the supposed thirty Taira-held provincial proprietorships actually numbered only twenty; and of these the majority were acquired after the 1179 coup. This suggests that in terms of both time and area the Heishi had far fewer opportunities than once suspected. Also, among the fewer than ten provinces held by the Taira for more than a brief period, only three—Wakasa, Echizen, and Noto, all in the Hokurikudō region—were in continuous Heishi possession from after 1160.[33] Most revealing of all is what happened in those three provinces, where security should have been greatest: within a year of the Gempei outbreak, the provincial officer class—nominally subordinates of the Taira—went en bloc over to the Minamoto.[34]

On the strength of this new information, it seems evident that before 1180 the Taira-held governorships and supragovernorships were possessed as part of the normal routine of late Heian governance; the Heishi simply held their logical share. Moreover, to the extent that they sought conversion of local officials to personal subservience, the program was evidently a failure. Proprietary provinces, a resource in land and political lever at court, were not conducive to a rapid accumulation of private vassals.[35]

The year 1180 was a momentous one for the Taira, embracing both spectacular successes and humiliating setbacks. On 2/21 Kiyomori saw his own grandson ascend the throne as emperor, and four months later (6/2) he moved the government itself to his "country estate" in neighboring Settsu Province. The rationale behind this

32. The originator of this revisionist view of the Heishi-held proprietary provinces is Professor Kikuchi Takeo, "Heishi zuryō hyō," *Sekai rekishi jiten* (Tokyo, 1956), 22:159–62.

33. Ibid.

34. See *Gyokuyō*, 1180/11/28, 1181/7/24, and 1181/9/2, 2:446, 518, and 525.

35. The ardor of the Heishi's pre-1180 effort is a key factor here, but one about which we know very little. It is certainly noteworthy that almost all of our data come from after 1180, including the traditional figures of "500 shōen" and "thirty provincial proprietorships."

latter move is significant. Contrary to what we might have assumed it did not derive from anxiety over weaknesses in the Taira's local base. In 1180/4 the prince Mochihito had issued a call to arms against the Taira, and it was by this dubious pretext that Yoritomo later justified his rebellion (see chapter 3). However, in the context of late spring and early summer local conditions had not yet become threatening. The Mochihito initiative was squelched on 5/26 and major rumblings in the east were still several months off. It is likely therefore that the prince's treachery was seen as reflective of the anti-Heishi animus then building within the capital city itself. The transfer to Fukuhara in Settsu was not for the purpose of broadening the Heishi appeal but rather indeed of narrowing it. By transferring governance away from Kyoto the Taira leader would be effectively isolating his central rivals.[36]

The bankruptcy of this policy became apparent only when the Minamoto launched their rebellion and then showed no signs of collapse. As quickly as the old capital had been abandoned it was now once again reoccupied. Consolidation (rather than isolation) became the new order of the day, and the Fukuhara episode was permanently ended. In the twelfth month Kiyomori even sought to reactivate the In–Heishi alliance. Go-Shirakawa was brought out of retirement and restored, however nominally, to his former position.[37] The strategy here was many-sided. Most important, the Minamoto were denied all chance of allying with the ex-emperor, and the authority of Kyoto's senior figure was once again placed at Kiyomori's disposal.

In the initial stage of war preparations the Taira leader made generous use of imperial commands.[38] The results, however, were not

36. For the move to Fukuhara see *Gyokuyō*, 1180/6/2, 2:413–14. In the period after 1179, Heishi high-handedness and accretion of land and office titles led to estrangement of peers in the capital. Plots such as the following developed: a report in *Gyokuyō* (1180/3/17, 2:386) that Onjōji, Enryakuji, and the "Nara priests" were conspiring to support the retired emperor against the Heishi. *Hyakurenshō*, 1180/6/20 and 8/16, p. 134, described the denouement—respective confiscations by the Taira of the shōen of Onjōji and Kōfukuji (Nara priests).

37. *Gyokuyō*, 1180/12/18, 2:453. Before this date there had been a "junior retired emperor," Takakura, who was evidently a Taira puppet.

38. A capture order was given for Yoritomo at the start of the ninth month, and two weeks later Taira Koremori was charged with conquering the "eastern rebels" (Kantō *zokuto*). *Hyakurenshō*, 1180/9/5 and 9/22, p. 134.

encouraging. For example, the outcome of a general conscription order to Noto, Tajima, Kii, and Sado provinces was only half successful. Two of these four Heishi proprietorships (chigyōkoku) failed to respond to this plea for commissariat rice (hyōranmai) and soldier levies (heishi).[39] But this, actually, was only one dimension of the problem; the Taira were beset suddenly with a whole host of difficulties. Most revealing was the trouble encountered even in garrisoning Kyoto. Capital proprietors bore so much resentment to the Taira that there was resistance to providing guards and supplies.[40] This in turn led to a Kyoto-wide inventory of servant houses to determine who, apparently, was holding back.[41]

With resistance to the Taira mounting on all sides, the Heishi were finally forced to innovate. Early in 1181 they established two new local control offices designed to expedite prosecution of the war. In 1181/1, Taira Munemori was invested with a military-police competence (sōkan) over the five central provinces (Kinai) and Tamba, Ise, Iga, and Ōmi.[42] Earlier defense pleas to the latter three on this list—all to the east of Kinai—had failed to prevent the advance there of Minamoto forces.[43] The sōkan appointment was undoubtedly aimed at blocking this Genji movement. A second reason for the introduction of the sōkan was Kiyomori's desire to create a long overdue personalized command system over the entire central region. With this objective in mind, the Taira leader, now in the final months of his life, chose to have his own son and heir invested with this new title.

The means used by the Taira sōkan to implement his new authority centered on an appropriation of the "pursuit and punishment" powers hitherto held by the separate offices (kokuga) in the nine

39. *Sankaiki*, 1180/12/10 in Kokumin seishin bunka kenkyūjo, comp., *Kokushi shiryōshū* (Tokyo, 1940), 2:10.

40. Examples cited in Ishimoda Shō, "Kamakura bakufu ikkoku jitō shiki no seiritsu," in Satō Shin'ichi and Ishimoda Shō, eds., *Chūsei no hō to kokka* (Tokyo, 1965), pp. 40–42. (Hereafter cited as Ishimoda, "Ikkoku jitō.")

41. *Gyokuyō*, 1181/2/20, 2:481.

42. See *Hyakurenshō*, 1181/1/8, p. 137, and *Gyokuyō*, 1181/1/19, 2:466. The only detailed study of this officer is Ishimoda Shō, "Heishi seiken no sōkan shiki setchi," *Rekishi hyōron* 107 (1959), pp. 7–14. (Hereafter cited as Ishimoda, "Sōkan setchi.")

43. See *Ishiyamadera Shozō Monjo*, late 1180 Takakura Jōō inzen, in *HI*, 8:3008, doc. 3940; and *Hyakurenshō*, 1180/12/1, p. 135.

provinces. As far as can be determined, he gained no lawful power over general provincial administration.[44] This meant that while Munemori was now ostensibly the supreme commander over all "government forces" in central Japan, he did not simultaneously become the region's special governor. An unrestricted right of levy, requisition, and general interference in the multiplicity of local governances had evidently not been sought.[45]

This deficiency in the sōkan was partly offset by the *sōgesu,* a province-level "steward-in-chief" for shōen. Actually, only one sōgesu is documented, that of Taira Moritoshi in 1181/2. Although this particular assignment was for Tamba Province to the west of Kyoto, it seems likely that similar investitures were also made in the contested provinces to the east.[46] Faced with critical shortages of soldier recruits, rice rations, and other provisions, the Taira hoped to use these appointments to coordinate on a provincial basis direct requisitioning efforts in private shōen. Their other objective, we may presume, was to open a channel for contact and possible vassalage ties with shōen officials.

There is no direct way to judge the effectiveness of either sōkan or sōgesu. Since the names of these two officials do not reappear, and since the shortages of men and supplies were evidently not allayed,[47] it seems likely that neither experiment succeeded. At any rate, the flight of the Taira in 1183 away from the central region suggests the final failure of all Heishi programs. Waging a major war using the capital as a base area ultimately proved unworkable.

Were the Taira merely victims, then? Was there any way for them to have surmounted their difficulties? Unlike Minamoto Yoritomo, who would capitalize on an outlaw status by simply seizing outright

44. Ishimoda, "Sōkan setchi," pp. 8–9.
45. It is interesting that to expedite Kyoto acceptance of this measure Kiyomori saw fit to cite a sōkan precedent from the year 731. Ibid., pp. 4–5.
46. *Gyokuyō,* 1181/2/8, 2:474. See Ishimoda, "Ikkoku jitō," pp. 36th ff. As early as the end of 1180, a Heishi commander called *tsuitōshi* ("subjugation officer") was sent to Kii Province south of the capital region to collect commissariat rice. Referred to in *Negoro Yōsho,* 1184/2 Kii no kuni Daidembōin shoshi ge an, in *HI,* 8:3119, doc. 4141.
47. *Gyokuyō,* for example, continues to allude to such problems, e.g., 1181/int. 2/6 and 3/6, 2:486 and 492.

the estate and provincial rights he desired, Kiyomori and his heirs could neither abruptly alter the central office structure on which their own authority largely rested, nor move too precipitately to convert the land system into a resource of war. In a sense it was a fatal dilemma: as protectors of order and the imperial system, the Taira could not simply set aside all precedents on behalf of raising, equipping, and rewarding troops—even though that was what the conditions of war clearly demanded. We should not be surprised, therefore, that the Heishi's levy and conscription orders were almost invariably channeled through traditional bureaucratic agencies.[48] Similarly, we find no evidence of a new approach to the problem of rewards that might have induced large numbers of armed men to abandon their fields in exchange for fighting in unfamiliar places.[49]

The meaning of the foregoing will become clearer as we proceed to explore the more advanced state of warrior development in eastern Japan, home region of the future bakufu. In the area known as the Kantō, greater local strength held the potential for a greater explosion of negative feeling against the very system on which the Taira depended. The Heishi were toppled as much by the new combination of resources tapped by the Minamoto as by their own inadequacies and links with the past.

48. Ishimoda, "Ikkoku jitō," pp. 41–47, provides much evidence to show that levies, both manpower and supply, continued to go through governors and provincial offices in the public sector, and proprietors and estate managers in shōen.

49. Warriors did fight as Taira, of course, but for a variety of private reasons. Details in chap. 3.

2 WARRIOR DEVELOPMENT IN
EASTERN JAPAN

When the Taira finally tried to organize a military alliance base in the provinces, they were hard pressed to shift outward from a locus of authority that had been centered in Kyoto for nearly a generation. It was the destiny of Minamoto Yoritomo to move in a different direction, to ride the crest of a wave of pressure that swelled out from the provinces rather than to stand against it. Thus, while the achievement of the Heishi proved transitory, the Genji drive to power left results of the most revolutionary kind. The outpouring of localism around the country, sparked initially by the Gempei War, set events on a course that would eventually erase all but the memory of Kyoto-centered authority.

The traditional view of the establishment of Minamoto rule has come from a single source, the *Azuma kagami*, a chronicle prepared in the late thirteenth century as an "official history" of the Kamakura regime.[1] Among the weaknesses of the *Azuma kagami* are a coverage of the Minamoto movement that begins with the first overt signs of war in 1180 and a tendency to place Yoritomo and a handful of key advisers largely alone in center stage. In fact, Yoritomo was not merely a charismatic figure able to gather support for an attack on the established order by the sheer force of his character. The movement he led had social and economic underpinnings and was fueled by a membership that, upon recognizing its potential in 1180, simply determined to challenge the old order. E. H. Carr has described this phenomenon in general terms:

To set up the popular picture of the individual in revolt against

---

1. Many editions of *Azuma kagami* exist. Page citations will therefore not be included here. (Hereafter cited in text and footnotes as *AK*.)

society is to reintroduce the false antithesis between society and the individual. . . . Revolutionary leaders of new movements owe their role in history to the mass of their followers, and are significant as social phenomena or not at all.[2]

Yoritomo must be seen as just such a figure, the scion of a famous family who emerged in 1180 as the expression of a deeply felt resentment against a political and economic system too long dominated by the court in Kyoto.

The Minamoto story, then, is intimately related to the nature of local government in eastern Japan and to the condition of the military families upon which the provincial system depended. Inasmuch as Yoritomo was formally designated as a rebel and enemy of the court in 1180, his unexpectedly rapid drive to power would be realized almost entirely through his private capacity as chief of a coalition of these elite warrior houses. Who these military families were and where their sources of power lay must therefore be our initial inquiry.

One of the difficulties of the Heishi organizational attempts in central and western Japan was that the provincial military units there were either too small to be of any consequence or too resistant to the advances of the governor agents (*mokudai*) sent out from the capital. In the east, to the contrary, there were large permanent garrisons centered in the provincial headquarters, seemingly just waiting to be coordinated by a private chieftain of sufficient stature. A major reason for this is that the provinces of the east probably at no point during the long Heian period were ever placed as fully under central control as those to the west. Families of local prominence were much more apt to maintain a semi-independent influence in their home areas. This condition was then compounded by a rising tide of lawlessness and resistance to public authority that ultimately forced each of the respective provincial offices (*kokuga*) to request permission to arm itself.[3]

2. E. H. Carr, *What Is History* (New York, 1965), p. 65. Carr continues, "Every society is an arena of social conflicts, and those individuals who range themselves against existing authority are no less products and reflexions of the society than those who upheld. . . . To describe Wat Tyler and Pugachev as individuals in revolt against society is a misleading simplification. If they had been merely that, the historian would never have heard of them."

3. The story of eastern semi-independence can be traced back to the difficulties

In the ninth and tenth centuries there thus emerged the three
well-known provincial enforcement posts of *kebiishi, tsuibushi,* and
ōryōshi. The first, which might be translated as "police captain," was
a permanent position with assignments made at the upper administrative levels. For example, kebiishi were appointed to each of the
districts (*gun*) within Musashi and Ise provinces.[4] The latter two
titles, both constableships, were conceived somewhat differently.
The earliest appointments were made only for the duration of emergencies.[5] The important point, however, is that the persons receiving
all three titles were provincial officials of the very highest rank. This
contributed to a portentous development. As nominally civilian
bureaucrats came increasingly to double as provincial military commanders, the original subordination of military office and status
under the imperial system began to unravel. Holders of vice-gover-
norships and similar titles were now permitted—indeed authorized
in the name of public peacekeeping—to recruit and attach to their
garrison local persons of military disposition and ability. By the
eleventh century the leadership group had taken up permanent do-
micile in the countryside and gained recognition as a distinctive
warrior elite. As a class, they were now called *zaichōkanjin*, resident
public officers.

It is essential to understand that these captains of provincial
society were not immediately a subversive element. They were not
Japan's answer to Europe's barbarian invaders. Indeed, a kind of
balance (or even partnership) was struck between titular governors,
who invariably remained in the capital, and this new class of resident

---

encountered in establishing court authority there in the seventh century. See
Inoue Mitsusada, "Ritsuryō taisei no seiritsu," *Iwanami kōza, Nihon rekishi 3,
kodai 3* (Tokyo, 1962), pp. 20 ff. Local interests had from the outset to be
accommodated. We should note, however, that the east vs. west dichotomy was
never absolute. E.g., the first three kokuga to "militarize" were not in the east
at all; they were in Nagato, Izumo, and Hōki, where, during the 860s, unchecked
piracy was making a shambles of local security. See Yoshimura Shigeki, *Kokushi
seido hōkai ni kansuru kenkyū* (Tokyo, 1957), pp. 666–67. Nevertheless, unlike in
the east where the arming of the kokuga merely exemplified the arming of the
larger society, in many parts of the west there was not a similarly regionwide
emergence of *bushi* (armed warriors).

4. Yoshimura, *Kokushi seido*, pp. 667–68. In other instances, there was but a
single kebiishi for the whole province.

5. This did not last. Both offices tended toward greater permanence, and some
became hereditary.

provincial officials. Governors came to seek from their provinces a secure flow of "public" revenues in place of a close, day-by-day control of administration.[6] Zaichōkanjin were willing to provide that income in return for recurrent investiture of centrally delegated titles and the freedom to turn local authority to private gain. The steady increase of village-level administrative units (*gō*) is a clear example of this. On their own initiative, resident officials would seek to acquire village headships (*gōshi shiki*) in return for which they would pay certain taxes. Higher authority in the capital had little involvement in the planning or execution of such projects.[7]

Thus the greatest warriors in the land had much to gain by working within the system. To have turned against the Heian polity would have been to undercut a major prop of their own provincial dominance. At the same time, discontinuities existed to augur ill for the future; the balance of interests was not always in harmony. A prime illustration of this is the misunderstandings that occurred between governors, whose tenures were short, and resident officials, whose titles and interests in land were fast becoming permanent. On the one hand, the jurisdictional leverage of governors sometimes led to power displays and dismissals of subordinates without apparent cause (see pp. 49–50). On the other side, the threat of such action emboldened public officials to breach their "contracts" with the center. Withholding income deliveries, or, more indirectly, commending public domain to a central estate-holder, were both common results.[8]

What is important to recognize is that the provincial system during Heian times never succeeded in disengaging itself from control by the center. Provincial warriors could not lawfully exceed their local spheres of activity since authority over land had to be shared

6. This does not mean that Kyoto simply abandoned all concern with provincial governance. The relative abundance of surviving documents both to and from the capital makes clear that governorships—despite the popular designation, *zuryō*, or "tax managers"—were not merely receptacles for income.

7. Toyoda Takeshi, *Bushidan to sonraku* (Tokyo, 1968), pp. 3–4.

8. For the governor of Echizen reproaching zaichōkanjin for levy seizures see *Daigo Zōjiki*, 1138/11/28 Echizen kokushi chōsen an, in *HI*, 5: 2023, doc. 2400. The governor here was acting on behalf of a shōen owner (the imperial house), who was probably his patron. Public-officer commendations survive in some numbers, e.g., that of the Chiba to Ise Shrine (see p. 48).

with those at court. It is within such a context that the "rise of the warrior" took place. Central and local remained essentially joined during the long incubation period of the Japanese fighting class.

Marc Bloch has stated with respect to Europe, "The most striking feature of the dominant families in the first feudal age is the shortness of their pedigrees."[9] As we have just seen, this stands in sharp contrast to the experience in Japan. Both the Seiwa branch of the Genji and most local officer families could trace their lineages back to noble origins in Kyoto. But the main Seiwa line had special advantages. Like its Ise Taira counterpart, the Seiwa could boast of a direct imperial family descent, whereas even the most exalted of the eastern province officer families of the eleventh and twelfth centuries were no more than offshoots—often fairly remote—of these Genji and Heishi trunk lines.[10] Similarly, whereas the Minamoto continued during this period to enjoy a succession of governor posts and/or Kyoto offices, local official families came to be identified with only single provinces. While a house of the latter type might have received its initial introduction to a province at the governor level, the titles it came to hold in heredity were invariably less exalted; to the Minamoto, Taira, or other middle-level nobles went the posts of governor (*kami*). Finally, while the Genji occasionally became recipients of unrelated commended land and supraprovincial peacekeeping responsibilities, provincial families enjoyed neither of these distinctions. Instead, they remained junior partners in central–local landholding arrangements and served as objects of recruitment under Minamoto command.

These distinctions between the Genji and the families who came to comprise Yoritomo's vassalage system can be viewed historically. We start with the careers of two of the most famous of all Minamoto chieftains, the late-eleventh-century Yoriyoshi and his son Yoshiie. In what was essentially a military campaign inspired by the Heian court, Minamoto Yoriyoshi was invested with the titles of governor

9. Bloch, *Feudal Society*, p. 284.

10. This branching can be best understood by examining both the Taira and Minamoto clans genealogically. A clear, streamlined version of the main branches can be found in Ōmori, *Buke*, I:412–21. For more detailed charts see Toyoda Takeshi et al., eds., *Dokushi sōran* (Tokyo, 1966), pp. 253 ff.

of Mutsu Province and "pacification general," and then ordered to bring the warlike families of northern Japan to heel. While Yoriyoshi in the resulting Former Nine Years War led numerous eastern warriors into battle, the initial recruitment order had been by Kyoto writ. In its original conception, therefore, the Genji leader's army was an imperial force with Yoriyoshi as its commander. The number of warrior units answering the call to arms from a feeling of personal loyalty to Yoriyoshi is believed to have been quite small.[11]

The creation of Japan's first regional vassalage system was an achievement of Yoriyoshi's son and heir, Yoshiie.[12] As a result of both the sustained mobilization of warrior families under Yoriyoshi and the decision by Yoshiie in the mid-1080s to wage a largely private campaign for mastery of the north, the component units under the latter's command came to be thought of (and to think of themselves) as housemen (ke'nin) of the Genji. The tie, however, was not enduring; Yoshiie's leading private forces into battle did not wholly dilute his fundamental role as a central noble.[13] Moreover, while the existence of a Genji corps of vassals during the final decades of the eleventh century was no doubt real enough, the passage of Yoshiie from the scene led to a rapid disintegration of a ke'nin system that as yet lacked a permanent bond. Inasmuch as each of the component warrior families had its own base area and had developed independently, the mutual rivalries of the past quickly resurfaced as individual bushi groups (bushidan) placed their own interests and integration ahead of those of any larger Genji combination. In the absence

11. Yasuda Genkyū, Bushidan (Tokyo, 1964), pp. 64–65. This is despite a literary account (the Mutsu waki) to the contrary.

12. Yasuda, Bushidan, pp. 51–63, discusses the inappropriateness of the label "vassal group" for the military units involved in earlier outbreaks of rebellion or lawlessness. Thus, for instance, military organization in both the Taira Masakado rebellion of 935–41 and Taira Tadatsune outburst of 1028–31 is considered as a "traditional" type: recruitment was by way of military units attached to provincial offices or by forced conscription of independent farmer families. Not all scholars agree with this view, e.g., Takeuchi, "Heishi shojōken," p. 5. While rejecting the traditional theory that Taira Masakado was Japan's first "feudal" chieftain of consequence, Takeuchi maintains that Masakado's opponent, Taira Sadamori, does deserve this distinction.

13. He eventually came to achieve the senior fourth rank, lower grade, an accomplishment that placed him just outside the highest nobility. Yasuda Genkyū, Minamoto Yoshiie (Tokyo, 1966), p. 196.

of dynamic leadership and the opportunity to fight side by side and then be rewarded as in northern Japan, all chance to perpetuate a viable Genji union was lost.

The court's issuance of decrees in 1091 and 1092 outlawing Minamoto receipt of commendations and establishment of shōen raises the question of whether Yoshiie had used this acceptance of lands as a primary basis for his vassalage system.[14] In other words, did the men enrolling as Yoshiie's vassals also become his tenants? Several considerations are relevant here. In the first place, the two prohibition orders seem to have been aimed less at Yoshiie's growing military strength than at his rise on the economic scale and the creation of technically unqualified shōen. The court saw its objective in terms of snuffing out a dangerous new precedent—the warrior leader who could also function as an independent "central proprietor."[15] Second, the basic motivation behind commendation to a nonresident figure like Yoshiie seems roughly akin to endowment acts directed at other nobles. Commending families—the extant documentation refers only to "farmers" (*hyakushō*)—would appear to have been seeking economic security from provincial tax collectors not membership in a military coalition. Finally, surviving records concerning Genji vassal houses suggest that the homelands of these warriors were either still in the public sector or in shōen holdings of proprietors such as the Fujiwara or (especially) Ise Shrine. We may conclude from this that Yoshiie's possession of commended land-shōen was only temporary and that very few of his vassals resided on new Minamoto proprietorships.[16]

A close examination of the condition of the Genji in the east at

14. The decrees are reproduced in Yasuda, *Bushidan*, pp. 134–35.

15. Professor Fujiki attributes to Yoshiie a fundamental desire to elevate his lineage to full stature as a *kemmon seika*. Fujiki Kunihiko, *Nihon zenshi 3, kodai 2* (Tokyo, 1959), pp. 261–62. Kemmon seika was the designation used for high noble families and central religious institutions, those qualified to possess shōen as proprietors (*ryōke*).

16. Yoritomo, in contrast to Yoshiie, clearly used the promise of economic protection as a means to win vassals. Whereas Yoshiie had seemingly sought wealth before men, Yoritomo neatly reversed this. For more on the debate over the quality of Seiwa Genji landholdings during the eleventh and twelfth centuries, see Yasuda Genkyū, "Kodai makki ni okeru Kantō bushidan," *Nihon hōkensei seiritsu no shozentei* (Tokyo, 1960), pp. 23–26. (Hereafter cited as Yasuda, "Kodai makki.")

the time of the Hōgen and Heiji disturbances will illustrate further
the "military–noble" dualism that would be part of Yoritomo's
inheritance a generation later. To understand the nature of the Minamoto military alliance in the mid-twelfth century, it is necessary to
amplify somewhat on the warrior band, or bushidan, concept. The
term itself was given the broadest usage: there were bushidan consisting of only single family collectives, as well as provincewide
combinations centering on one of the great public-officer houses.
In most cases, however, there remained a core identification with the
founding family, normally a lineage that had opened to cultivation
the lands on which its extended membership now stood as the
dominant force. In those instances in which such families commended
their holdings to a central proprietor, they normally became the
military locus of the shōen resulting from their act. Smaller families,
whether actually related or not, were compelled to identify with the
shōen-wide bushidan of this dominant warrior house. On the other
hand, the warrior groups forming in the vast tracts of land that remained technically public were more apt to be absorbed by hereditary
district officers (gunji) or by the major provincial office function-
aries.[17]

Internally, most bushidan demonstrated little mutuality between
the chieftain and his "kinsmen vassals"; the family head (in other
words, the bushidan leader) exercised a more peremptory control
over housemen than did his German war-band counterpart. In the
former case, superior prestige stood as the prime requisite for leadership; in the latter instance, companions shared equal status. Moreover, the familial aspect of the relationship in Japan clearly outweighed any feudal considerations: during Heian times a true
beneficiary system—economic benefits in return for loyal service—
developed only very slowly. As long as the patriarch remained in
close physical proximity to his membership, there was simply little
incentive to raise expectations by promising rewards. But in fact no
single pattern ever prevailed. For instance, on those occasions when
(for whatever reason) a chieftain's authority was preempted by a
cooperative arrangement between coequal branches, a different kind

17. The clearest exposition on early bushidan development is Yasuda, *Bushidan*, pp. 13–141.

of alliance appeared, called *tō*, or leagues. These warrior groupings were, in effect, bands of virtually independent bushidan who, by virtue of a common ancestry, fought when necessary as a collective force.

We should attempt to picture, therefore, an eastern Japan in the mid-twelfth century composed at the highest social level of bushidan of various shapes and sizes. Into this milieu came Minamoto Yoshitomo, who as first son of the Seiwa Genji scion, Tameyoshi, abandoned the capital in the period after 1140 and took up residence in eastern Japan's Sagami Province. His immediate objective was to revive the Genji union, in disarray since the time of his great-grandfather, Yoshiie. The obstacles Yoshitomo encountered and the techniques he was compelled to use will tell us much about the provinces in which his son, Yoritomo, would come to build his alliance after 1180.

Of primary significance is the fact that although the alliance fashioned by Yoshitomo extended in a highly irregular pattern over large sections of the east, the heartland region from which he drew his support consisted of only four provinces, Sagami, Musashi, Shimōsa and Kazusa. Sagami, which had earlier enjoyed a close association with Minamoto Yoshiie, had now to be resubordinated by Yoshitomo after several decades of relative inattention. Many of the erstwhile Minamoto ke'nin fell quietly into line but others apparently did not. For example, in 1144, Yoshitomo, leading a military force of more than 1,000 horsemen, is known to have invaded a recalcitrant area in Sagami under the control of a warrior house named Ōba. The Ōba family, as long-time residents of their Sagami homelands, had commended a portion of Sagami's Kōza Gun to Ise Shrine in 1117 while retaining, in typical fashion, the essence of actual local control. Ise became honke while the Ōba chieftain became gesu, or estate manager. Soon thereafter, however, a series of challenges to the new domain's exempt status were initiated by persons within the Sagami provincial office. In order to counteract this effort, the Ōba and Ise found it necessary to travel the full gamut of appeals under the late Heian legal process. Working through a hierarchy of well-placed intermediaries, several Ōba petitions made their way to the pinnacle of authority—the ranking noble counselors at court. Decrees handed down by the latter confirmed the estate's exemption from provincial levies and, indirectly, the validity of the Ōba's status as hereditary administrators.[18]

By the mid-1140s, Yoshitomo's sole recourse was to join with discontented local officers in a blatantly illegal military venture against the Ōba region. His invasion was successful, but the resulting legal test was easily won by the Ōba. Appealing anew to higher authority, the Ōba gained a series of condemnations of Yoshitomo and once more were restored to their hereditary estate position.[19] The story does not end there, however. For unexplained reasons, the family's humiliation in 1144 did not prevent the Ōba heir from joining with Yoshitomo twelve years later in the Hōgen encounter.[20] It was only in 1180 that the Ōba leaders showed they had not forgot their dispossession a generation earlier. The chieftain of that house spurned Yoritomo and initially cast in his lot with the Heishi (*AK* 1180/8/23, 9/3, etc.).

More typical of the bushidan in Sagami was the Yamanouchi of Kamakura District; with less apparent friction, it aligned itself with Yoshitomo. As lawfully recognized local possessors by virtue of a commendation of traditionally held land to a central institution, the Yamanouchi had become the dominant influence in the resulting Yamanouchi Estate, centering on the modern Kamakura city. Inasmuch as Yoshitomo chose to make his own headquarters in this district, the Yamanouchi, a small bushidan, quickly fell under his sway.[21]

Yoshitomo, however, did not restrict his attention to shōen-type bushidan such as the Ōba and Yamanouchi. Construction of a provincewide system necessitated the parallel submission of the larger bushidan, which had grown up around provincial officer lineages. In this category fall the Miura family of later Kamakura period fame. It is noteworthy that this house, which joined Yoshitomo in the 1144

18. *Ōba Mikuriya Komonjo*, 1134/int.12/23 Sagami kokushi ge an, in *HI*, 5:1957, doc. 2312; and 1141/6, in *HI*, 5:2054–55, doc. 2245.

19. Ibid., 1145/2/3 Kan senshi an, in *HI*, 6:2145–46, doc. 2544, and 6:2146–50, docs. 2545–48. For further details on the Ōba and Yoshitomo see Nishioka Toranosuke, *Shōen shi no kenkyū*, (Tokyo, 1966), 2:639–46.

20. Ōmori, *Buke*, 1:425.

21. Yasuda, *Bushidan*, p. 94.

assault on the Ōba domain, was itself ranged on both sides of the public–private land and title ledger. In addition to a homeland region that had been converted into a "centrally owned" estate (Miura-no-shō), the family exercised a provincewide policing authority (*ken-danken*) and a responsibility for general tribute and tax collection. The Miura were honored additionally with hereditary possession of the assistant governor title (*suke*). And yet, while the Miura were obviously at a level of authority far above that of the Ōba and Yamanouchi, they were never able, on the model of two or three public-officer families in other provinces, to construct a province-wide hegemony in Sagami. For Yoshitomo, this meant that instead of having to work *through* the Miura to establish a level of control over the various bushidan of Sagami, he would be in a position to serve as the center of an integrated alliance in which the separate warrior chieftains would participate individually as his own ke'nin.[22]

When we turn to Musashi Province we find an important variation of the Sagami integrated alliance pattern. In Musashi there had come to exist a complex of bushidan leagues on the tō model discussed above. In the absence of a dominant chieftain (*sōryō*) through whom Yoshitomo could work, the Genji leader enrolled as his personal vassals the separate bushidan leaders from within the various Musashi warrior leagues.

In Shimōsa and Kazusa we find that a wholly different set of circumstances confronted Yoshitomo. At some earlier date a single local officer family (an offshoot of the Taira) had divided into two parts and taken up separate residence in these two provinces. The resulting Chiba and Kazusa houses each came to possess high-level provincial titles, and each was ultimately able to fashion a bushidan alliance whose contours roughly coincided with the boundaries of their respective provinces. Although the means used by Yoshitomo to win the support of the Kazusa remain moot, it is highly revealing that in the case of the Chiba, Yoshitomo used his superior status to establish a claim to homeland regions belonging traditionally to Tsunetane, the Chiba leader. Further details of this episode will be related shortly. For now, it is only important to note that Yoshito-mo, in order to gain control over the combined bushidan strength

22. Ibid., pp. 96–97.

of both Shimōsa and Kazusa, was obviously compelled to work from the top through the two major scions there, Tsunetane and the Kazusa chieftain, Hirotsune.[23]

By these various methods Yoshitomo ultimately gained control of four provinces. But there were other provinces in the vicinity of Sagami, his base area. Why, it might be asked, did Yoshitomo fail to spread his influence throughout the entire Kantō region? One obvious reason appears to have been his decision at some point during the late 1140s to return to the capital, evidently to give attention to that neglected part of his career.[24] He thus absented himself at least temporarily from the east. An even greater obstacle to Yoshitomo's expansion would seem to have been the pretensions of other Genji branches that they, and not Yoshitomo, were the legitimate spokesmen for the Minamoto in their respective provinces. In Hitachi, for example, both the Satake and Shida proved strong enough to resist subordination by the Yoshitomo line of the Minamoto until 1180–81, when Yoritomo simply invaded that province and destroyed these reluctant kinsmen.[25] The conditions in Shimotsuke and Kōzuke are even more interesting. Yoshikuni, one of the sons of Minamoto Yoshiie, settled in Shimotsuke in the early twelfth century and came to exercise great influence there. Upon his death in 1155 on the eve of the Hōgen Disturbance, Yoshikuni's line divided into two branches. It is possible that even before this development, his first son, Yoshishige, had already moved into Nitta Gun of neighboring Kōzuke Province. This would have made him a contemporary and likely competitor of Yoshitomo.[26] Once

23. Yasuda, *Bushidan*, pp. 99–100. A generation later we will find Yoritomo moving to depose this same Hirotsune as the only means of making direct contact with Kazusa Province's component warrior units.

24. Actually, we do find scattered representation from other provinces. For lists of the known warriors who joined with Yoshitomo in the 1156 Hōgen fighting see Ōmori, *Buke*, 1:424–26, and Yasuda, "Kodai makki," pp. 38–39, n. 4. In addition to the four major provinces, others represented in this list are Ōmi, Owari, Izu, Awa, and Shimotsuke. For a discussion of the evidence—mostly circumstantial—regarding Yoshitomo's physical whereabouts, see ibid., p. 31.

25. See Yasuda, "Kodai makki," pp. 33–34, 40, for the rise of the Satake and Shida in Hitachi.

26. Ibid., p. 35.

there, he either inherited from his mother's side an already established private domain, or supervised the opening and then commendation (to the regent's line of the Fujiwara) of a new estate. Whatever the actual case, it is known positively that in 1157 Yoshishige was appointed gesu (manager) of Nitta-no-shō, adopting as his surname the name of the district he now came to dominate.[27] In a parallel move, Yoshikuni's second son, Yoshiyasu, inherited his father's base area of Ashikaga-no-shō in Ashikaga Gun, Shimotsuke, as well as another holding in the same province.[28] We see in these sequences the origins of the famous Nitta and Ashikaga families who would play a major role almost two centuries later in the destruction of the Kamakura bakufu.

The significance of these Seiwa Genji branches for Yoshitomo was that there existed in the 1150s Minamoto collaterals that, if they could not claim to represent the main line of that illustrious house, could at least marshal a sufficient prestige to win local converts and stand aloof from Yoshitomo's efforts at subordination.[29] This was especially true of Ashikaga Yoshiyasu, who possessed, in addition to his expanding bushidan in Shimotsuke, both a membership in the In's guards and the important title of police captain (kebiishi) for the capital city. Thus, in the Hōgen skirmish, while Yoshitomo led a force of some 200 troops on behalf of the emperor's faction, Ashikaga Yoshiyasu fought on the same side but as the independent commander of 100 of his own mounted warriors.[30]

The picture in Shimotsuke was further complicated by the presence of a fully distinct family using the same Ashikaga surname. Descended from the Fujiwara and based in the same Ashikaga Gun, this second house became a bitter rival of the Minamoto Ashikaga. A final complication in Shimotsuke was the existence of a provincial official family, the Koyama, which was the main line from which

27. This investiture document appears in *Masaki Monjo*, 1157/3/8 Saemon no kami ke mandokoro kudashibumi, in Kōzuke kenykūkai, comp., *Masaki komonjo* (Maebashi, 1938), p. 15. For the debate over Yoshitomo's initial contact with this area, see Nishioka, *Shōen*, 2:617.

28. Yasuda, "Kodai makki," p. 35.

29. Minamoto Yoritomo, as we shall see, would spend virtually the entire decade of the 1180s in an effort to bring to heel such Genji collaterals.

30. Nishioka, *Shōen*, 2:623.

the Fujiwara-related Ashikaga had earlier broken off. Since the Koyama made the competition for hegemony over Shimotsuke a three-sided affair, such internecine struggle made that province a poor prospect for any uniform take-over by Yoshitomo. Even the latter's tenure as Shimotsuke governor during the mid-1150s appears to have had no noticeable effect.[31]

In addition to the mixed reception that Yoshitomo's efforts encountered in Shimotsuke, it will be helpful also to inquire into the failure of the well-endowed public officer Koyama house to achieve a provincial hegemony. The various assets of this family constitute a fairly impressive list: (1) a long residence in Shimotsuke as evidenced by the Koyama's alleged possession over many generations of the provisional assistant governor post (*gon no suke*); (2) provincewide enforcement authority in the form of a hereditary constableship (*ōryōshi shiki*); (3) local proprietorship over vast stretches of arable land in the region of the provincial capital; and (4) a sizable bushidan organization[32] On the minus side were the two Ashikaga families—one a recent offshoot of the Seiwa Genji and therefore virtually impossible to subordinate; the other, one of its own branches, which happened to be in possession of land tracts rivaling those of the main line itself. The Koyama's emergence as the dominant house in Shimotsuke would therefore have to await the outbreak of the Gempei War and early alliance with Yoritomo.

The fact that Minamoto Yoshitomo did not construct a vassalage system extending comprehensively over more than just a handful of provinces can thus be attributed to divisions among the localized

31. It is known that Yoshitomo's main rival in the capital, his father Tameyoshi, possessed at least several ke'nin of his own in Shimotsuke. A pair of shōen officers in a Fujiwara-owned domain in Shimotsuke are recorded as having been vassals of Tameyoshi. Fujiki, *Nihon zenshi*, 3:254. A document of 1153 is signed "Shimotsuke governor Yoshitomo." *Sonkeikaku Zō Buke Tekagami*, 1153/8/27 Minamoto Yoshitomo ukebumi, in *HI*, 10:3885, doc. 5023. A record of 1161 refers to the recently deceased Yoshitomo as the "former Shimotsuke governor." *Ichiki Monjo*, 1161/1 Minamoto Yoshimune kishinjō an, in *HI*, 7:2514–15, doc. 3121. The precise dates of Yoshitomo's Shimotsuke governorship do not seem to be known.

32. Ishii Susumu, "Kamakura bakufu ron," in *Iwanami kōza, Nihon rekishi 5, chūsei 1* (Tokyo, 1962), pp. 93–94. (Hereafter cited as Ishii S., "Bakufu ron.")

Genji branches as well as to other competing warrior houses. But even more, families in the east simply had not yet discerned that Kyoto's estate-holders might be vulnerable to a united warrior front. Bushidan in the Kantō were still ranged primarily against one another.[33] To a certain limited extent alliance with the "military–noble" Yoshitomo had taken these houses farther, providing at least a foretaste of regional coalescence. But it is doubtful whether the enrolling families or Yoshitomo himself had more than the dimmest awareness that organization of this type held great potential. The day had not yet come when families in the east would be choosing to play for higher stakes, seeking under the Genji umbrella a protection against the capital city itself.

The issue that would eventually push the eastern military houses to see Kyoto as an obstacle was, of course, already evident; it was a matter of land and land rights. The authority to make judicial settlements concerning land, confirm inheritances, invest local managers, and perform other executive functions remained with centrally based absentee interests. In other words, despite Kyoto's visibly declining capacity to enforce its decisions, the decisions themselves, or rather, their resulting documentation, were still considered indispensable.[34] This meant that the exercise of power without authority—such as Yoshitomo's effort in 1144 against the Ōba Estate—rarely led to more than temporary gains. Herein lay the fundamental weakness of even the most influential bushidan leaders. Without a direct channel to some ranking patron in the capital, a Kantō chief had no hope of providing his men with anything more than their physical security By himself, he was unable to guarantee their lands. An adequate level of local land legitimation, normally meaning the power to block governors, was reserved for those whose writs of

33. E.g., an 1172 dispute over Kōzuke Province's Sonoda Estate between Nitta Yoshishige (from neighboring Nitta-no-shō) and the local head of Sonoda. Nishioka, *Shōen*, 2:620.

34. Thus in the Sonoda case referred to in n. 33 the local chief of this Ise Shrine estate petitioned the court through Ise for a judgment against Nitta Yoshishige's violations. While it is not known whether the imperial state council, which ultimately assumed jurisdiction in the matter, ever succeeded in bringing the two sides to Kyoto, a victory for the plaintiff is assumed, and with it a quashing of the Nitta's effort at local aggrandizement. Ibid.

investiture and exemption would exceed in authority the tax assessments of provincial magistrates. We see here the basic rationale for land commendations to the center.

It should be realized, then, that initially this endowment relationship between prominent local landholders (*ryōshu*) and central proprietary receivers was of distinct advantage to the former. The transaction, involving incorporation of commended areas as shōen held by new central owners (*ryōke*), provided the most effective means by which local families might detach homelands from governor office purview. On the other hand, donors might pay a considerable price for such release; a change in status to shōen custodian often left them vulnerable to the willful use of executive powers by ryōke.[35] Nevertheless, at least in the short run, these newly appointed managers of shōen acquired relief from provincial levies and entrance and enhanced dominion over estate residents.

Evidence of both these post-commendation benefits exists in some abundance. For the former, we refer once again to the homeland region of the Ashikaga branch of the Genji, Shimotsuke Province's Ashikaga Estate. This domain is believed to have received its formal incorporation in 1142, just at the time that Yoshitomo was beginning his activities in the Kantō.[36] Commendation had been to Anrakujuin, an In-controlled central chapel whose patronage could be expected to yield protection of a high order. A pair of documents from the 1150s reveals the vaule of such support in actual practice. The first is an In's office decree of early 1156, addressed to the local managers of all Anrakujuin shōen. These managers are advised to pass on any information regarding violations by governors or their agents; a prohibitory judgment would quickly follow. At this very time the governor of Shimotsuke was none other than Minamoto Yoshitomo, Ashikaga Yoshiyasu's rival for influence in that province.[37] The second document is an 1159 imperial state council decree, Kyoto's most prestigious edict, granting to various itemized

35. These powers (listed on p. 45) could be so abused as to lead to an actual dispossession of an original commender. This is what happened to the great Chiba family of Shimōsa. See pp. 48–53.

36. Nishioka, *Shōen*, 2:629.

37. *Anrakujuin Komonjo*, 1156/3 Toba In-no-chō kudashibumi, in *HI*, 6:2341, doc. 2834. For a reference to Yoshitomo's governorship see *Heihanki*, 1156/7/5, reproduced in Ōmori, *Buke*, 1:385.

Anrakujuin shōen (of which Ashikaga-no-shō is specified as one) an immunity from interference by governors and other state agencies.[38]

Concerning the enhancement of authority over local dwellers, comparison can be made to the condition of such persons before and after establishment of a shōen. As long as these people remained resident on lands that were technically public, the governor retained some level of jurisdiction over them. Governor and ryōshu regularly clashed on this issue, as both sides hoped to dominate peasant labor and resources. All this normally changed after a region became shōen. The warrior commender, now with his local possessory rights clarified, might henceforth be able to impose on tenant dwellers his own "rental" levies (*kajishi*).[39] Shōen administration, tax collection, and the opportunity to convert the workers of the land into a servile population were the hoped-for rewards of commendation to Kyoto.

This pattern was, of course, not universal in eastern Japan. Indeed, the region's geographical remoteness, reputation for instability, and relative underpopulation actually worked to inhibit central enthusiasm for incorporating shōen there. For provincial landholders also, it was often more advantageous simply to retain key domains in a public land form. But shōen establishment did continue to grow, showing that when circumstances were right, the reciprocal acts of commendation upward and immunity granted downward could serve an important initial purpose for warriors.[40] Both sides profited from this central–local partitioning of authority, function, and revenues.

Troubles in the system, however, were never far below the surface.

38. *Anrakujuin Komonjo*, 1159/9/29 Dajōkan chō an, in *HI*, 6:2470–71, 3029.

39. This arrangement is spelled out in a commendation document of 1146. See *Ichiki Monjo*, 1146/8/10 Shimōsa no kuni Taira Tsunetane kishinjō, in *HI*, 6:2187–88, doc. 2586. For a treatment of "land rent" and other aspects of commendation, see Uchida Minoru, "Heian makki ryōshusei kenkyū no isshiten—shiryōshu to shōen ryōshu to no kankei," *Rekishigaku kenkyū* 233 (1959): 46–49.

40. F. W. Maitland, *The Constitutional History of England* (London, 1963), pp. 149–50, has admirably described this unevenness between patterns of landholding and systems of protection (relevant to England): "Commendation meant different things in different cases. . . . No legislation had turned the smaller owners into tenants of other men's lands or even compelled them to have lords—the change had been brought about by the private acts of individuals and the result . . . is intricate and confused."

Commendation and shōen incorporation not only failed at times to prevent governor agent entrances and tax assessments, but failed as well to continue to satisfy. We see this most clearly in the case of the Chiba house. The succession of buffetings absorbed by this great family provides a fitting backdrop for 1180. A land guarantee system so disdainful of power realities could hardly survive indefinitely.

The Chiba, at one with the great public-officer families of the east, held a large portfolio of local administrative titles and the land rights associated with them.[41] Yet the Chiba's history shows that it was constantly obliged to seek prestigious connections with a central proprietor. Our earliest reference is to Shimōsa Province's Soma District, which was passed in heredity in 1126/6 to the new Chiba family scion, Tsuneshige. Soma, held by the Chiba for some six generations, had gained exemption from provincial levies (*kokuya-ku*) due to the efforts of Tsuneshige's uncle, who in addition to having assumed the district chieftainship himself had made Tsune-shige his adopted son. In 1126/10 Tsuneshige's own inheritance (as well, presumably, as Soma District's newly exempt status) was given legal confirmation by the office of the governor.[42]

Unfortunately, we do not know precisely what prompted the next move, but in 1130 the Chiba leader took the customary step of commending a major share of his family's heritage to a central lord, in this case, Ise Shrine. Three copies of Tsuneshige's statement of alienation were forwarded to Ise for countersignature; one was retained on permanent deposit and the other two were sent on to the new "operating proprietor," shrine officer (*kannushi*) gon negi Arakida Enmei. It was stipulated that Enmei would receive the estate's annual tax payments. On the next level was a "supervisor"

41. For the Chiba genealogy and data regarding the family's various titles, see Takeuchi Rizō, "Zaichōkanjin no bushika," *Nihon hōkensei seiritsu no kenkyū* (Tokyo, 1955), p. 32.

42. All this information is drawn from *Ichiki Monjo*, 1146/8/10 Shimōsa no kuni Taira (Chiba) Tsunetane kishinjō, in *HI*, 6:2187–88, doc. 2586. The Ichiki document collection appears in consecutive arrangement in Nishigaki Seiji, comp., "Kaburaya Ise Hōki," *Tōkyō gakugeidai fuzoku hō kenkyū kiyō*, vols. 4 and 5 (1966 and 1967). This particular document, which is the collection's most important record, is in 4:19, doc. 7.

(azukari dokoro), a certain Minamoto Tomosada who is not further identified. Finally, beneath Tomosada was the original commender, Chiba Tsuneshige, who was to receive both investiture as gesu and recognition of his right to extract "land rent" (kajishi) from the domain's local residents. The shiki titles at all levels were designated as being permanent and hereditary for their recipient families. The entire transaction was then given official approval by the governor: a decree of 1130/12 recognized Tsuneshige's local managership (gesu shiki) over Soma Estate, while also acknowledging the Chiba head's ongoing chieftainship (gunji) over Soma District.[43]

The question of motivation for Tsuneshige's 1130 act is unclear. Certainly more was at stake than his avowals of piety[44] and his expressed wish to promote greater shrine prosperity (see note 43). Inasmuch as the governor's office had given its willing approval to the entire transaction, there was no reason to perceive danger from that quarter. (Within a few years, however, this would change.) The most likely goal for Tsuneshige—aside from solidifying his control over local residents—was a desire to freeze the inheritance within his own line. A rivalry would soon develop between Tsuneshige's son and his adoptive father's true son, Tsunezumi.

An event of five years later suggests that this was indeed Tsuneshige's motive. In 1135, just nine years after Tsuneshige's own inheritance, he passed his managership over Soma Estate to his lineal son, Tsunetane.[45] But this entire protective effort proved ineffective when, without warning in mid-1136, the new Shimōsa governor acted to void the commendation release granted by his predecessor six years earlier. Claiming that taxes had been withheld from "public fields," he proceeded to place Tsuneshige under arrest. A fine was imposed some days later, with the governor's deputy's (mokudai) arranging also for the assignment over to his chief of

43. *Ichiki Monjo*, 1130/6/11 Taira (Chiba) Tsuneshige kishinjō an, in *HI*, 5: 1871–72, docs. 2161–62, and 1130/12 Shimōsa no kuni chōsen an, doc. 2176, p. 1879.
44. Referred to in ibid., 1146/8/10 Taira (Chiba) Tsuneshige kishinjō, 6:2187–88, doc. 2586.
45. Ibid. The title that was transferred is referred to here as *jinushi*, an equivalent of gesu.

two unit areas within Soma. Tsuneshige and his son were forced
to put all of this in writing.[46]

What happened over the next few years is not known, but it was
during this general ebb period for the Chiba that Minamoto Yoshitomo came upon the scene. In 1143, by exploiting the "false words"
(*fugen*) of Tsunetane's rival, Tsunezumi, and by extracting from
Tsuneshige some further documents of release, Yoshitomo was
able to place under his own control the entire Soma area.[47] In 1145,
he even went so far as to commend the region to Ise Shrine and to
receive for himself its gesu post.[48] Where Tsunetane fits into this
new development is unclear, although two conjectures are possible.
Since we know that in 1146 Tsunetane (1) received from the governor's office Soma's gunji post in return for payment of a huge
indemnity and (2) re-commended Soma Estate to Ise, gaining the
gesu post for himself (see note 44), it is evident that this took place
either with or without Yoshitomo's blessing. If the former, we may
assume that in return for Tsuneshige's pledge of vassalage Yoshitomo simply gave up his own gesu claim of the year before; as we
know, Tsunetane fought under Yoshitomo's command in the Hōgen
Disturbance just a decade later.[49] If the latter, we must assume that
Tsunetane, faced with this new competitor for his homelands,
simply bowed to the governor's ransom demands and "bought
back" his family's district headship. As the gunji of record he then
simply ignored Yoshitomo's commendation and gained Ise's acceptance for a gesu title of his own. At some later point the two
rival gesu of Soma Estate made peace, one becoming the follower of
the other.

The terms of Tsunetane's 1146 contract renewal with Ise were
much the same as his father's agreement of sixteen years earlier. The

46. Ibid. There is no indication that Tsuneshige had passed his gunji post to
his son, Tsunetane, in 1135. Hence (perhaps) the governor's decision to move
against the Chiba elder, his nominal subordinate.

47. Described in ibid.

48. *Ichiki Monjo*, 1145/3/11 Minamoto bō kishinjō an, in *HI*, 6:2150–51, doc.
2549. Although the name Yoshitomo does not appear in this document, it does
in the 1146 record cited in n. 44. It is certain that the unnamed "Minamoto"
here was Yoshitomo.

49. Yasuda, "Kodai makki," pp. 38–39, n. 4.

same Arakida Enmei (Masatomi) was made proprietor (ryōshu), with the gesu post and land rent going as before in heredity to Tsunetane and his descendants. The only apparent difference was that the original supervisor's post (azukari dokoro) was now made the permanent possession of an agent sent out by the shrine (see note 44).

Unfortunately, not a single reference survives regarding conditions in Soma during the 1150s. We know only (as mentioned above) that Tsunetane and Yoshitomo fought together as soldier and commander in 1156. In 1160, Yoshitomo was killed in the Heiji Disturbance, thereby sparking a new round of challenges to the Chiba managership. First to join this effort was Minamoto Yoshimune, of unknown origin, who issued a commendation document of his own in 1161, bidding for possession of Soma's deputyship (azukari shiki). Criticizing Tsunetane's "violations" and the general neglect of services to Ise Shrine, he stated that he would defend the estate against the treacherous acts (akugyaku) of followers (rōjū) of the rebel (dai muhonnin) Yoshitomo. The implication, presumably, was that Tsunetane was a Yoshitomo follower. Yoshimune justified his claim by asserting that the Chiba's release documents from 1136 had been passed to him by the son of the governor from that period. To complicate matters still further, his act of commendation was directed to Ise's Outer Shrine (Gaigū), which meant in effect the suggestion of a new candidate for ryōshu.[50] In other words, parallel to the rivalry developing between Tsunetane and Yoshimune, a higher level "proprietor's conflict"—eventually between the Inner and Outer shrines—was also being set in motion. Within a month of Yoshimune's act of commendation, a pair of tax documents shows that it was now he who was performing Soma's managerial duties.[51]

Recognizing this obvious threat, Tsunetane jumped to his own defense. In a legal brief of the same month (1161/2) we see him recounting the history of Chiba possession over Soma and then offering his own service to both the Inner and Outer shrines. In

50. *Ichiki Monjo*, 1161/1 Minamoto Yoshimune kishinjō an, in *HI*, 7:2514–15, doc. 3121.

51. Ibid., 1161/2 Minamoto Yoshimune ukebumi an, docs. 3142–43, p. 2525.

another brief (1161/4) he offered details on how he had lost Soma now for the third time.[52] According to this account, a year before, in the wake of the Yoshitomo "rebellion," the deceased Genji leader's land portfolio had been confiscated by an act of the Shimōsa provincial office. Soma was apparently included, giving rise to a Tsunetane complaint that Yoshitomo had not in fact been Soma's legal holder. This had led to a governor's directive that the province's resident officers (*zaichō*) proceed with an investigation. The order was carried out, but for unknown reasons a judgment could not be reached. At this juncture the case was transferred to Kyoto, where the Minister of the Left conferred with an official of Ise Shrine in a further effort to work out a settlement. A decision was reached to the effect that Soma would be converted into an immune estate, henceforth owing services to both shrines.

The timing and background for this resolution cannot be entirely understood,[53] but it was evidently at this point, as noted above, that Minamoto Yoshimune rushed in to make his commendation offer. He not only bested by one month a similar gesture by Tsunetane (notes 50 and 52), but seems to have sealed his victory by giving special attention to newly assumed financial burdens. As an indication of the enormous leverage exerted by central proprietors under such circumstances, Yoshimune actually increased the rate and bulk of his tax payments between 1161 and 1165.[54] In competition with Chiba Tsunetane for the Soma management authority, Yoshimune had gained Ise's endorsement by posing as the highest bidder.

Further detail is available on the Chiba and their incapacity to

52. Ibid., 1161/2/27 Shimōsa gon no kami Taira (Chiba) Tsunetane ge an, doc. 3139, pp. 2522-23; and 1161/4/1 Shimōsa gon no kami Taira (Chiba) Tsunetane shinjō an, doc. 3148, pp. 2527-28. The other losses were to the Shimōsa governor in 1136 and to Minamoto Yoshitomo in 1143-45.

53. E.g., a document of 1166 seems to offer a somewhat different explanation: the governor himself, after seizing control of Soma in 1160, moved to grant it a public immunity as an estate belonging to the "two" Ise Shrines. He based his action on the release document that had been extracted from the Chiba by his predecessor in the 1130s. Ibid., 1166/6/18 Daijingū gon negi Arakida Akimori kishōmon an, doc. 3395, p. 2674.

54. Compare the figures in ibid., 1166/6/3 Minamoto bō kishōmon an, docs. 3392-94, pp. 2673-74, with those of 1161 cited in n. 51.

hold on to their homelands, but we have seen enough to draw some important conclusions. First, despite an unmistakable rise in local lawlessness, contention over land remained essentially within a legal framework. Documents might be compelled, forged, or stolen, but the mere fact that judgments regarding land possession were based on written records tended to keep the basic hierarchy of interests intact. Second, to the very eve of the Gempei War, the system remained weighted in favor of those at the center, or those with the strongest central connections. Ise was not merely the passive recipient of commended income from land whose executive privilege remained close to the soil, but became instead the final arbiter over which among the contending parties would serve as its representative. By retaining, as did all central holders, a power to legitimize, Ise was able to improve its own financial arrangements while denying with impunity Soma Estate's traditional local owners. Third and last, the Chiba episode proves that a warrior family, no matter how large its bushidan or how impressive its provincial offices, was simply unable under the Heian system to gain immune control over full-sized estates. Local titles were important for a family's rise to local prominence, for its organization of a local following, and for its acquisition of a limited "local possession" over land. Independent local proprietorship in the sense of total immunity and total control was as yet a contradiction in terms.

Under circumstances such as these, a family such as the Chiba had two options open to it in its search for landed security. It could rely on commendation to the center, a decision that might enhance local influence for a time but at the expense of continued submission to the traditional power structure. Or it could search out localized sources of protection such as that afforded by military organization. Neither device, however, provided the Chiba with the degree of land protection that it desired. While the one, commendation, had proved ineffectual against summary dispossession by a governor,[55] the other, bushidan coalescence, simply bypassed the central monopoly of legitimizing privilege entirely. Even the appearance of Yoshitomo in the east and Kiyomori in the west offered little more than a temporary amelioration. For neither figure conceived of any final

55. It can be argued that the Chiba were dispossessed in the early 1160s by the shrine proprietor to whom they had gone for protection a generation earlier.

advancement of his (or his vassals') interests apart from Japan's single locus of authority, the capital city and its institutions.[56]

What therefore must have begun to loom ever larger in the minds of great warriors everywhere was the unbridgeable legal gulf between the limited authority they might aspire to and the level of full proprietorship (and consequent right of local interference) that even the most effete courtier could claim merely by virtue of his noble rank.[57] To make matters worse, a bloc concept of shōen possession was already much in evidence. Increasingly throughout the twelfth century we find central owners issuing single edicts to all their estates, as if these domains had now become uniformly held[58] On the receiving end of such directives were Japan's elite fighting men, proud warriors who were expected to allow their domains to serve as ongoing sources of absentee revenue. Disobedience, as noted, was always possible, but this kind of noncompliance with proprietary demands could easily be self-defeating. Withdrawal of ryōke patronage and the transfer to others of central legitimation meant an end to lawful possession.

As the foregoing clearly reveals, then, the day had not yet come when a thoroughly self-contained provincial authority system would exist to provide fighting men with an *alternative* to dependence on the capital. Not until the 1180s would the bakufu appear with its capacity to guarantee not only lives, as had the older bushidan, but livelihoods deriving from land as well.

With the knowledge of what the Minamoto were ultimately able to do by way of creating an independent military regime after 1180, it is interesting to reflect on why it was the Taira who emerged as victors a generation before them. On the surface the Minamoto might have seemed a more likely choice than the Heishi to have

56. Conditions in pre-feudal Merovingian Europe were quite different. In the words of one scholar, "It was less the judicial order than the distribution of power that determined the structure of institutions" (Walter Schlessinger, "Lord and Follower in Germanic Institutional History," in Frederic L. Cheyette, ed., *Lordship and Community in Medieval Europe* [New York, 1968], p. 84). The Heian polity, by contrast, had become more elastic but was still largely intact.

57. According to Nakada Kaoru, *Shōen no kenkyū*, (Tokyo, 1948), pp. 60–61, possession of a ryōke proprietary shiki required a rank of at least third level on the court scale of eight ranks. It was a distinction that no person from the provinces could remotely hope to obtain.

58. E.g., a document of 1139 shows the In's office issuing a blanket decree to

gained military dominance in the capital. Inasmuch as it was in the east that bushidan construction and dissatisfaction with central interference had proceeded farthest, should not Yoshitomo have been able to best Kiyomori? How did the Taira chieftain succeed in 1160 in eliminating as contenders for power both Yoshitomo, who was killed, and the remainder of the Genji mainline, which was scattered and sent into exile?

The Taira victory in 1160 should be considered within the context of the brevity of their period of ascendancy. In terms of the political realities of the mid-twelfth century it was the Heishi, actually, who enjoyed several key advantages over the Genji. In the first place, from 1153 Kiyomori was the head of a lineage whose greatest single asset became its internal cohesion. By contrast, father and son— Minamoto Tameyoshi and Yoshitomo—fought on opposite sides in the Hōgen Disturbance and thereby irremediably weakened their great family. Locally, this internal division within the Genji is illustrated by the refusal of branch Minamoto lines in the east to submit to Yoshitomo.

Second, the Taira were fighting for Go-Shirakawa, a choice that proved to be a major advantage. Although Kiyomori, as will be recalled, was not apparently rewarded in lands after 1156, he was granted the governorhsip of Harima and the assistant governor-generalship of Kyushu. In contrast, Yoshitomo found that his years in the east and defection from his father had left him largely isolated in the capital. He received no governorships after the Hōgen Disturbance, and indeed may have been divested of the one such office, Shimotsuke, that he did hold. Yoshitomo was forced to content himself with a promotion to the headship of the "Stables of the Left."[59] At court, in other words, his Heishi rival, Kiyomori, gained a clear upper hand.

---

the managers of all imperial estates. An equal amount of land in each domain was to be set aside as payment fields (*kyūden*) for a Buddhist priest. Not only were regular taxes to be paid, but the recipient priests were to have their directives obeyed concerning emergency levies. All managers were to heed this order from the In's chancellery. *Anrakujuin Monjo*, 1139/7/28 Toba Jōō In-no-chō kudashibumi an, in *HI*, 5:2031, doc. 2411.

59. Evidence adduced earlier shows Yoshitomo holding that governorship at least for the period 1153–56. That he was granted no additional governorships is demonstrable from his posthumous appellation of "former governor of Shimotsuke" (see nn. 31 and 37). For his Stables of the Left title, see *Heihanki*, 1156/7/17, quoted in Ōmori, *Buke*, 1:389.

Finally, the struggles of the 1150s in Kyoto were essentially of a political cast despite the fact that they were resolved by force of arms. This suggests that the deeper-running social developments in the east and west were simply irrelevant to the turn of events in the capital in 1156–60. Inasmuch as the forces that fought in the Hōgen and Heiji wars probably numbered fewer than 1,000 men in total, it simply did not matter as yet that the social context in eastern Japan far outstripped that of the west in terms of warrior growth and local resentments.

The brevity of the Taira period of rule can be similarly explained. We have seen that while Kiyomori did seek to organize local families, haphazardly at first and with determination after 1180, his "regime" can in no way be considered "class-oriented." The alliance with the In and the absence of internal disunity under Kiyomori's family headship served as the Taira's major underpinnings. By contrast, in spite of the Minamoto's total eclipse during this period, when revival did come it would develop quickly and be permanent. The Minamoto movement would be buttressed by a clear class identification. Thus, with the passage of a generation, many of the same warriors who had avoided joining with Yoshitomo in the latter's effort to outpace both his father and Taira Kiyomori at court, would now in 1180 support Yoritomo, as a new Genji leader raised entirely fresh goals. The outbreak of the Gempei War would signal a decision on the part of the great eastern bushidan to seize the initiative and establish an independent regime. Here was a movement that the Chiba as well as countless other warrior families could easily identify with. It was only a matter of time before the Kyoto-centered hegemony of the Taira would give way to the Minamoto-led bakufu of eastern Japan and, ultimately, of the country as a whole.[60]

60. Robert Lopez has described this phenomenon in Europe: " . . . to become masters of the West the Franks needed only to find a leader and learn how to obey him" (*The Birth of Europe* [New York, 1967], p. 84).

PART 2:
THE GEMPEI WAR,
1180–1185

3 THE ESTABLISHMENT OF
KAMAKURA POWER

In the wake of the Heiji Disturbance the five surviving sons of
Minamoto Yoshitomo were scattered and sent into exile. The eldest,
thirteen-year-old Yoritomo, was placed under the supervision of a
minor collateral of the Taira, the Hōjō family of Izu Province.
Seventeen years later (1177), Yoritomo was permitted to marry the
daughter of Tokimasa, his Hōjō captor. In hindsight, both of these
decisions proved critical. The Kantō, where Izu was located, was the
future site of the bakufu and the area historically associated with
the Minamoto. And the Hōjō, with whom Yoritomo had now
united, would later emerge as the bakufu's most influential family.
Why, in view of such developments, had the Taira taken steps that
would contribute to their own demise?

Kiyomori's perceptions are at the heart of this issue. In 1160
when he made his decision to exile, Yoshitomo's death and limited
success in the Kantō were both fresh memories. The years that
followed saw nothing to challenge this: the Genji displayed no
political activities at all. In this context, Yoritomo's marriage into a
minor branch of Kiyomori's own clan may well have been considered
a positive development. The Minamoto, now absorbed into the
Taira, would be further neutralized.

The Hōjō background reinforces this view. The absence of reliable
data on Tokimasa's forebears suggests that his family was much
smaller than some warrior houses elsewhere in the Kantō. It is
noteworthy, for example, that while Izu was a proprietary province
of the Taira, its deputy-in-residence was an appointee sent out from
the capital: Tokimasa had not been entrusted with this important

authority[1]. Nor do we know whether his family even had access to the provincial office. The Izu headquarters (kokuga) would have been the normal starting point for military organization. It was in such an environment that the heir to the Genji spent almost a generation. The period 1160–80 was a time of total eclipse for the Minamoto, with no realistic prospects for revival.

A new decade, however, was to bring a new world to Japan. Within several years the Heishi would be gone, the unity of Kyoto's authority permanently shattered, and a new regime—the bakufu— hurrying to pick up the debris of countrywide governance. It is to this fascinating story that we now turn.

The tale begins in 1180/4 with the dissemination of a call to arms against the Heishi by a disaffected prince left out of the imperial succession; Kiyomori's own infant grandson had just ascended the throne as the new emperor, Antoku. We should note, concerning this call, that it took cognizance of the disarray within the Minamoto camp: it was directed not just to the Genji of the eastern circuits, but to all warrior bands (*gumpei*) in the east, as well as to anti-Taira temples such as Onjōji and Kōfukuji. (AK 1180/4/27 and 5/27). This suggests that there was little way of knowing whether Yoritomo would, or even could, mount an antigovernment rebellion. The question indeed was a difficult one. From one angle the timing was propitious. The Taira take-over of the previous year and the anti-Heishi call to arms were both expressions of a deep rift at court. The central polity was vulnerable. On the other hand, the year 1180 marked the completion of two decades of total Minamoto quiescence. Even before that, Yoritomo's father had spent several years in the east, producing a band of only several hundred fully reliable men.[2] With this as background, what likelihood was there that Yoritomo could achieve success?

1. Tokimasa's alleged descent from a Taira-surnamed vice-governor of Kōzuke (*AK* 1180/4/27) cannot be corroborated. For speculations on the pre-1180 Hōjō, see Satō Shin'ichi, "Kamakura bakufu seiji no senseika ni tsuite," and Takeuchi Rizō, "Zaichōkanjin no bushika," in Takeuchi Rizō, ed., *Nihon hōkensei seiritsu no kenkyū*, pp. 97–98 and pp. 37–38.

2. This is the estimate, at any rate, that has come down to us for Yoshitomo at the time of the Hōgen Disturbance. It should be remarked, however, that the figure refers only to those forces that the Minamoto leader was able to call to the capital. See pp. 39–45.

The Genji leader took several months to make his decision. During this time he sent out quiet overtures to houses he thought might support him. Finally in the eighth month he declared formally against the Taira by announcing a disengagement of the east and advancing the prospect of an autonomous warrior government. The results, as we know, were nothing short of astonishing. By the final months of 1180, the son of Yoshitomo was overlord of forces already numbering into the tens of thousands.[3]

This is not to imply, however, that the eastern provinces all caught fire simultaneously or with an identical intensity; nor was there a one-sided rush to the Genji standard. The matter of fighting as Taira or Minamoto involved careful assessment. For example, the condition of a family's possession over its homelands was probably of first concern. Hence the decision of Chiba Tsunetane and others like him to join with Yoritomo early on (*AK* 1180/6/27, 9/4). As we will see in a moment, alliance with the Minamoto was to lead to an innovative, locally based system of land confirmations for traditional holdings. On the other hand, there were obviously families whose local position was agreeable enough to warrant a posture of neutrality, or even of support, for the existing order. If confronted with a choice, such families probably chose at first to identify with the centrally based Heishi.[4] In neither case was loyalty to Yoritomo or Kiyomori the paramount concern.

A family's internal circumstances also played a part in determining its political alignment. Rivalries among branch lines or between a main line and its branches frequently helped to decide the issue.

3. Minoru Shinoda has suggested that the warrior response to Yoritomo's overtures was actually slow and disappointing (*The Founding of the Kamakura Shogunate, 1180–1185* [New York, 1960], pp. 48–59). But this judgment is valid only if one views events in the short compass of day-by-day recruitment. Taken in its broader context, the warrior response of 1180 was entirely without precedent. See, e.g., *AK*'s figure of 200,000 men (however inflated) by 10/18, just two months after the start of war. Most of *AK*'s entries for the period 1180–85 are translated by Shinoda in his valuable study.

4. Before very long, however, even houses that had initially opted for the Taira were switching sides and becoming members of the Genji. Yoritomo's physical presence in the east and his success in attracting the region's greatest houses made it more and more difficult to sustain a pledge of loyalty to the Heishi. For details on this point, see Mass, "The Emergence of the Kamakura Bakufu," in Hall and Mass, eds., *Medieval Japan*.

Such was the case, for example, in the Koyama–Ashikaga rivalry referred to earlier. In 1180 the Koyama joined the Genji while the Ashikaga sided with the Heishi (*AK* 1181/int.2/23). In other locations it was interfamily rivalries that affected the choice. At a slightly later stage the Kōno and Nii, long-time rivals in Shikoku's Iyo Province, appear to have divided on that basis between the Genji and Heishi. For these two houses the Gempei War took on the character of a civil war within Iyo Province.[5]

It is clear in any event that the sudden possibility of major rebellion in 1180 brought tensions of a diverse type to the surface. The Gempei War in that sense was not so much a confrontation between two warrior leagues as the setting for a national upheaval—a many-sided opportunity for venting long-suppressed frustrations and securing quick benefits. It is all the more significant, therefore, that from this potentially destructive release of energies, Yoritomo was able to find a common denominator of interests to bolster his rise to power. Moving quickly beyond the mere preparation for war, he set out to establish a new system of political organization. In rapid fashion this would lead to both secession of the eastern provinces from central control and the start of a process of title confirmation on behalf of men joining his movement. In this way Yoritomo was able to tailor the Minamoto drive of 1180 to fit the most deep-seated desires of his major followers.

From 1180/8, when the war officially began, to 1183/10, when Yoritomo's authority in the east received its initial recognition from the court, events centering on the Minamoto band passed through several relatively discrete stages.[6] An initial six-month period of outright lawlessness began when Yoritomo ordered direct military action against the Taira deputy in Izu. As a symbol of the centrally dominated authority system, this agent of a Heishi proprietary governor was summarily executed by Genji forces. Two days later on 1180/8/19 (*AK*) Yoritomo announced that, based on the authori-

5. Tanaka Minoru, "Kamakura jidai ni okeru Iyo no kuni no jitō goke'nin ni tsuite," in Takeuchi Rizō hakushi kanreki kinenkai, comp., *Shōensei to buke shakai*, p. 275. (Hereafter cited as Tanaka, "Iyo.")

6. These stages are expertly analyzed in Ishimoda Shō, "Kamakura seiken no seiritsu katei ni tsuite," *Rekishigaku kenkyū* 200 (1956): 2–16. (Hereafter cited as Ishimoda, "Kamakura Seiken.")

zation he had received from Prince Mochihito, he was assuming full jurisdiction over "all public and private lands in the east," in other words, over the entire Kantō region and beyond. Yoritomo and his followers had gone on record that the court-centered authority usurped by the Taira was no longer operable for the east. It was to prove a momentous declaration.

Almost as if to underscore his point, Yoritomo proceeded to issue on the same day the earliest known of his personal documents: an announcement to the resident officers (*rusudokoro zaichō*) of the Izu governor's headquarters that the management authority (*sata shiki*) of a certain administrative unit (*gō*) was now being granted (literally, "commended") to Mishima Shrine. Residents of that unit were to take heed and obey.[7] Not only had Yoritomo thus affixed his signature to a public document, but in his very first act he had asserted prerogatives over the land and tax system which, from the viewpoint of the Taira and the court, clearly constituted an illegal seizure of Kyoto-based powers.[8]

The Genji leader, of course, was motivated by the immediate desire to build up a military following. In order to achieve this goal he attempted something entirely new. In return for an oath of allegiance to himself, Yoritomo promised to protect through personal confirmation whatever an enlisting vassal considered to be rightfully his own. Taira Kiyomori, by contrast, had never conceived of such a step, preferring instead to gain promotions and land confirmations for his men by working through traditional channels. For Yoritomo,

7. *Mishima Jinja Monjo*, 1180/8/19 Minamoto Yoritomo kudashibumi, in *HI*, 9:3782–83, doc. 4883. Mishima Shrine is recorded (*AK* 1180/10/21) as having received other Izu lands from Yoritomo. A record of 1183 is similar to that of 1180/8/19: a directive to the Izu provincial office that Mishima Shrine receive tax exemptions for dependent families, etc. *Mishima Jinja Monjo*, 1183/3/17 Minamoto Yoritomo kudashibumi, *HI*, 8:3029, doc. 3976.

8. Asakawa Kan'ichi observed forty years ago that "Yoritomo's rule of the east during the period of the rebellion necessarily involved a wide infringement of the established rights of the domainial lords. . .   Before [a] more orderly process of development could begin, precedents of general intervention with the domainial customs had been established by Yoritomo in the first lawless period" (Asakawa, "The Founding of the Shogunate by Minamoto-no-Yoritomo," reprinted in *Land and Society in Medieval Japan* [Tokyo, 1965], p. 286).

the outlaw,[9] this new form of largesse was entirely without cost. The rights and titles, which he was now offering to underwrite, neither belonged to him in a personal sense nor properly were under his jurisdiction. But this was not all. Alongside the confirmatory privilege that Yoritomo arrogated to himself, the Minamoto leader assumed a virtually unrestricted right of military confiscation. He thus was afforded an opportunity to guarantee what was already held and to grant anew what was desired. It was a program with obvious appeal, especially since it seemed to offer both a distribution and a strengthening of local rights and offices without recourse to Kyoto authority.

It should be recognized that there were natural limits to the type of power that Yoritomo was proposing to exercise. Positive acts would be required to make explicit the Minamoto chieftain's announced accession to governance over the east. As a figure now at war with the Heishi protectors of the central polity, Yoritomo was denied advancement or his interests through the usual means: he was compelled to stress only what could be acquired by the local application of force or persuasion.[10] It was an approach to the exercise of power whose very simplicity, involving bypassing Kyoto entirely, made it so attractive.

The foregoing can best be illustrated by data found in the *Azuma kagami* entry for 1180/10/23. In this entry we read of twenty-four meritorious vassals being rewarded either by confirmations of original holdings (*honryō ando*) or by the disposal of new grants (*shin'on*). The diversity of the bequests is what is most striking: alongside the confirmation of the Miura family's assistant governorship over Sagami Province, we find other housemen receiving villages in the same province and in one case a full shōen. Evidently, few if any limits were imposed on the size or category of benefices that could be distributed.[11]

9. Yoritomo had been so designated within two weeks of his declaration of authority over the east. *Hyakurenshō*, 1180/9/5, p. 134.

10. As a political exile, Yoritomo had long before been stripped of all ranks and titles. It would seem to follow, therefore, that he held no lands in 1180, at least none with Kyoto's sanction. Only those units that had been confiscated would have been available for distribution to vassals. A number of such cases exist, e.g., *AK* 1181/int.2/28, which refers to bequests in Hitachi, Shimotsuke, and Kōzuke.

11. At the opposite end of the scale can be found confirmations of a warrior's

How Yoritomo conceived of these activities in conjunction with his own role is a difficult question. Did he consider himself permanent lord over the Kantō, a status justifying his seizure and free distribution of land? Or did he view his purpose as one of an indefinite superintendence of the region pending some future settlement with the court? Looking ahead, it is clear that Yoritomo never surrendered any of the public governance he had seized in the early stages of the war. Only in the shōen sector would Kyoto owners (after 1184) receive a partial restoration of their former authority. The issue concerning Yoritomo's initial self-image and purpose must therefore be considered inconclusive. Only the method and impact of his policies are fully clear. The actions taken by the Minamoto lord were done so independently of the central polity in order to win the support of the great warrior houses of the east.

Yoritomo's ability to utilize the agencies of the imperial provincial system proved particularly valuable in extending his power. This endeavor required the enticement of public-officer families such as the Chiba, Koyama, Miura, and Kazusa as a necessary first step. Without these great provincial bushidan in Yoritomo's camp the administrative expertise and local contacts needed to rule an entire region would have been largely lacking. It will be recalled that in the Kantō shōen penetration had been slow and uneven, with a majority of lands remaining in the public sector. Privatization had taken place not in spite of, but within, the provincial structure. With the headquarters (kokuga) in each province continuing to function as the major centers of government in the east, Yoritomo determined during 1180–81 to make their possession his primary objective.

Assuming control over each of the Kantō kokuga was apparently a relatively easy procedure. We have already noted the forceful take-over in Izu. The same action occurred in Suruga, just to the west (*AK* 1180/10/1, 13, 14). It was in Shimōsa and Kazusa, however, that the basic pattern seems to have taken form. The Chiba and Kazusa, respectively the major public-officer houses in those two provinces, were called on by Yoritomo to eliminate all persons sent out from the capital and to take provincial matters in their own

---

most fundamental possession, the home in which he lived. See, e.g., *AK* 1182/12/30. Also, *Kasokabe Ke Monjo*, 1184/7/29 Minamoto Yoritomo ando kudashibumi, in *HI*, 8:3141, doc. 4187, which cites a "confirmation of a residence" (*hontaku ando*). This document may, however, be a forgery.

hands.[12] Here was a mandate to which a house such as the Chiba, victimized several times at the hands of absentee interests, would be naturally responsive.

Certain variations on this general model might appear. Awa, for example, had no dominant public-officer house through whom Yoritomo would be obliged to work; the Genji leader simply assumed direct control. Thus, early in 1181 we see him issuing a governor's-type fiscal exemption for a favored shrine to the unnamed provincial officials of Awa (*AK* 1181/2/10). By now these men had probably become his vassals. It was, indeed, only in Hitachi Province that Yoritomo encountered difficulties of a sustained nature. As late as 1184/4/23 (*AK*), we find him politely requesting the entrenched provincial deputy to grant one of his vassals a special tax immunity. What is clear from this appeal is that, despite a successful Genji offensive against the same Shida and Satake houses that a generation earlier had refused to submit to Yoshitomo, Yoritomo in 1184 had not yet won control of that province's headquarters. Not until later that year would Hitachi come to be numbered as a Genji-controlled province, seemingly the last of the strictly Kantō provinces to be so categorized.[13]

The destruction in 1180–81 of the Genji-related Satake and Shida families reveals the disunity that continued to plague the Minamoto clan itself. In later chapters we will see that such disunity remained endemic and was only resolved by Yoritomo's systematic elimination over a period of fifteen years of various Genji collateral lines. In this initial period, however, open defiance by blood-related Genji lines was limited to a few outstanding examples. In general, it can be said that most of the Minamoto branches, even those in parts of the east far from the Kantō, pledged (though sometimes tardily) at least nominal allegiance to Yoritomo.

The case of Yoritomo's cousin, Kiso Yoshinaka of Shinano, can be cited to show that the intrafamily jealousies that had prevented Yoshitomo from expanding into certain provinces were still present,

12. *AK* 1180/9/1, 13. By 1181 such confrontations between central agents (*mokudai*) and local officers (*zaichō*) had spread to the Hokurikudō region facing the Japan Sea. See n. 21.

13. *AK* 1184/8/13 describes continued disturbances in Hitachi while *AK* 1184/11/12 notes that the province's local notables (*jūnin*) had finally become the vassals of Kamakura.

if now temporarily less apparent. From the outset Yoshinaka expected a minimal level of direction from Yoritomo. We know that in the early stages of the war Yoshinaka was engaged in organizing activities in Kōzuke, Shinano, and the Hokurikudō chain[14] but was restive with his subordinate status within the Genji hierarchy (*AK* 1180/12/24). Yoritomo's concern with this state of affairs must have been strengthened when Yoshinaka began issuing under his own seal confirmatory documents on behalf of local warrior lands. It was the practice just inaugurated by Yoritomo, lord of all the Genji. Evidence of such an act can be found as early as 1180/11/13 in Yoshinaka's home province of Shinano.[15] After expanding his activities into Hokurikudō, we see him confirming in 1182/2 an Etchū Province village in the form of a gesu management authorization. No such documents have been discovered for other Minamoto leaders, whether close relatives or major vassals.[16]

This is not to suggest, on the other hand, that Genji kinsmen such as Yoshinaka failed to play a highly significant role in the anti-Taira effort that was at hand. In fact, the simultaneous rising of Minamoto-related families in the provinces just east of the capital, in the area known as Chūbu, was probably the key factor in determining the military pattern of the war and resulting political configuration. A glance at the sequence of main force encounters clearly suggests this. After the rout of Genji forces at Ishibashi in Sagami during the first days of the war,[17] the next major battle (during the tenth month of 1180) took place in Suruga, to the *west* of the Kantō. Not only had Yoritomo in two months' time succeeded in destroying or neutralizing virtually all Heishi partisans in the

14. See *AK* 1180/10/13, 12/24, and 1181/9/3, 4.

15. *Ichikawa Monjo*, 1180/11/13 Minamoto Yoshinaka kudashibumi, in Shinano shiryō kankōkai, comp., *Shinano shiryō* (Nagano, 1968), 3:65.

16. The gesu authorization is referred to in *Kanazawa Toshokan Shozō Monjo*, 1262/3/1 Kantō gechijō, in Seno Sieichirō, ed., *Kamakura bakufu saikyojō shū*, (Tokyo, 1970), 1:125, doc. 106, 1. 10. (Hereafter cited as *KBSS*.) I exclude the various war period documents issued by Kamakura agents on behalf of Yoritomo.

17. *AK* 1180/8/23. This battle was largely a provincial civil war among the major contending families of Sagami, a phenomenon that became a pattern in other provinces. Nonindigenous Heishi forces—troops drawn and dispatched from central Japan—were not involved at Ishibashi. Mass, "The Emergence of the Kamakura Bakufu."

Kantō,[18] but from the tenth month on he shifted the war permanently away from the main Genji base.

It is interesting that both sides seemed to find this agreeable. For Yoritomo such freedom from the threat of external attack meant that he could turn his attention almost exclusively to internal consolidation. For the Heishi and the court, Chūbu now became the main area of interest. A contest resulted between the Taira and the two Minamoto generals there, Yoshinaka and Yukiie. Indeed, many of the Taira's initial war policies seem keyed to Yukiie, whose base was closest to the capital. The sōkan and sōgesu appointees discussed in chapter 1 are cases in point. So also was a court decree of late 1180 that directed shōen owners in adjacent Ōmi to protect "barriers and roads," to prohibit travel for all save members of the Heishi, and to beware of "Ōmi traitors."[19] The Gempei War in the period before 1184 was largely staged between the central Taira and Chūbu-resident Minamoto who were only nominally the vassals of Yoritomo.

The fury of anti-Kyoto actions unleashed from various quarters probably surprised the court and Yoritomo equally. In many regions of Japan there appears to have occurred a sudden outpouring of lawlessness, unprecedented in both its violence and scope. The war was assuming national overtones. In Kyushu, for instance, local rebels set fire in 1181 to the Heishi-controlled government-general of Kyushu (dazaifu),[20] while two weeks later warrior chieftains from Higo and Bungo led six hundred men against a Taira force of two thousand (*AK* 1181/2/29). In Hokurikudō, the Taira's ranking agent in Noto was expelled in 1181/7 by local residents. This incident in particular reveals the nature of these actions as outbursts of indigenous origin unprompted by any actual relationship with the Kantō.[21] What is important, however, is that this did not deter use of the Minamoto tag anyway. Identification as "Genji"

18. This refers to families actively supporting the Taira. Even Yoritomo's victorious foe at Ishibashi, the Ōba family of Sagami, had now surrendered. Most houses that initially chose a Heishi labeling were now scrambling to be accepted as Genji. Ibid.

19. *Ishiyamadera Shozō Monjo*, late 1180 Takakura Jōkō Inzen, in *HI*, 8:3008, doc. 3940.

20. *Gyokuyō*, 1181/2/15, 2:478.

21. *Gyokuyō*, 1181/7/24, 2:518. Parallel examples can be cited, e.g., in Wakasa,

was fast becoming the pretext for resistance to all constituted authority.[22]

As yet, Yoritomo had no way of controlling such developments outside his own home region. But even within the Kantō some of these same tendencies toward unrestrained violence were clearly on the rise. It was Yoritomo's own grip on events that was now, in a sense, being challenged. Ironically, therefore, the Minamoto leader was compelled to halt much of the antiestablishment lawlessness he himself had worked so hard to incite just a short time earlier. The danger in the Kantō no longer came from "Taira," but rather from Minamoto who were acting like common outlaws.

Several important decisions followed. One was a policy of relative noninvolvement in the Chūbu then being organized by Yoshinaka and Yukiie. As long as Yoritomo's kinsmen continued to recognize his own chieftainship, the Genji leader could afford to devote most of his attention to consolidating authority at home. Toward this aim, Yoritomo took steps to tighten control over his men by establishing a vassal control bureau called *samurai dokoro*. This was the agency name long used by the great central estate-holders for their military retainers. Also during this period the Genji leader ceased his movements across the Kantō and settled down to establish a permanent headquarters. Because of his family's long association with Kamakura District in Sagami Province, ground was broken there during the tenth month of 1180 for creation of some physical expression of this new concentration of local authority. Henceforth when Yoritomo prohibited local outrages, authorized fiscal exemptions, assigned new lands, or issued orders to "public officials," he would be doing so from a stationary base area that he could legitimately call his capital.[23]

Echigo, and Echizen provinces. Ibid., 1180/11/28, 1181/7/1, and 1181/9/2, and 9/9, pp. 446, 510, and 525–26.

22. As we will see in chap 4, the unauthorized invocation of Yoritomo's name became especially common during 1184–85, with momentous results.

23. For examples of these activities see (in order) *Sonkeikaku Shozō Monjo*, 1180/10/18 Minamoto Yoritomo gechijō, in *HI*, 10:3908, doc. 5066; ibid., 1180/11/8 Minamoto Yoritomo kudashibumi, 9:3783, doc. 4884; *Kashima Jingū Monjo*, 1181/3 Minamoto Yoritomo kishinjō, 8:3019, doc. 3961; and *Mishima Jinja Monjo*, Minamoto Yoritomo kishinjō, 9:3783, doc. 4885. According to *AK* 1180/10/21, Yoritomo's principal advisers urged securing the

A second stage in the creation of this eastern warrior regime is marked by the beginning of efforts to make contact with the court. The initial period of usurpation of governance now gave way to attempts to gain Kyoto approval of the new status quo. A Yoritomo petition of 1181/8 was in this vein. The Genji leader asserted that he was not a rebel or traitor to the court and that his deepest desire was to subjugate the imperial house's true enemies. He went on that, much as in the past when Genji and Heishi served the court, the two families should now divide administrative responsibility for eastern and western Japan respectively. Yoritomo concluded his appeal with a promise that provincial governors might continue under court jurisdiction.[24]

We must consider the rationale behind this unusual offer by Yoritomo to share a national authority with the Taira.[25] Of immediate interest is that the Genji chief, even a year into the war, did not see the central Taira's destruction as his primary objective. Only later, after the court's censure of his movement had been lifted and after Yoritomo's own horizons had been raised to national level, did he finally "discover" his enemy and move to destroy its leadership. In 1181, two concerns were probably paramount. First, the Genji chief may have felt the time opportune to begin his expansion into the eastern provinces' Chūbu sector. Acceptance of his division proposal promised to cut short Taira claims there as well as Yoritomo's dependence on Yoshinaka and Yukiie. Second, however one interprets Yoritomo's "usurpations" of 1180–81, the Genji lord was obviously aware by now that autonomy within the imperial fold, not independence and isolation, would be the most effective way to gain permanence for his regime. All thoughts of a separate sovereignty, presuming any existed, were now abandoned.

Kantō before considering expansion. In this we see reflected the desires of men who had staked everything on establishing a self-sufficient, independent government.

24. *Gyokuyō*, 1181/8/1, 2:519. For this summary see Iida Hisao, "Kamakura jidai ni okeru chōbaku kankei," *Rekishi kyōiku* 11.6 (1963): 42–43, nn. 1 and 2. (Hereafter cited as Iida, "Kamakura jidai.")

25. It should be noted that the entire account may be apocryphal. No other source, including *AK*, makes any mention of this Yoritomo overture. Nevertheless, most scholars accept the episode at face value, despite the fact that *Gyokuyō* is known for its chronicling of unsubstantiated rumors.

Central governorships, shorn of their executive authority, were not inconsistent with Yoritomo's actual control of eastern province governance.

The negative outcome of the sequence is most interesting. While many of Kyoto's proprietors expressed a willingness to enter into an arrangement by which they hoped conditions might return to those of an earlier day, the Taira leadership rejected the plan outright. For its part, any abandonment of the court's quarantine of the Kantō posed great dangers.[26] The Heishi, due to their many excesses against central-owner rights in the provinces and their inability to secure the Chūbu, had become themselves the objects of strong criticism.[27] By contrast, the Genji, despite their initial posture of rebellion, now seemed better equipped to protect Kyoto and its interests. Some elements in the capital must have realized that Yoritomo, with his broad warrior backing and assumption of governance in the Kantō, was not of the same mold and disposition as courtier generals of the past. However, there were others, especially religious proprietors, who undertook a steady, if covert, campaign to promote direct court–Kamakura relations.[28] Over the next two years, the Taira continued to resist all talk of a compromise settlement.

The period from 1181 to 1183 can thus be characterized in several ways. It was a time of military stalemate between the main forces of the Minamoto and Taira, but also one of constant confrontation

26. This seems to have been a deliberate policy, e.g., exclusion of the Kantō from a general levy imposed to defray temple repair costs for the Kōfukuji. *Gyokuyō*, 1181/3/21, 2:496.

27. For details of Heishi excesses, see Ishimoda, "Ikkoku jitō," pp. 39 ff. In regard to Chūbu, see, e.g., a document of 1182, which refers to the total stoppage of annual taxes from an Echizen Province estate. This was the result of a communication breakdown due to the war. *Daigo Zōjiki*, in Asakawa, *Land and Society in Medieval Japan*, Japanese section, p. 11. An even more explicit example contains a reference to the total lapse of communication with Noto Province since the outbreak of the "great rebellion" in 1180. *Kujō Ke Monjo*, 1183/10/19 kan senshi, in *Toshoryō sōkan, Kujō ke monjo* (Tokyo, 1972), 2:45, doc. 295.

28. Yoritomo's letters to these religious institutions included both a promise to restore the flow of rents from eastern holdings and a statement of respect for the court. At the same time, they were also a tacit assertion that Yoritomo was indeed the ruler of the Kantō: only he could guarantee that region's shōen. Ishimoda, "Kamakura seiken," pp. 8–9.

locally between those choosing to fight under these labels. Simultaneously, it was a period of quiet persistence by Yoritomo in his effort to gain a hearing at court, yet a time during which the Genji chieftain sought more eagerly to establish his standing as permanent lord of the Kantō. These and other anomalies were brought to the surface in mid-1183. In the seventh month of that year, Chūbu forces under the leadership of Kiso Yoshinaka and Minamoto Yukiie poured into Kyoto and immediately changed the entire complexion of the war. Since the Taira had fled the capital without a fight, ostensibly this was a victory for both the Minamoto cause and the court, the latter having now been released from the dictatorial Heishi yoke. Within a matter of weeks, however, there was growing disenchantment with these new military occupiers of Kyoto. Yoshinaka seemed clearly intent on imposing his own military rule over the court and on seizing for himself the mantle of chieftain over all the Genji. Yoritomo now stood in danger of being isolated by a new protector of the central polity, this time from within his own movement.

What is remarkable under these conditions is that even as Yoshinaka and Yukiie were rapidly beginning to gather up prestigious court titles, high provincial offices, and an accumulation of confiscated Taira shōen,[29] the embattled Minamoto chieftain refused to be drawn into a competition for traditional central rewards. Yoritomo was evidently playing for higher stakes, a supposition borne out by negotiations with the In for his own government's guarantee of shōen in the Kantō and Hokurikudō.[30] These discussions were soon allowed to embrace the elimination of Yoshinaka[31] and Kamakura's assumption of the protector's role for the entire region east of the capital. In 1183/10, an imperial decree was issued that authorized Yoritomo to perform certain public responsibilities in

29. Within a matter of days, Yoshinaka was made Director of the Left Horse Bureau (*Sama no kami*), governor of Echigo (subsequently governor of Iyo), and possessor of some 140 confiscated domains. Yukiie was made governor of Bingo (subsequently governor of Bizen) and holder of 90 land units. *Hyakurenshō*, 1183/8/10, 16, p. 144.

30. Ibid., 1183/7/30, p. 143.

31. By the beginning of the ninth month we find references to the despair in Kyoto over Yoshinaka's tactics, as well as to a growing desire to call in Yoritomo as his replacement. *Gyokuyō*, 1183/9/5, 2:627.

defense of the traditional order. It was a seminal turn of events, somewhat unreal in view of Yoritomo's having been cast for most of his life in the roles of political exile and then outlaw. But it was a development that would lead in short order to countrywide expansion of Kamakura's interests and authority.

Most important was the fact that Yoritomo now gained an open channel to an "expanded east."[32] Faced with a Yoshinaka–Yukiie power bloc that included the capital region and much of the Chūbu,[33] the Genji lord hurried to assume control in his new jurisdictional area. For the first time, he launched a major military thrust well beyond the Kantō. Yoritomo's brother, Yoshitsune, was chosen to lead this expedition, and within a matter of days a push down the Tōkaidō corridor brought the young commander to Ise Province at that circuit's western extremity. Although Yoshitsune proceeded to announce Kamakura's assumption of rule over this Heishi stronghold, Yoshinaka was clearly intended as the primary audience. The latter, feeling justifiably threatened, quickly countered by sending there some forces of his own.[34] A little later the harried Yoshinaka decided to act even more boldly. He offered to make peace with the Taira and to join Heishi forces in an attack on the Kantō. However the Taira rejected this overture and Yoshinaka found himself with only one remaining option. Taking advantage of his military oc-

32. Precise terms of the edict are discussed on pp. 74–77.

33. In the central region's Izumi Province, for example, proof exists of Yukiie's political influence, even though he is not known to have held formal title there: an 1183/12 reference to a "Bizen governor's notation" (Bizen *no kami gedai*) on a peasant appeal regarding a temple's claim to certain Izumi lands. Quoted in *Kumeidadera Monjo*, 1248/12/15 Kantō gechijō, in Osaka fu kyōiku iinkai, *Kumeidadera monjo* (Osaka, 1959), doc. 2, p. 15, ll. 1–3. A slightly earlier reference shows Yukiie in Izumi after suffering a military setback at the hands of Taira forces: *Hōryaku kanki*, 1183/11/12, in Gunsho ruijū, zatsu bu, 16 (Tokyo, 1901), p. 701. As for Chūbu, a court decree of 1183/9 (for example) refers to outrages committed in an Echizen estate by a certain "police captain" (*kebiishi*). A document of several months later shows the latter to have been an agent of Yoshinaka. *Ninnaji Monjo*, 1183/9/27 Go-Shirakawa In-no-chō kudashibumi, in *HI*, 8:3102, doc. 4107; and *Ninnaji Monjo*, 1184/5 Go-Shirakawa In-no-chō kudashibumi, in Tanaka Minoru, comp., "Ninnaji monjo shūi," *Shigaku zasshi* 68.9 (1959), p. 75. (Hereafter cited as Tanaka, "Ninnaji monjo.") In Chūbu's Tōsandō sector, *AK* 1184/2/21 reveals a Yoshinaka land confirmation occurring in 1183/8.

34. *Gyokuyō*, 1183/int.10/27, 2:646.

cupation of the capital he pressured the court into branding Yoritomo once more as a rebel. This was in the twelfth month, and the
Genji chief reacted immediately. For reasons not entirely clear in
view of Yoshinaka's commanding presence in central Japan, the
advance westward of Kantō forces now proved irresistible. Yoshinaka's securing from the court the title of "barbarian subduing
great general" (*sei i tai shōgun*) did little to stem this progress, and
within a matter of days the Minamoto personage, who in many ways
had done more than Yoritomo to ensure a Genji victory over the
Heishi, was hunted down and killed. The way was now free for
Kamakura to seek a final subordination of the east and, beyond
that, to begin laying plans for an expansion into western Japan.[35]

Before turning to this search for new horizons, it is necessary to
comment briefly on the specific issues raised by the several versions
of the 1183/10 edict. Unfortunately, the original text of the decree
has not been preserved, and hence confusion exists over its content
and intended significance.[36] The substantive points, however, can
be summarized as follows: (1) central proprietorship of shōen either
in Tōkaidō and Tōsandō, *or* in those two circuits plus Hokurikudō,
was to be restored, with Yoritomo's assistance, to its antebellum
condition; and (2) should there be any in those regions who failed to
obey, they were either to be hunted down by order of Yoritomo,
or dealt with by him as he saw fit.[37]

These discrepancies have led to intense speculation among
scholars. In virtually all cases, however, the major concern has
been with the *type of authority* being released by the court, not with
the decree's actual results. Thus the legal character of Yoritomo's investiture, rather than the drive into Chūbu and beyond, has
drawn most attention. There are two schools of thought on the

---

35. After Yoshinaka's death in 1184/1 Yoritomo was able to turn in earnest
to an elimination of Heishi remnants in provinces such as Ise. See *AK* 1184/3/22
for a Kamakura vassal, Ōi Saneharu, on a military venture in Ise against Heishi
elements there. Also *AK* 1184/5/15, 7/5, 7/18. As for Yukiie, he had broken with
Yoshinaka just in time. Two years later he would join with Minamoto Yoshitsune
in still another Minamoto rebellion against Yoritomo's leadership.

36. The four extant versions, all different, appear in *Gyokuyō*, 1183/int. 10/13,
20, and 22, 2:642, 645, 646; and *Hyakurenshō*, 1183/int. 10/14, p. 145.

37. Ishimoda, "Kamakura seiken," pp. 12–15.

"public" aspects of the decree. If, according to the first view, Yoritomo was being authorized to hunt down and capture recalcitrants, then his assignment was merely that of a constable officer under imperial command. The In had succeeded in reducing Yoritomo's powers by ingeniously maneuvering the Kamakura chieftain into guaranteeing the flow of eastern shōen rents. The second view holds that Yoritomo was actually being granted an independent administrative authority over the east, an event of such importance that it marks the establishment of the Kamakura bakufu itself. For the one group, then, the 1183 edict brought Yoritomo securely within the imperial fold; for the other, the decree constituted nothing less than the birth of dual government in Japan. The argument, it is plain, reduces to one of legal definition.[38]

What has been largely lost in this debate over constitutional issues is that the decree's implementation bears directly on its importance. How Yoritomo interpreted and used the edict cannot be neglected. A major question, then, is how the nature of Kamakura's activities changed after 1183/10.

It is highly significant that governance in the Kantō—where we might have expected the greatest change—shows no difference at all: the format and content of Yoritomo's pronouncements remain entirely the same. A case in point is an 1184 order to the Hitachi

---

38. The omission of Hokurikudō in all but the earliest *Gyokuyō* entry (see n. 31) is explained, simply enough, in terms of the pressure brought to bear on the In by that region's major figure, Yoshinaka. The point is a minor one, however, since the court (whatever the edict's final form) chose to apply in Hokurikudō the decree's principle of restoring to rightful owners the original substance of shōen proprietorships. We see this from the very moment of the edict's issuance, i.e., an 1183/10 directive to Noto Province mandating that one Wakayama Estate be returned, as of old, to its legal owner, the Kujō house of Kyoto. *Kujō Ke Monjo*, 1183/10/19 kan senshi, in *Kujō ke monjo*, 2:45, doc. 295. Within a matter of months, anyway, representatives of the Kantō would be exercising a jurisidiction in Hokurikudō roughly akin to that in Tōsandō and Tōkaidō. Leading spokesmen for the two views are Ishii Ryōsuke, "Kamakura bakufu no seiritsu," *Rekishi kyōiku* 8.7 (1960): 5 ff (view 1); and Satō Shin'ichi, *Kamakura bakufu soshō seido no kenkyū*, (Tokyo, 1943), chap. 1, pt. 1 (view 2). [Hereafter cited as Satō, *Soshō seido*.] A number of variations on these two main themes also exists. For a review of the main arguments, see Uwayokote Masataka, "Kamakura seiken seiritsu ki o meguru kingyō," in *Hōseishi kenkyū* 11 (1960): 175-81.

official class assigning public taxes from three gō-level administrative units to Kashima Shrine[39] The lord of Kamakura had been making bequests of this type from the very beginning of his movement when he was still an outlaw.[40] The importance of the 1183 edict evidently lies elsewhere.

In fact, as we have noted, the decree opened the way for a penetration of the Chūbu region and beyond. This activity was not merely military; Kamakura governance was extended westward. On 1183/10/10 Yoritomo issued a new kind of document—a pronouncement in which the various lands of a central proprietor, the Kamowake Ikazuchi Shrine of Kyoto, were ordered freed from Heishi interference and resulting losses. In the past, Yoritomo had issued decrees on behalf of religious institutions, but the affected shrines had always been local.[41] All this was now changed: within a matter of months the bakufu would be involved in the defense of centrally held domains in many parts of the country.[42]

Nor did this involvement remain limited to "cease and desist" type directives on the model of the Kamowake shrine-protection order cited above. While edicts of this genre naturally predominated,[43]

39. *Hanawa Monjo*, 1184/12/25 Minamoto Yoritomo kudashibumi, in *HI*, 8:3157, doc. 4222.

40. E.g., *Mishima Jinja Monjo*, 1180/8/19 Minamoto Yoritomo kudashibumi, in *HI*, 9:3782–83, doc. 4883. Also, *Sonkeikaku Shozō Monjo*, 1180/12/28 Minamoto Yoritomo kudashibumi, in *HI*, 10:3909, doc. 5068.

41. *Kamowake Ikazuchi Jinja Monjo*, 1183/10/10 Minamoto Yoritomo kudashibumi, in *HI*, 8:3102–03, doc. 4109. Past decrees were issued, for example, to Mishima Shrine in Izu (n. 40); Kashima Shrine in Hitachi (*Kashima Jingū Monjo*, 1181/10 Minamoto Yoritomo kishinjō, in *Ibaragi ken shiryō, chūsei hen 1* (Mito, 1970), doc. 367, p. 239—not in *HI*); and Katori Shrine in Shimōsa Province (*Katori Jingū Monjo*, 1181/10 Minamoto Yoritomo kishinjō, in *HI*, 8:3027, doc. 3971). I have found no comparable examples for local Buddhist institutions.

42. The actual term "bakufu" appears only later, but I use it here simply to designate "the government of Kamakura." In Chinese history, "bakufu" had connoted the military headquarters of a person achieving the title of "captain of the guards," a title that Yoritomo himself received from the court and then resigned in 1190. Although the term "bakufu" is found in *AK* from about this time (e.g., 1191/3/3), this chronicle is a much later work. Precisely when the term came into use is not clear.

43. E.g., an 1184 Kamakura admonition against outrages committed on all shrine and temple lands in Hokurikudō: *Tōdaiji Monjo* 1184/7/2 Kantō migyōsho an, in *HI*, 8:3130, doc. 4158.

the bakufu also began to involve itself in judicial matters. A decree of 1184/4/3 shows Yoritomo as mediator in an Iga Province (Chūbu) dispute between two central proprietors. After examining the documentary evidence, the bakufu leader awarded the contested domain to Tōdaiji Temple.[44] Here, then, was a development entirely without precedent—a noncentral military figure serving as final judge in a proprietary dispute between high-ranking absentee owners. We can find no hint of such authority being delegated to Yoritomo by the 1183/10 court edict. Rather, what is shown here is a growing paralysis in Kyoto, along with Kamakura's eagerness to fill the void of defaulted governance. The legal limits of Yoritomo's court-granted authority, whatever they might have been, were simply outpaced. Much the same occurred in western Japan, as we shall now see.

During the early months of 1184 the court sought to define for the west as it had for the east the proper boundaries of Kamakura responsibility. In the first of two edicts, Yoritomo was directed to destroy the Heishi; in the second, he was authorized to suppress warrior outrages, now countrywide.[45] But such investiture, coming at a time of deepening national crisis, proved less a restraint than a channel and license for promoting bakufu interests. Control of the country's military and police affairs, along with Yoritomo's eagerness to accept westerners as vassals, enabled the bakufu to make rapid contact with lands and men in areas far from its home base. It was during 1184–85 that Kamakura's status as a countrywide warrior organization became essentially set.

The war itself was the main rationale for the bakufu's advance into western Japan. What is important, however, is that the main-force fighting remained largely incidental to Kamakura's aggrandizement of power. For example, Settsu Province, site of the well-known Genji victory at Ichinotani (1184/2), never became a bakufu stronghold. In fact, the earlier reluctance of the Gempei armies to face one another was still present. Stalemate set in once again and continued until a sudden quickening of the tempo early in 1185. After a series

44. *Kashiwagi Shi Shozō Monjo*, 1184/4/3 Minamoto Yoritomo kudashibumi, in *HI*, 8:3125, doc. 4147.
45. The two edicts, dated 1/26 and 2/19, are recorded in *Gyokuyō*, 1184/2/23, 3:13.

of lightning (and now legendary) military maneuvers Yoshitsune, youngest brother of Yoritomo, caught the main Taira generals at sea in the historic Battle of Dannoura.[46] The Gempei War, slow and plodding throughout, ended in spectacular fashion in the third month of 1185.

Of greater interest to us are the ways in which, during this same time period, Kamakura established an influence in western Japan that would outlast the war. The two major means adopted were suppression of local disturbances and the gaining thereby of a permanent interest in affected areas, and conversion to vassalage of a region's ranking warrior families.

In order to coordinate its campaign against local outrages the bakufu, with court approval, established an agency in Kyoto in early 1184. Under the supervision of Minamoto Yoshitsune, this first Kamakura office beyond the east acted as a kind of clearing house for complaints of violence brought by central owners. There is a question concerning this agency's territorial range: the sources yield data on only six provinces.[47] But even if this sphere had been dictated by Kyoto, the seminal importance of Yoshitsune's presence and function is hardly diminished. From his headquarters in Kyoto, he issued patents of guarantee in his capacity as representative of the bakufu, not appointed official of the court[48] Related to this is the fact that every one of the known Yoshitsune decrees was in defense of a central religious institution. Kamakura was developing a policy of making itself indispensable to the most amenable segment of capital society (see note 28).

46. The course of the war from 1184 is expertly handled in Shinoda, *The Founding of the Kamakura Shogunate*, pp. 85–100. For Yoshitsune's exploits and the legends that have grown up around them, see Helen Craig McCullough, *Yoshitsune, A Fifteenth-Century Chronicle* (New York, 1966).

47. See Tanaka Minoru, "Kamakura dono otsukai kō," *Shirin* 45.6 (1962): p. 12, for the extant references to Yoshitsune's Kyoto-based activities. The provinces affected were Tamba, Settsu, Kawachi, Kii, Izumi, and Ōmi—all to the immediate west of Kyoto, save Ōmi, which bordered the capital city on the east.

48. With one exception, Yoshitsune's given name is all that appears; no court titles are affixed, and there are no references to desist orders "in compliance with the will of the In." For details, see Mass, "The Emergence of the Kamakura Bakufu."

Early in 1185, in advance of the final military drive against the Taira, Yoshitsune was ordered to leave Kyoto and meet the enemy in battle. Two vassal officers, Kondō Kunihira and Nakahara Hisatsune, were sent to the capital as his replacements. In several ways their arrival signaled an expansion in the activities of the bakufu's central office. First, we find a handful of references to a range of involvement now inflated to eleven provinces.[49] Also, the two men themselves represented a neat combination of pen and sword: Nakahara is depicted as the scribe, while Kondō is portrayed as a warrior stalwart (*yūshi*) standing at the ready to use force (*AK* 1185/2/5). Finally, the two men were kept sufficiently busy by their duties to warrant Yoritomo's sending them six assistants (*AK* 1185/5/25).

The problem lies in how these duties should be understood. With their "outrage prevention" function there is no argument.[50] Upon receipt of a complaint the two deputies would issue a decree and dispatch a military contingent to the areas being attacked. Professor Yasuda, however, goes farther. Basing his conclusion on a pair of entries in *Azuma kagami,* he posits a full judicial and administrative competence for the central region.[51] The phrases themselves are clear enough—"the judging of general suits in the central region" (entry one), and "the judging of commoner suits and an investigative capacity in the central region and adjacent provinces" (entry two). Yet there is doubt as to whether this condition had been agreed to by the court, in other words, formalized. Erosion and diversification of central authority were the main processes at work. Thus as instability cut an ever-deeper path across Japan in 1185, the bakufu's Kyoto commissioners found themselves *necessarily* in contact with a wider spectrum of both appeals and persons. As we shall see in chapters 4 and 5, this broadened responsibility was eventually

49. *AK* 1185/2/5, 1185/12/6, and *Gyokuyō*, 1185/12/27, 3:127. Precisely which eleven provinces is not clear, although evidently the court had now moved to define a jurisdiction, rather than to leave this to chance.

50. *AK* 1185/2/5 suggests that warriors everywhere were seizing war supplies (*hyōrō*) under pretext of fighting the Heishi. The extant Kondō–Nakahara documents are discussed in Mass, "The Emergence of the Kamakura Bakufu."

51. Yasuda Genkyū, *Jitō oyobi jitō ryōshusei no kenkyū,* (Tokyo, 1961), pp. 163–64, citing *AK* 1185/5/25 and 6/16.

eschewed. For the time being, however, Kamakura was assuming, with great relish, an ever larger share of countrywide governance.[52]

In attaining his second objective, creation of a national vassal corps, Yoritomo encountered special problems in the west. This region was, first of all, unfamiliar to him and distant from his capital. The receipt of personally offered oaths of loyalty, the usual practice for new housemen in the Kantō, was thus consistently denied him; the Kamakura lord never ventured beyond his own home area. This set the stage for a dual approach to the matter of houseman (*goke'nin*) rewards and esteem. Despite a policy formally inviting all westerners (including Heishi) to become vassals of the Minamoto,[53] the men accepted into this status remained essentially foreigners to their new chieftain. As such, they came to be treated in discriminatory fashion: few ever received the confirmatory land documents they had been promised, and those of major prestige in their home provinces were often later subjected to ouster attempts. The bakufu's policy was demonstrably one of extensive vassal enrollment in the west, but the intention from the outset was to have as many easterners as possible in positions of command.

Among Yoritomo's major western commanders were his brothers, Noriyori and Yoshitsune, and his trusted vassals, Doi Sanehira, Kajiwara Kagetoki, and Tachibana Kiminari. All appear to have been engaged in vassal recruitment on behalf of the bakufu. In

52. Thus we see Yoritomo making high-level public official appointments in provinces where he had no authority (e.g., the constableship [*ōryōshi*] of Iwami: *Hagi Han Masuda Ke Monjo*, 1184/5 Kajiwara Kagetoki [a Yoritomo deputy] kudashibumi, in *HI*, 8:3137, doc. 4175) and shōen assignments in estates he did not own (e.g., gesu and *kumon* managerial titles in a Settsu Province shōen: *Aida Jirō Shūshū Eisha Monjo*, 1184/5/18 Minamoto Yoritomo kudashibumi, *HI*, 10:246, supp. doc. 245). We see him also ignoring legal channels by allowing his deputies to issue directives to western province public officers entirely outside Kamakura's jurisdiction (e.g., in Nagato Province: *Nagato Sumiyoshi Jinja Monjo*, 1185/9/7 Minamoto Noriyori kudashibumi an, in Takeuchi Rizō, comp., *Kamakura ibun* [hereafter *KI*], 1:4, doc. 4.

53. See *AK* 1184/3/1 and 1185/1/6. Some scholars doubt the authenticity of the Yoritomo pronouncements contained in these two entries. In practice, certainly, there were never the blanket enrollments that the oratory (here aimed at Shikoku and Kyushu) seemed to promise. Yet even with this qualification, there is no reason to question Yoritomo's fundamental desire to inflate his regional band to national proportions.

Shikoku, for example, Tachibana, assigned to Sanuki Province, is recorded as having sent to Kamakura a list of submitting warrior houses. On 1184/9/19 (*AK*), Yoritomo replied by directing these new housemen to obey Kiminari's command. Less than a month later, Minamoto Noriyori made grants to meritorious bushi in Aki Province in western Honshu (*AK* 1184/10/12). An additional three weeks brought Genji armies to Suō: a document of 1184/10/30 shows Noriyori confirming a district chieftainship there.[54] Doi Sanehira was also active in western Honshu. In addition to his appointment as shugo for Bitchū, Bizen, and Bingo (see chapter 4), we see a reference to Doi in Izumo: an edict of early 1186 cites prior decrees (*kudashibumi*) by Yoritomo and Sanehira granting an important shrine headship to a prominent local figure.[55] It is possible that under his own seal Doi had enrolled the recipient as a vassal of Kamakura. But it was Kajiwara Kagetoki, one of Yoritomo's most trusted comrades, who clearly took the lead in promoting houseman enrollments. Contemporary records show him as active in a variety of tasks in diverse regions of the west.[56] It is a late Kamakura document, however, that is most explicit: this record of 1324 asserts that while there were western province houses not in possession of original Kamakura investitures, these families commonly held proof of houseman status by virtue of private Kagetoki letters (Kagetoki *no hōsho*).[57]

In terms of the favorable outcome of the war, the bakufu's programs in the west must be considered successful. With some

54. *Tōkyō Daigaku Shiryō Hensanjo Shozō Monjo*, 1184/10/30 Minamoto Noriyori kudashibumi, in *HI*, 10:3917, doc. 5090.

55. *Senge Monjo*, 1186/2/9 Taira no ason kudashibumi, in Shimane ken, comp., *Shinshū Shimane kenshi, shiryō hen 1* (Hirata, 1967), p. 194.

56. In addition to his Harima and Mimasaka "shugo" assignments (p. 97) and his constableship (with Doi Sanehira) for the central provinces (*kinkoku no sōtsuibushi: AK* 1185/4/26), Kagetoki is known to have been active in Iwami (*Hagi Han Masuda Ke Monjo*, 1184/5 Kajiwara Kagetoki kudashibumi, in *HI*, 8:3138, doc. 4178), and in Bitchū (*Jingoji Monjo*, 1184(?)/10/18 Kajiwara Kagetoki shojō, doc. 4211, p. 3151), among other places. Likewise, his activities— belying his titles—were not always on the side of lawfulness. E.g., his condemnation for outrages in Kyoto's home province of Yamashiro: *Tanimori Monjo*, 1185/5/1 Kantō gechijō, doc. 4225, p. 3175.

57. *Hiromune Monjo*, 1324/12/21 Kantō gechijō in *KBSS*, 1:375, doc. 302.

important reservations,[58] the same can be said of Kamakura's desire to lay the groundwork for a permanent network of men and an enduring share of western province governance. A closer look at how this infiltration process unfolded in different provinces will clarify these points.

It should be stated initially that western military bands were usually small, weakly organized, and subject to the constraints of the Kyoto-controlled estate system. As a result, the bakufu found that recruitment of shōen-defined bushidan did not pay off in the passage of whole areas into Kamakura's orbit of power. Vassal enrollment from larger (and more amenable) administrative units would have to be tried. In this context thinking came to focus on the various provincial offices.

Iwami, at the western end of Honshu, is one of the few provinces for which ample materials survive. The half dozen or so extant records from 1184–85 can be summarized as follows. First is a pronouncement of 1184/5 by the Kamakura deputy, Kajiwara Kagetoki, to the effect that Masuda (Fujiwara) Kanetaka had just been appointed Iwami constable (ōryōshi); Kanetaka was to exercise command over that province's Kamakura housemen. This was followed by a letter of the same date informing both Kanetaka and the Iwami vassals that a Kamakura investigator would be dispatched shortly to ascertain the loyalty of all new Genji. Third is a Minamoto Yoshitsune decree, also of 1184/5, in which the Iwami vassals are promised rewards in return for fighting and destroying Taira. Constable Kanetaka was to command this operation. Next is a Kajiwara Kagetoki directive ordering all military types—provincial guards (kondei), Kamakura housemen, local officials (zaichōkanjin), and Kanetaka—to cross into adjacent Izumo and destroy Heishi rebels. Fifth is a Minamoto Noriyori decree of half a year later confirming Kanetaka's possession (chigyō) of twenty-one itemized

58. Bloch, *Feudal Society*, p. 147, reminds us that in Europe "homage could not be offered or accepted by proxy." In western Japan, by contrast, the lord–vassal relationship was reduced to the promise, often unfulfilled, of a document (not land) grant. This meant that while Kamakura succeeded initially in gaining its foothold, it left the door open for future resentments and instability. Unrewarded Kamakura housemen would play a major role, e.g., in the abortive Jōkyū War attempt to overthrow the bakufu in 1221.

Iwami land units. Last is a Yoshitsune document of 1185/6 further confirming Kanetaka's tenure (*shintai ryōshō*) over rights (*shoshiki*) in various land parcels.[59]

What do these records tell us about the bakufu effort in Iwami?[60] The pattern indeed was a familiar one. Kamakura had identified the leading warrior in a province and moved to win his allegiance. This was accomplished by making Masuda Kanetaka constable and by placing him in command of all provincial forces. The relationship was then sealed by issuing documents guaranteeing all Masuda holdings. Kamakura stood to gain from such an effort in several ways. Agents from the east would exercise command over a remote area's most prominent public officer. This in turn would facilitate conversion of other persons to vassalage and permit entrance, through the medium of newly enrolled housemen, into the public land system. A by-product might well be reward openings for trusted easterners.

The important wedge here was not legal, court-ordained authority, but private power over public figures, in short, a maximizing of the military–feudal nexus. Yoritomo's deputies were as free to attempt an advancement of bakufu interests as private power and local conditions would permit. It is precisely this individuality of circumstance that helps to explain the invasion order into nearby Izumo. Apparently, no Masuda-level house was present to receive bakufu investiture as provincial constable. In the absence of indigenous support, Yoritomo's generals had no choice but to order interdiction of Heishi forces by loyalists from neighboring Iwami. An unrelated 1184 record shows bakufu weakness in Izumo from a different angle. In response to an appeal from a local shrine, Kama-

59. *Hagi Han Masuda Ke Monjo*, 1184/5 Kajiwara Kagetoki kudashibumi, in *HI*, 8:3137, doc. 4175; ibid., 1184/5 Fujiwara Yoritane hōsho, 8:3138, doc. 4176; ibid., 1185/5 Minamoto Yoshitsune kudashibumi, doc. 4177; ibid., 1184/5 Kajiwara Kagetoki kudashibumi, doc. 4178; ibid., 1184/11/25 Minamoto Noriyori kudashibumi, 8:3155, doc. 4128; and ibid., 1185/6 Minamoto Yoshitsune kudashibumi, 8:3180, doc. 4262. This series of documents appears also in *Shinshū Shimane kenshi, shiryō hen 1*, pp. 540–42.

60. In a private conversation, Seno Seiichirō of Tokyo University has expressed some doubt concerning the authenticity of these documents. However, since neither *HI* nor *Shinshū Shimane kenshi* (nor any secondary material known to me), raises this point, I have decided to use them freely.

kura confessed, in effect, its inability to control rapacious warriors. Instead of moving against these elements, it admonished shrine officers to pay attention to shrine affairs, and to refuse all orders issuing from outlaw-minded warriors misusing Yoritomo's name.[61]

Before leaving Iwami, recent calculations show that the public–private paddy-land distribution greatly favored the former (837.6 *chō* to 638.4 *chō*). This meant that even well into the twelfth century it was the provincial office that played the major role in Iwami governance. The Masuda dominated that headquarters, which explains the bakufu's offer of vassalage and willingness to confirm Masuda holdings.[62] Iyo in Shikoku was another province with a dominant provincial office.[63] But here control was in the hands not of one family, but of two; a local contest would have to be resolved before Kamakura influence could penetrate. The story of Iyo in the 1180s is thus one of civil war—fought under Genji and Heishi labels—between long-standing resident officer rivals, the Kōno and the Nii.[64]

Of initial interest is that the Kōno's triumph did not come until late in 1185. This suggests that local struggle and bakufu expansion in Iyo were not keyed to the main Gempei fighting: the Taira defeat had come some months before. The final resolution, indeed, occurred in a most interesting way. Difficulties within the Minamoto hierarchy, and between Kamakura and Kyoto, ultimately determined the outcome. Events began on 1185/8/16 with Yoshitsune's appointment as Iyo governor (*AK* 1185/8/29). While Yoritomo had himself been responsible for this recommendation, a growing rift between the two brothers caused the Genji chief to seek a reversal.

61. *Kitajima Monjo*, 1184/10/28 Minamoto Yoritomo kudashibumi, in Kitajima Hidetaka, comp., *Izumo Kokuzō ke monjo*, pp. 1–2. (Not in *HI*.)

62. These holdings constituted an interest in nearly one-third of Iwami's total cultivated acreage. Kobayashi Hiroshi, "Iwami no kuni Masuda shi no ryōshusei ni tsuite," in Yasuda Genkyū, ed., *Shoki hōkensei no kenkyū*, p. 133. (Hereafter cited as Kobayashi, "Iwami.")

63. In Iyo, there were only 37 shōen compared with a public sector of 14 *gun* and 71 *gō*. Also, of the 29 known jitō in thirteenth-century Iyo, 19—or more than half—had their tenures in public land. Tanaka, "Iyo," pp. 261–62.

64. The Kōno's early opposition to the "Heike" (i.e., the Nii) is recorded in *AK* 1181/int.2/12. The Kōno leader's status as a leading "public official" (*zaichō*) is noted in *AK* 1181/9/27.

The In, however, had other ideas; he refused at first to grant Yoritomo's request.[65] This led Kamakura to shift its strategy: if Yoritomo could not legally end his brother's governorship, he would move to siphon away its substance. On 10/17 the bakufu leader appointed the Kōno and their followers to a series of administrative jitō posts. The logic behind this maneuver is expressed in the diary *Gyokuyō*: "Because of jitō being appointed, [Yoshitsune] has not been able to discharge provincial affairs." We may assume, based on this description, that most or all of Yoritomo's appointments were over units of public land.[66] The essence of Yoshitsune's authority would thereby have been absorbed by district- (*gun*) and township- (*gō*) level figures owing loyalty to Kamakura.[67]

A provincial office and attendant public land had thus once again played an important role in extending bakufu power. In Iwami, the major public-officer house had been invested by Kamakura with the title of constable (*ōryōshi*). In Iyo a year later a different title was used but with roughly similar effect. It was an experience that yielded important lessons. Not only were the subgovernor organs of provincial administration shown to be capable of new direction from afar, but the Kamakura power to grant, not merely to confirm, offices had proven its workability in western Japan. It was an awareness that would lead in time to the bakufu's assumption of an appointment right over shugo and jitō.

65. Incidents such as this were probably a major reason why Yoritomo eventually eschewed governorships as a technique for advancing bakufu interests. Appointments and dismissals were all made by the court, which could block or delay Kamakura's recommendations. In later years the only governorships retained by the bakufu were in eastern Japan, dominated in any case by Kamakura, and in Bungo Province, gateway to Kyushu.

66. *Gyokuyō*, 1185/10/27, 3:105. Specifically the account speaks of retainers (*rōjū*) being appointed by Yoritomo to Heishi-confiscated areas in Iyo. Evidently, the rōjū were the Kōno and their followers, and the seized areas came from the public officer Nii.

67. It is arguable that Yoritomo's authority as Iyo provincial proprietor was what allowed him to make jitō appointments into public land. This view is based, however, on the assumption that Yoritomo's proposal of a candidate for governor meant, ipso facto, that he was now provincial proprietor. The headnote in Ehime kenshi hensan iinkai, comp., *Ehime ken hennen shi* (Matsuyama, 1960), 2:161, makes this assumption, for example. Actually, the *AK* entry (1185/8/29) to which the headnote refers leaves the question entirely open.

Wakasa Province provides another case study. Although technically in Hokurikudō, this province was closely associated with
Kyoto due to its proximity to the capital. Even so, much as in the
more remote areas of Iwami and Iyo, Wakasa possessed a large
public sector, roughly half the cultivated acreage. The province was
similar to Iwami and Iyo in another respect; it was largely controlled
by its resident public-officer class.[68] By winning the support of the
leading family of Wakasa, the Inaba, the bakufu succeeded in
making contact with still another provincial headquarters.

This process began soon after the outbreak of the Gempei War.
In 1180/11, powerful resident officers (*yūsei no zaichō*) in Wakasa
joined forces with anti-Heishi elements in nearby Ōmi.[69] This is
noteworthy for two reasons. First, Wakasa had been a Heishi
proprietary province from the early 1160s; as such it had received
Taira governors for almost twenty years, though to obviously little
effect.[70] Second, the Inaba and their subordinates joined forces
with the Chūbu Genji. There is nothing, in other words, to link these
houses immediately with Kamakura. After 1183, as we know, the
bakufu extended its power into Hokurikudō. But although we read
that Kamakura agents were active in Wakasa from 1184,[71] we
cannot be sure just how extensive this authority now became. The
Inaba were certainly vassals of Yoritomo's by this juncture, and to
that extent Kamakura could exert pressure and expect support. But
the Inaba, as subsequent events show, never developed into true
Kamakura stalwarts.

The clear obstacle to both Heishi governance and early bakufu
control was a family of unique local power and influence. Much of
this strength derived from Inaba Tokisada's headship of Wakasa's
tax office (*saisho*). It was Tokisada's responsibility to oversee the
tax collection for 1,140 chō of public rice land. Even more significant was the Inaba's vast private holdings, some 800 chō, or

68. Tanaka Minoru, "Kamakura bakufu goke'nin seido no ichi kōsatsu—
Wakasa no kuni jitō goke'nin o chūshin to shite," in Ishimoda and Satō, eds.,
Chūsei no hō to kokka, p. 282. (Hereafter cited as Tanaka, "Wakasa.")

69. *Gyokuyō*, 1180/11/28, 2:446.

70. Takeuchi Rizō, "Heishi seiken ron," *Nihon rekishi* 200 (1965): 47.

71. *Jingoji Monjo*, 1184(?)/4/4 Minamoto Yoritomo shojō, in *HI*, 8:3125,
doc. 4184.

roughly 37 percent of the full provincial total. The heaviest concentration, as expected, was in public land near the provincial capital.[72] The Inaba were not of course "proprietors" over these extensive fields; absentee personnel, especially the governor, held formal title.[73] But the standing of Tokisada relative to other provincial officers leaves little doubt that he was the supreme local figure in Wakasa. It was Tokisada who held the "acting governor's" post (*gon no kami*), and the Inaba whose provincial salary fields (*kyūden*) came to 40 percent of the full public total.[74]

In Wakasa, our information permits us to make broad inquiries into the condition of the men who became Kamakura vassals. Characteristically, the majority of the eleven provincial officer families became housemen of Kamakura—at least six directly, with the Inaba acting as go-between for the others.[75] A military register of 1196 lists a total of thirty-three former Genji and Heishi houses in Wakasa, and a later record confirms the existence of "more than thirty" housemen initially.[76] What is important is that more than half of these may have been pre-1180 dependencies of the Inaba: some twenty-six of the thirty-three names listed were settled in the two Wakasa districts (gun) where Tokisada held his land rights. The third of Wakasa's three districts showed a different configuration but with probably the same result. In an area with a heavy preponderance of public land, the Inaba exercised sway through control of the province's tax apparatus.[77]

72. Tanaka, "Wakasa," pp. 256–58.

73. The actual control enjoyed by the Inaba (or Masuda, et al.) over their "many holdings" is one of the great unanswerables. Obviously, the same incompleteness of authority was operant for western houses as for their Kantō counterparts.

74. *Wakasa no kuni shugo shiki shidai*, entry for 1196/9/1, in *Shinkō gunsho ruijū* (Tokyo, 1930), 3:107. The 40 percent figure is cited by Tanaka, "Wakasa," p. 267.

75. Ibid., pp. 267–68.

76. *TōjiHyakugō Monjo*, 1196/6 Wakasa no kuni goke'nin (?) chūshin an, in *KI*, 2:191–92, doc. 854. Why these houses are listed as "former Genji and Heishi" (*sakizaki no Gempei ryōke*), rather than Kamakura vassals (goke'nin), is not clear. *Tōji Hyakugō Monjo*, 1245/6 Wakasa no kuni goke'nin sojō an, in Tōkyō Daigaku shiryō hensanjo, comp., *Dai Nihon shiryō*, ser.5 (Tokyo, 1973). 19:38. (Hereafter cited as *DNS*.)

77. Tanaka, "Wakasa," p. 281.

It is possible, then, that in Wakasa it was the leading members of the Inaba bushidan who had, *en bloc*, become vassals of Kamakura. In this regard Wakasa was not alone. In Iyo, half or more of the enrolling housemen are thought to have belonged to the private allegiance group of the Kōno.[78] This may suggest a larger pattern in provinces possessing a dominant resident officer. But there is another conclusion. The bakufu had clearly succeeded in extending its influence into western Japan, enrolling housemen both individually and in groups. At the same time, however, it is far from certain that Yoritomo gained a lord's control over many of his new vassals. Families such as the Inaba potentially blocked the way. In later years a further stage of consolidation would be required.

While Kamakura thus benefited from the initial conversion of great magnates, clear difficulties were anticipated for the future. In other provinces more direct methods of expanding bakufu power were employed. The range of techniques shows considerable ingenuity, and it will be useful to refer briefly to several of these.

In Sanuki, for example, public officers were enlisted as vassals but immediately subjected to a commander sent from the Kantō. The special circumstance here appears to have been the absence of a dominant native house: Fuji Sukemitsu was merely the first among relative equals of the fourteen enrolling Sanuki families.[79] Elsewhere, a shugo-denominated officer was sent out from the east. These cases will receive special treatment in chapter 4. In Hokurikudō, a Yoritomo deputy was appointed to oversee the government offices (kokuga) in each of the separate provinces.[80] Finally, in Kyushu, a variety of devices was tried:[81] (1) in late 1185, Kondō and Nakahara, Kamakura's co-deputies in Kyoto, were sent to Kyushu with responsibility for curbing and adjudicating local outrages (*AK* 1185/7/12); (2) infiltration of that region's special administrative head-

---

78. Tanaka, "Iyo," p. 274.

79. Tanaka Minoru, "Sanuki no kuni jitō goke'nin ni tsuite," in Hōgetsu Keigo Sensei kanreki kinenkai, comp., *Nihon shakai keizai shi kenkyū, kodai-chūsei hen*, (Tokyo, 1968), pp. 369–82. (Hereafter cited as Tanaka, "Sanuki.")

80. *Ninnaji Monjo*, 1184/5 Go-Shirakawa In-no-chō kudashibumi, in Tanaka, "Ninnaji monjo," p. 75. For a discussion see ibid., pp. 76–77 and Ishii Susumu, "Heishi-Kamakura ryō seikenka no Aki kokuga," *Rekishigaku kenkyū* 257 (1961): 8–11. (Hereafter cited as Ishii S., "Aki.")

81. Bakufu expansion into Kyushu is detailed in chap. 6.

quarters, dazaifu, was begun, and a Kyushu deputy was sent out from the east; (3) the governorship of strategic Bungo Province was acquired by Kamakura in late 1185, and retained permanently (*AK* 1185/12/6); and (4) special "supra-jitō" (*sōjitō*) posts were distributed to trusted easterners. Assignments were to land units in which indigenous Kamakura vassals had received regular jitō investiture.

To conclude our picture of bakufu expansion into western Japan, a word must be added concerning areas that did not submit to extensive Kamakura infiltration. That there were various provinces in this category is not surprising, especially since much of the central and western region had experienced widespread shōen formation. This tended to reduce the sphere of the provincial officialdom, which invariably constituted the group most receptive to bakufu overtures. On the other hand, this does not explain why, for example, Wakasa with its roughly 50–50 public–private land ratio produced the Inaba family, while Bizen with a comparable division yielded no similarly prominent house.[82] Whatever the reasons for such contrasting histories, the absence of powerful warriors in Bizen seems clearly to have slowed bakufu progress there. Bizen's government headquarters—and with it the province as a whole—continued to be run by agents sent out from the capital, and by minor indigenous officers who had not become Minamoto vassals.[83]

By the end of 1185 Kamakura had succeeded in extending its influence across much of Japan. From a movement that had begun in the east with Kantō-based warriors offering their support to a regional figure, the Minamoto drive had now inflated to full country-

82. Although acreage statistics are not known, the number of public and private land units is thought to have been forty-four each. See Hall, *Government and Local Power*, pp. 155 ff.

83. This is not to say that Yoritomo was never party to the intrigue surrounding Bizen. When the provincial proprietorship over Bizen was transferred to Tōdaiji in 1193, Yoritomo took a keen interest in who the governor appointment would fall to, i.e., who would be given jurisdiction over the provincial office. The result, however, was a victory for Tōdaiji: Ichijō Yoshiyasu, Yoritomo's Kyoto-resident brother-in-law, was named governor, but actual "provincial authority" (*kokumu*) was placed in the hands of Chōgen, agent for Tōdaiji. Kanai Madoka, "Kamakura jidai no Bizen kokugaryō ni tsuite," *Nihon rekishi* 150 (1960): 41–42.

wide proportions. Yoritomo, its leader, was not only the most
powerful man in Japan by the end of the war, but was also the head
of the bakufu, a warrior-controlled regime owing little to central
authority. The progress of these extraordinary developments,
summarized below, marks the coming to maturity of autonomous
local power.

Yoritomo and his band of followers started the decade with a
campaign to secure the Kantō from central interference. The converse of this effort was a Yoritomo offer, simple but revolutionary,
to legitimize all warrior holdings under his own name. He and his
men would rule the east themselves, bypassing all court-centered
authority. A period of initial jockeying took place among various
local families, but by the end of 1180 most of the Kantō had become
at least nominally Genji.

The next two years were spend constructing a new capital and
consolidating Kamakura's governance; what main-force fighting
occurred against the Taira was left to Minamoto bands with origins
in the Chūbu. During this same period other sections of the country
were caught up in the new spirit of rebelliousness. Taking up arms
against one's private enemies lent to the violence a specter of social
upheaval and unprecedented national crisis. Most dramatic was the
upsurge in encroachments against absentee authority. In an ironic
twist of fate, the Minamoto as instigators of this new local license
were soon to be called on by Kyoto for assistance in restoring the
country to peace.

In 1183, Yoritomo's Genji headship was suddenly threatened by
the appearance at court of a rival who, like Yoritomo himself, saw
his kinsman, rather than the now-expelled Heishi, as the more
logical enemy. Kamakura was quick to respond, securing from the
court the 1183/10 In decree, and moving troops westward for the
first time. Yoshinaka, the challenger, was eliminated early in 1184,
and Yoritomo was free at last to undertake new goals. Abandoning
his earlier scheme to divide the country's local administration
between his own regime and the Heishi, he now sought final destruction of the latter and a permanent establishment of his power
countrywide.

In western Japan, where the eastern-based bakufu did not enjoy a natural constituency, special policies had to be devised. For example, a certain measure of cooperation with the court and capital proprietors became useful: a number of documents survive showing Yoritomo or his agents issuing prohibitive decrees against warrior outrages. Such efforts, of course, greatly favored bakufu interests. Not only was Kyoto demonstrating its abject dependence on Kamakura power, but Kamakura was assuming governmental responsibilities everywhere by taking a positive stand against lawless behavior. To a considerable degree such a posture was at variance with the natural desires of indigenous warriors. But Yoritomo was not offering freedom of encroachment, rather only patents of guarantee. This promise of enhanced security over land was apparently enough to win the support of fighting men in most provinces.

The particular configuration of Kamakura power in a given area was a product of various factors. In some instances, bakufu influence was channeled through a dominant resident official; in others, it was more direct. What is important is that the expansion process itself depended less on any sanction from the court than on a combination of bakufu resourcefulness and a growing local disorder. The greatest emphasis was on the control of men.

The bakufu in mid-1185 stood as the dominant political and military force in Japan. Victorious in a countrywide civil war and possessing warriors numbered as its vassals in virtually every province, the regime of Yoritomo could point to accomplishments that fighting men only a few years earlier would not have thought possible. Inevitably, comparisons must have been made between the Taira's road to power at court, followed by rapid demise in the recent war, and the unprecedented successes and seemingly unlimited potential of a Minamoto movement that had held back from subordinating itself to the traditional power structure. What was most significant was that Kyoto had indeed been largely bypassed: noncentral sources of authority were proved sufficient not merely to legitimize private landholding—the objective in 1180— but also to provide warriors with a justification, or "right," to discharge governance in areas far from their homelands. By 1185 easterners were carrying out governmental tasks in western Japan, a lesson that could hardly have been lost on the country's absentee owners, sedentary themselves in the capital for hundreds of years. Japan's "age of military houses" was now beginning.

At the same time, it had also been revealed that warriors without rewards and without organizational controls to keep them in check were more apt to abuse than use for constructive purposes their newly acquired powers. The story of the wartime shugo and jitō (especially the latter) will help us to understand these simultaneous and disparate trends.

4 SHUGO AND JITŌ BEFORE 1185

Traditional historians of Japan cite 1185 as the year in which the Kamakura shugo and jitō were first instituted. A description in the *Azuma kagami* of a court order authorizing bakufu control of both officer types has served as validation for this claim.[1] However, the emergence of these two figures is certainly more complex than this account would have us believe. According to *Azuma kagami*, a court edict rather than a gradual "historical" evolution was at the origin of both offices. The account also binds shugo and jitō into a unitary birth, thereby locking them into the same framework. The following discussion will challenge these ideas. Not only must we examine the offices separately, but we must delve back into the war period and even earlier for their origins.

The Heian period had no officers called shugo.[2] There were, of course, provincial constables—the kebiishi, ōryōshi, and tsuibushi referred to in chapter 2—but these narrowly conceived imperial police offices bear little resemblance to the highly versatile private shugo of Gempei War Japan. To complicate the problem of origins still further, there is a hiatus of sorts from late in 1185—the very time that shugo were supposed to have appeared—to the 1190s.[3] From 1192 we see the emergence of the institutionalized "Kamakura shugo," a figure much different from his 1180s predecessor. Recent

1. The key entries are 1185/11/12, 28, 29, and 12/6—easily *AK*'s most famous sequence. See n. 88.
2. The term *shugo* ("to protect") had long been used as a verb, especially in reference to native virtue, the gods, or shrines. See, e.g., *Kōkokuji Monjo*, 1138/3/25 Sa Kon'oe gon no chūjo Fujiwara Kimiyoshi kishinjō, in *HI*, 5:2016, doc. 2384.
3. Very little is known of shugo during the second half of the 1180s; certainly, there was no sudden creation of a comprehensive shugo network as implied by the *AK* rendition of the famous court decree. See chap. 8.

Japanese scholars have dealt with this distinction by calling the
1180s group "*sōtsuibushi*," a title actually found in some texts. In
this view, sōtsuibushi were transitional figures from whom the true
shugo soon evolved.[4] Unfortunately, this approach ignores entirely
the usage in our sources of the two terms: most 1180s materials
refer to "shugo," while those that do not, involve us in a hopeless
round of contradictions.[5] This suggests that the real distinction
is not one between titles; it is one involving duties. As we shall see,
the shugo of the war years were emergency figures operating under
no explicit framework, while their post-1192 namesakes exercised
rights carefully limited by law.[6]

Our earliest reference to shugo is the 1180/10/21 (*AK*) posting,
allegedly under this designation, of two Yoritomo vassals to the
provinces of Suruga and Tōtomi. Several considerations are relevant
here. First, we must recall the progress of the war late in 1180. The
tenth month—after the Fujigawa battle in Suruga—was when Genji
and Heishi decided to pull back and eschew further direct confrontation. Suruga and Tōtomi were chosen as a western buffer area for
Yoritomo's Kantō-based movement, with housemen Yasuda Yoshisada and Takeda Nobuyoshi appointed as provincial commanders.
It is likely, under these circumstances, that the assignment was
viewed functionally. Even if we assume accuracy in *Azuma kagami*'s
hindsight use of the term "shugo," we should not admit a *title*;
instead, "protection of a province" was assigned to a warrior who
only later came to be thought of as that province's "protector." This
was the route followed by other emergent titles—a fusion of re-

4. The clearest account of sōtsuibushi in the 1180s is Yasuda Genkyū, *Shugo
to jitō*, (Tokyo, 1964), pp. 22–42.

5. E.g., while we find extant documents of 1184–85 referring to shugo, an 1185
entry in *Hyakurenshō* (1185/6/19, p. 151) notes that all bakufu sōtsuibushi had
now been canceled by order of the court. Or again, *AK*'s late 1185 entries concerning Yoritomo's countrywide shugo privilege, and *Masu kagami*'s similar
reference using the designation "sōtsuibushi" (Iwanami Bunko edition, 1931,
p. 28). Or finally, an *AK* reference to Ōuchi Koreyoshi as shugo of Iga Province,
and a documentary citation of two years later to Koreyoshi as Iga Province
sōtsuibushi (*AK* 1184/3/20, and *Tada-In Monjo*, 1186/11/25 Ōe Hiromoto hōsho
an, in *KI*,1:116, doc. 195).

6. The present chapter takes the shugo story only through 1185. For the later
period, see chap., 8.

sponsibility with holder, leading to eventual recognition and more generalized application as a shiki (office). In the case of shugo, the requirements of war and a growing awareness of the advantage of a concept not subject to Kyoto definition combined to accelerate a process that normally took generations.

The nature of the Suruga and Tōtomi responsibilities is revealed in a complaint to Yoritomo by one of the two "shugo," Yoshisada of Tōtomi. The refusal of local persons to provide laborers for construction of fortifications was complicating his provincial protection duty.[7] This suggests a pacification–recruitment–requisitioning function for these first "shugo." It also brings to mind the timing and duties of the Heishi-appointed special officer (sōkan) described in chapter 1. The comparison cannot be extended, however. The sōkan was placed jurisdictionally *above* the separate governors, only to find that his authority was too indirect for optimum mobilization through the provincial headquarters. Yoritomo by contrast could simply intrude his authority without regard for governor sensibilities. Taking advantage of his status as an outlaw, the Genji leader dispatched two of his vassals to Tōtomi and Suruga, giving each the assignment, if not the actual title, of "shugo."

The only other possible reference to shugo for the period before 1184 appears in an 1180/11 entry in the fictional war tale *Gempei seisuiki*. Listed alongside the names of the Suruga and Tōtomi assignees just discussed are Chiba Tsunetane and Kazusa Hirotsune of Shimōsa and Kazusa provinces.[8] An actual shugo title seems even more doubtful here. In addition to the general unreliability of our source, the name "shugo" does not itself appear. Similarly, a formal shugo designation would have been superfluous to an already lustrous genealogy: Chiba and Kazusa had long been dominant in their respective provinces by virtue of offices held within the traditional hierarchy. As we shall see, almost without exception the shugo during these years were nonindigenous warriors sent by Kamakura generally for the purpose of gaining a foothold in non-Kantō areas. It is therefore more likely that the *Gempei seisuiki*

7. *AK* 1181/3/3. "Shugo" is used in this entry as a verb.
8. Cited in Satō Shin'ichi, *Zōtei-Kamakura bakufu shugo seido no kenkyū* (Tokyo, 1971), p. 67. (Hereafter cited as Satō, *Zōtei-shugo seido.*)

reference to Chiba and Kazusa alludes not to their investiture as shugo, a new concept, but rather to their mandate, discussed in chapter 3, to seize full and unhindered control from the headquarters (kokuga) in their respective provinces.

The reappearance of shugo in 1184 coincides with the initial push westward of the Kamakura regime. By this juncture the simple defense responsibility of Yasuda and Takeda would no longer avail, given the new geographical environment and changed complexion of the war. A development into something at once more complex and flexible would have to be combined with a status, or "name," for bakufu officers in provinces near the capital. Information on planning and background has unfortunately been lost. All we know is that during 1184 a handful of men came to be called "shugo": Doi Sanehira over Bitchū, Bizen, and Bingo; Kajiwara Kagetoki over Mimasaka and Harima; Teshima (or Toshima) Aritsune over Kii; and Ōuchi Koreyoshi over Iga.[9]

Doi's authority over Bitchū is described in *Azuma kagami* as that of a Kamakura agent (*otsukai*) exercising administrative responsibility (*rimu*) in or for that province. Specifically, we see him reappointing a number of persons to the shiki rights earlier seized from them by the Heishi.[10] This activity is not new to us. In a variety of contexts, Yoritomo, through proxies, was confirming holdings in western Japan, and accepting warriors into vassalage.

For Bizen, the nature of Doi's authority is expressed in *AK* 1184/12/16: Yoritomo is described as ordering Doi, then present in Bizen, to investigate the validity of a claim by that province's Kibitsu Shrine regarding restoration of certain lands lost during the war. It is noteworthy here that a western province shrine would already be appealing for assistance directly to Kamakura. Even more striking is that Sanehira, after conducting his investigation, was apparently free to settle a dispute involving a proprietary claim. The traditional direction of legitimation was being inverted.

9. Hayashiya Tatsusaburō, "Chūsei shi gaisetsu," in *Iwanami kōza, Nihon rekishi 5, chūsei 1,* p. 20. This list is well known, but the shugo themselves have not been exhaustively studied.

10. *AK* 1184/3/25. However, a document of some months later shows not Doi, but Kajiwara Kagetoki, involved in a land-confirmation case in Bitchū Province: *Jingoji Monjo,* 1184(?)/10/18 Kajiwara Kagetoki shojō, in *HI,* 8:3151, doc. 4211. Evidently, the lines of jurisdiction were not sharply drawn.

Doi's involvement in Bingo Province is not recorded directly. We know only that he and Kajiwara had been granted shugo authority in the five most easterly Sanyōdō provinces (*AK* 1184/2/18), and that the latter figure held responsibility for Harima and Mimasaka.[11]

Our information on the two Kajiwara provinces is hardly clearer. For Harima, a reference at the time of Kajiwara's fall from grace in 1200 suggests his earlier shugo authority there; the years of this tenure are not specified (*AK* 1200/2/22). A war-period link between Kajiwara and Harima does exist, however, though not in the context we might expect. A document of 1185/4 accuses Kajiwara of committing lawless encroachments in that province, one of the very activities that shugo were supposed to suppress.[12] This may have had something to do with another vassal's receiving the Harima shugo assignment later in 1185, though Kajiwara was subsequently reinstated.[13] Data on Mimasaka comes entirely from the period after 1185. Kajiwara's holding of that shugo authority is cited in the *Azuma kagami* entry for 1187/12/7.

Looking ahead to the authorized responsibilities of the true shugo of post-1192, we see no hint here of either limited policing for certain crimes, or the drawing up of special guard registers for Kamakura housemen.[14] But neither do we find the construction of buffer fortifications by military "shugo" such as in Tōtomi and Suruga in 1180. Instead, the significance of Doi and Kajiwara as shugo lies in their buttressing of provincial offices and governorships made moribund by the war. There appear, indeed, to have been *no* restrictions on the practical range of their involvement; public and private sector might equally be in their debt, as well as local and central interests. Kamakura was once again proving its indispensability far from home.

The handful of materials on the Teshima house of Kii constitutes our richest source on any Gempei War period shugo.[15] At the same

11. Satō, *Zōtei-shugo seido*, pp. 164, 168.

12. *Kamowake Ikazuchi Jinja Monjo*, 1185/4/29 Go-Shirakawa In-no-chō chō, in *HI*, 8:3174, doc. 4244.

13. Satō, *Zōtei-shugo seido*, pp. 153–54. For more on this 1185 replacement, see p. 101.

14. See chap. 8. This was the extent of the shugo's lawful competence, later called *taihon sankajō*.

15. As with so many of the documents from 1180–85, possible doubt exists as to their authenticity. The materials themselves are Tokugawa period copies of

time, the Teshima themselves loom as an exception to the otherwise uniform practice of denying shugo status to a native warrior family. The scion, Aritsune's, "acting governor" title (*gon no kami*) marks him as a resident provincial officer of the very highest level.[16] Why the bakufu should have called its man in Kii as shugo when comparable western officers were given either no title (the Inaba of Wakasa) or accorded only a traditional post (the Iwami Masuda's ōryōshi post) will never be known.[17] We can only reiterate (however unsatisfactory this explanation) that war-period shugo should not be judged by the more uniform standards of their later namesake.

The documents themselves shed considerable light on the tangle of competing authorities in wartime Kii. Of interest to us is the focal position occupied by Aritsune in his capacity as shugo and acting governor. The particular incident described here concerns Teshima violations of a war requisitioning exemption for Dempōin Temple lands. The governor of Kii, helpless in the face of his subordinate's

---

records no longer extant. Most scholars, however, accept these Teshima documents as entirely genuine.

16. For these references see (1) *Negoro Yōsho*, 1184/8/24 Oribe no kami Kagemune hōsho, in *HI*, 8:3146, doc. 4201, (Teshima gon no kami dono), and (2) *AK* 1186/3/26 (Kii gon no kami Aritsune). Some scholars have assumed that Aritsune was not in fact a native of Kii, but rather part of the Kasai family in the Kantō's Musashi Province: e.g., Hotta Shōzō, ed., *Azuma kagami hyōchū* (Tokyo, 1944), 2:132. The link here is a contemporaneous Teshima Kiyomitsu, "acting governor" of Musashi (Teshima gon no kami Kiyomitsu: see Fuzambō, comp., *Kokushi jiten* [Tokyo, 1940], 2:472.) This unusual likeness of name, however, appears merely coincidental, for several reasons: (1) Aritsune does not appear in Fuzambō's genealogical chart of the Kasai; (2) the Kasai are not known to have had any relationship with Kii, much less an "acting governorship" over that province; (3) the gon no kami title was invariably a distinction held by a native house; (4) at the very moment that Aritsune was "acting governor" in Kii, the Kasai scion (followed by his son), was "acting governor" in Musashi; and (5) Aritsune continued to be associated only with Kii, even well after the war (*AK* 1190/5/29 and 1191/10/2).

17. Actually, there is no positive evidence that the Teshima were in fact assigned as shugo *by the bakufu*. None of our references to Aritsune as shugo issued from Kamakura itself; they either came from Kyoto or were used locally in Kii. All historians, however, have assumed that the Teshima were the bakufu's shugo appointees. E.g., Satō, *Zōtei-shugo seido*, p. 189. But no one, to my knowledge, has really studied this family.

encroachments, complained to the In that Aritsune alone among
resident officials (zaichō) was refusing to honor Dempōin's immunity.[18] The In's headquarters, responding to this appeal, decreed
that produce (shotō), soldier (heishi), and commissariat (hyōrō)
levies were not to be imposed against that temple's lands. The edict
was addressed to the provincial officers of Kii.[19] The governor added
his own exhortation, sending a directive to the Kii "absentee office"
(rusudokoro) to the effect that the shugo (shugonin) Aritsune was to
cease his unlawful levies.[20] This combined pressure from retired
emperor and governor induced Aritsune to make a reply. The exemption order, he asserted, was already in force and would continue
to be observed. The only levies that Dempōin lands would be
subjected to were musterings of Kamakura housemen (goke'nin)
and others with the capacity to fight.[21] This final remark is worth
underscoring: the shugo of Kii was now on record as saying that
while assessments in kind would not be collected under pretext of
war, prominent residents on Dempōin estates could be recruited.
Warriors, vassal and nonvassal, were seemingly to be placed under
the bakufu's expanding command system.

One of the clearest lessons to emerge here is that those denomi-
nated as shugo were obviously left much to their own devices; their
local circumstances and integrity as vassals determined the character
of their duty performance. In Iga Province, for example, the shugo
Ōuchi Koreyoshi became enmeshed in a proceeding that resulted
in his dictating an administrative settlement to that province's
headquarters.[22] In his edict of 1184/9, Koreyoshi judged that nonresident cultivators of a Tōdaiji estate were to have their tax-exempt

18. Negoro Yōsho, 1184/8/5 Kii kokushi Fujiwara Norisue ukebumi an, in
HI, 8:3142, doc. 4189.
19. Ibid., 1184/8/8 Go-Shirakawa In-no-chō kudashibumi an, doc. 4191,
p. 3142.
20. Ibid., 1184/8/8 Kii kokushi chōsen an, doc. 4192, pp. 3142–43. The term
shugonin (literally, "protector person") suggests the title's emergent status. The
diary Gyokuyō chronicles this transition from use strictly as a verb (e.g., 1180/3/
18, 2:386); to use three years later as a noun (bushi no shugo, 1183/11/15, 2:654).
21. Negoro Yōsho, 1184/8/29 Kii no kuni shugo Teshima Aritsune ukebumi
an, in HI, 8:3147, doc. 4204.
22. AK 1184/3/20 records Koreyoshi's appointment as shugo.

status reinstated to help defray the costs of repairs to that temple. The domain in question had earlier been seized by the Taira.[23] The main point of this episode is that Koreyoshi was engaging in an activity subsequently barred to all shugo; he was interfering directly in provincial affairs. This fact is duly recorded in a notation to our document, added later: Koreyoshi was not the governor (*kokushi*), according to this addendum, but was exercising provincial affairs (*kokumu*) anyway. Tōdaiji had evidently directed its appeal in mid-1184 to the only authority in Iga capable of granting it redress.

Another side to these wartime shugo was their tendency to act as disrupters rather than preservers of stability. Teshima in Kii and Kajiwara in Harima have already been noted. But there was a more ominous trend, indicated by the rise of "unofficial" shugo. As we will see shortly, the most conspicuous development along these lines occurred with jitō. However, by war's end the shugo title was also appearing in a context of general adversity. The following excerpt showing a Yoritomo guarantee of thirty-nine Iwashimizu Hachiman Shrine lands in twelve provinces, demonstrates this:

> . . . These domains have been the divine lands of Hachiman Shrine-Temple for a very long time. In recent years, however, due to the campaign against the Heike, *shugo-type fighting men*[24] have been withholding annual tax rice, have been collecting commissariat tax, and have been causing traditional religious expense tributes to be late. . . . Who midst the four seas would neglect shrinely virtue? . . . Such outrages are to cease. . . .

A document of several months later is even more explicit: now we see a specific reference to outrages being committed by "shugo persons" (shugonin).[25]

Several references survive to shugo appointed by Kamakura

23. *Tōnan'in Monjo*, 1184/8/9 Ōuchi Koreyoshi kudashibumi an, in *HI*, 8:3143, doc. 4193.

24. The phrase is "*shugo no bushi tō*." (See the *Gyokuyō* citation in n. 20 for these terms reversed: "*bushi no shugo*," warrior shugo.) Another possibility is that a comma should replace the "*no*." Hence, "shugo and bushi," rather than "shugo-type bushi." This quote is from *Iwashimizu Monjo*, 1185/1/9 Minamoto Yoritomo kudashibumi an, in *HI*, 8:3159–60, doc. 4227. (My emphasis.)

25. *Kamowake Ikazuchi Jinja Monjo*, 1185/4/29 Go-Shirakawa In-no-chō kudashibumi, in *HI*, 8:3174, doc. 4244.

during 1185. Unhappily, they exhibit little pattern. Our knowledge of the first in this group comes from a document issued almost 150 years later. As part of the final campaign against the Taira, Kōno Tokihiro of Musashi Province was posted as sōtsuibushi to Tajima, west of the capital.[26] The rationale here was obviously military. A different kind of shugo (shugonin) was oppointed to Tsushima, an island off the coast of Kyushu (*AK* 1185/5/23). The holder of this assignment, Kawachi Yoshinaga of Kai Province (*AK* 1180/10/13), was little more than a frontier guard. Still another shugo context emerges in 1185/8 in Harima Province. Here the title was granted (on the surface at least) as a reward. While probably an embellishment of what really happened, the *Azuma kagami* describes Shimokabe Yukihira's being queried as to which province he would like assignment as shugo. The reply was Harima (*AK* 1185/8/24). We can speculate on the larger significance of this appointment. The Gempei War had ended in 1185/3, and three months later, according to one account, the country's sōtsuibushi were all abolished.[27] The provinces, however, were far from stabilized—as witness the lawless acts of the Harima shugo, Kajiwara Kagetoki, during the fourth month (see notes 12 and 13). The present authorization of 1185/8 may thus have represented a shugo restoration in a province torn by instability. Our final reference to a shugo holder in 1185 does not help us on this point; still another shugo context reveals itself. In an 1185/10 entry from *Azuma kagami*, a certain Yamauchi Tsunetoshi decries an assault on his Ise Province shugo headquarters (*shugosho*) by forces loyal to Yoshitsune.[28] It seems likely that this shugo had been posted to coordinate consolidation efforts in a province with strong Heishi ties.

It is clear from the foregoing data that Kamakura did not con-

26. Cited by Satō, *Zōtei-shugo seido*, p. 138. See nn. 5 and 27 for the sōtsuibushi–shugo problem.

27. *Hyakurenshō*, 1185/6/19, p. 151. There is no way to establish the validity of this version of events. E.g., we may wonder why *AK* fails to mention any mid-1185 cancellation of shugo (sōtsuibushi). Most scholars, however, accept the *Hyakurenshō* account as genuine, even while they are at pains to explain it. See Yasuda, *Shugo to jitō*, pp. 27–30, and Hotta, *Azuma kagami hyōchū*, 1:269, editor's note.

28. *AK* 1185/10/23. Evidently, this was part of Yoshitsune's campaign late in 1185 to gather troops for his struggle against Kamakura.

ceive of a countrywide deployment of uniform provincial officers under the title of shugo.[29] Although such a development was delayed
until the 1190s, the shugo of Gempei War Japan do have a significance. For the most part, placements were made in provinces adjoin-
ing or ringing the capital region. These were areas normally under
strong central influence, however incapacitated at the moment.
This meant that in order for Kamakura to acquire a permanent
interest it would have to send in external commanders; there existed
no prominent native officer houses whose conversion to vassalage
could be used as an initial stage in this process. An interesting
configuration emerges here: in no province receiving an easterner as
shugo do we find a major resident magnate. Conversely, in no
province possessing a Masuda- or Inaba-level family do we identify
a shugo.[30] For the period under examination, these two forms of
extending bakufu influence seem mutually exclusive.[31]

Regarding, finally, the problem of whether to view these wartime shugo as forerunners of their later institutionalized namesakes,
no definitive answer can be given. Certainly they shared a title name
and appointment unit, the province. But if we are to conceive of the
"Kamakura shugo" as an outgrowth of an earlier counterpart, it
must be with the realization that the post-1190s shugo had a *narrower*
rather than a *wider* range of activity. These later figures were born
not from the conditions of helter-skelter bakufu expansion and
collapsed local governance, but from the more relaxed circumstances
of the reconstruction period that followed.

The origins of jitō, like shugo, are shrouded in mystery and
controversy. A handful of competing theories exists, but an eclectic
approach, reflecting the sources, seems clearly warranted. The
theories, at any rate, must be noted.[32]

29. Every known reference to shugo during 1180-85 has been cited. I have
found three other references, but in documents that are clearly forgeries: *Kokuzō
Kitajima Ke Monjo*, 1164/11/5 Tokimura watashijō, in *Izumo Kokuzō ke monjo*,
doc. 1, p. 1; *Itōzu Monjo* 1180/9/1 Minamoto Yoritomo kishinjō an, in *Ōita
ken shiryō* (Ōita, 1960), 1:59-60; and an unnamed document collection, c. 1185/1
Kawachi no kuni Tsūhōji ureijō, in *HI*, 8:3158-59, doc. 4226.

30. The Teshima scion of Kii was himself made shugo.

31. We will note in chap. 6 that indigenous houseman magnates were later
subordinated (or jettisoned) in deference to Kantō-sent shugo.

32. I am indebted to C. J. Kiley for valuable suggestions on the origins of jitō.

The most common approach to jitō origins is the one appearing in most Western-language histories. The post is viewed from its thirteenth-century position of dominance within shōen, and the conclusion is drawn that earlier jitō were managerial or agential tenures with roots in these same central proprietary domains.[33] A related view, also emphasizing a shōen framework, postures these pre-Kamakura jitō less as officials of the center than as "local magnates" (ryōshu) whose lands have been incorporated into shōen. Jitō represented one category of prominent military land commenders.[34] A third theory rejects entirely the private domain "apprenticeship" of jitō implicit in the two previous views. Stressing instead the "public sector" origins and character of jitō shiki, this third approach posits a provincial office genealogy for both the post and its holders. A major argument here is the absence of Heian-period jitō in shōen belonging to religious institutions.[35]

One of the first things we note when we go back to the Heian record is that the jitō shiki has a short history. Unlike the gesu and azukari dokoro posts with which it is often compared, the earliest known example of jitō connoting a land title pre-dates the bakufu by only thirty-odd years. The relative novelty of this shiki name would add to its attractiveness during the crisis years of the 1180s. The term itself, of course, is much older, and the earliest surviving instance of its use appears in a document of 896.[36] As used in that ninth-century record, the term "jitō" simply designates a local family's land; it was this context that continued largely intact into the twelfth century.

At the same time, from the end of the eleventh century we begin to find the term appearing as part of a set phrase—a provincial or private-estate official "going to the jitō" (jitō ni nozomu) for purposes

His approach to the problem, while different from my own, should be carefully considered. See his "Property and Political Authority in Early Medieval Japan" (Ph.D. diss., Harvard, 1970), chap. 6.

33. Shinoda, Founding of the Kamakura Shogunate, p. 132.

34. Yasuda, Jitō oyobi, chaps. 1 and 2.

35. Uwayokote Masataka, "Jitō genryū kō," Shisō 12 (1957): 19–33. While generally supporting Uwayokote, an excellent survey of basic approaches to the jitō problem is Ōae Ryō, "Jitō shiki o meguru shomondai," Hōkei gakkai zasshi 13.4 (1964): 26–32.

36. Cited in Uwayokote, "Jitō genryū kō," p. 23, and Yasuda, Jitō oyobi, p. 24.

of settling a dispute, marking off the boundaries of a shōen, or conducting some other important administrative task.[37] As examples we cite the following: (1) A Kyushu government-general (dazaifu) investigator (*jikkenshi*) being sent in 1089 "to the jitō" of a Chikuzen Province shōen in order to interrogate persons of long residence; (2) an Iga Province agent and temple proprietor agent returning "to the jitō" of a troubled domain in order to assess the failure of a harvest; (3) the resident officers (zaichō) of Shimōsa Province performing an investigation in 1160 of the "jitō" (lands) once held by Chiba Tsunetane; and (4) in 1144, an Owari governor office's agent being sent "to the jitō" in order to set a shōen's boundary markers.[38]

From such case examples it is evident that as late as the 1160s "jitō" had not yet entirely shed its original meaning of "land" or "site." Such a development, however, had clearly begun. During these middle decades of the twelfth century the term came to be used for the first time in a true shiki context. What prompted this transformation (beginning before the rise of the Taira) can only be guessed at, though several processes were doubtless involved. For one thing the connotation of "local area" must have hardened as administrative agents made constant official sojourns "to the jitō." The emphasis then shifted from a site to be visited on official business to those in possession of that site; these latter were now themselves called jitō. Another side to this complex development was the growing use of jitō in connection with older, fully recognized office titles. Caught up in the procedure of land-rights clarification, "jitō" eventually gained entrance itself into the shiki lexicon.

37. First pointed out by Uwayokote in "Jitō genryū kō," p. 24. A controversy has developed between Uwayokote and Yasuda over the type of officials being sent "to the jitō." Uwayokote asserts that they were almost always "public" officials, while Yasuda sees no limitation. Yasuda appears to have the better of this argument (*Jitō oyobi*, pp. 24–26). As an alternative to the phrase "jitō ni nozomu," the words "jitō ni tsukawasu" [sending to the jitō] sometimes appear.

38. (1) *Tōnan'in Monjo*, 1089/9/20 Dazaifu kumonjo kenchū an, in Takeuchi Rizō, comp., *Dazaifu-Dazaifu Tenmangū shiryō* (Dazaifu, 1969), 5:409, l.11, 411; (2) *Tōdaiji Monjo*, 1158/4 Iga no kuni zaichōkanjin tō gejō, in Nakamura Naokatsu, comp., *Tōdaiji Monjo* (Osaka, 1945), doc. 282, pp. 259–60, l.10; (3) *Ichiki Monjo*, 1161/4/1 Shimōsa gon no kami Taira (Chiba) Tsunetane shinjō an, in *HI*, 8:2527–28, doc. 3148, ll. 10–11 (the phrase here is somewhat different: "jitō o jikken"); and (4) *Engakuji Monjo*, 1144/10/20 Owari kokushi chōsen an, in *Kamakura shishi, shiryō hen* (Kamakura, 1956), 2:4.

The view that the jitō right had roots deep in the Heian period may have been unwittingly fostered in this country by Professor Asakawa of Yale. In his *Documents of Iriki* (p. 92) he presents a translation of a record describing a jitō shiki, without noting that in fact this is the earliest known document of its kind. The document, a petition of 1147, shows a Kyushu provincial officer, who was also a shōen official, requesting confirmation by Shimazu Estate's civil proprietor of a village-level jitō shiki.[39] The prominence of the petitioner as well as the size, character, and location of Shimazu, are all of considerable interest here.[40] For example, it is certainly significant that this and several other early jitō appeared in the remote hinterland of Kyushu, while the Kantō reveals no holders of this title until the mid-1170s (see p. 111). Second, it is noteworthy that Tomo Nobufusa was a ranking official within both the public- and private-office hierarchies, and that the village he claimed under jitō right was part of a district (Iriki-In) owing public and private taxes.[41] The jitō title was evidently sought as a title worthy of the region's leading local notable, yet one that would simultaneously convey or bridge the mixed status of the land unit in question.

The jitō right in this case had a secondary side. Perhaps because of the title's newness, it revealed in practice a certain weakness. We see this in two contexts. First in regard to the estate proprietor, the Fujiwara succeeded in denying Nobufusa's request for jitō reconfirmation over a second village; the title was assigned instead to the Fujiwara's own resident deputy (*mokudai*).[42] The Tomo's

39. In Japanese, *Iriki-In Monjo*, 1147/2/9 Satsuma no kuni Iriki-In benzaishi bettō Tomo Nobufusa ge, *Iriki.*, Japanese section, pp. 53–54. Tomo Nobufusa was tax or "finance" agent (*benzaishi*) of Iriki District, Satsuma Province and also administrative officer (*bettō*) of Shimazu-no-shō.

40. The gigantic Shimazu Estate, a proprietorship of the Fujiwara, extended over the greater part of the three southernmost provinces of Kyushu. Shimazu-no-shō was unique in size and infinitely more complex in structure than any other shōen. Asakawa, *Iriki*, pp. 3–8, provides a brief introduction in English; in Japanese, there is a voluminous literature, with the many writings of Gomi Katsuo (Kagoshima University) outstanding.

41. This mixed public and private land (*yose-gōri*) is described in Asakawa, *Iriki*, p. 92.

42. This was also in 1147. The incident seems roughly analogous to the eastern Chiba's post-commendation loss of their homelands. The jitō and gesu rights of the Tomo and Chiba, respectively, were compromised by a central legitimizer.

remaining jitō shiki was witness to the second form of pressure. During the Gempei War this village inheritance was violated by a succession of Taira vassals. After outright seizure by one Heishi member, a second appears to have assumed the jitō right by virtue of his superior ranking in the provincial (not shōen) hierarchy.[43] We are reminded again of the mixed essence of this Iriki district jitō post.

A somewhat different jitō-related sequence is recorded in an inheritance document of 1156. A land unit in Kii Province in central Japan had been received from an original holder by Tankei, who in turn commended the area to the court. Incorporation as shōen followed, with Tankei and his descendants receiving permanent investiture as jitō. At the time of the present writing (1156), Tankei was passing this inheritance to a younger brother, Sōken.[44] This episode exhibits a standard commendation–confirmation (local–central) partitioning of interests over a piece of land; dozens of similar transactions can be noted involving gesu or azukari dokoro titles. The difficulty comes when we look at what happened in the next generation. In Sōken's own will of 1175, nothing is changed from the earlier document except the name of the post being transferred: hoshi, the normal jurisdictional title for a small unit of public land, is used instead of jitō.[45] Had the jitō title then given way to hoshi? While speculative, it is probable that both shiki names were now being used to convey the area's dual commitment: revenue and/or service obligations were being paid to shōen owner and provincial treasury. At the same time, the existence of two titles—one recognized by the Kii headquarters, the other by the estate proprietor—probably served as a double guarantee.

A pair of records from 1152 and 1165 reveals a case in which a jitō right seems to have had a gesu shiki added to it.[46] The two documents are nearly identical local appointment decrees (man-

43. This figure was revenue agent (benzaishi) of Satsuma district (Kōri) within which Iriki District (In) was located (Asakawa, Iriki, p. 95; Iriki-In Monjo, 1183/8/8 Shimazu no shō bettō Tomo Nobuaki ge, ibid., Japanese section, p. 53).
44. Kanjōji Monjo, 1156/11/21 Sō Tankei shiryō yuzurijō, in HI, 6:2354, doc. 2857.
45. Ibid., 1175/8/19 Sō Sōken yuzurijō, in HI, 7:2873, doc. 3702.
46. Umezu Monjo, 1152/2/13 and 1165/5/6 Chikugo no kuni Kitano Tenmangū Dengaku mandokoro shiki buninjō, in HI, 6:2291 and 7:2651–52, docs. 2752 and 3357.

dokoro shiki) cosigned by a ranking official of the Tenmangū Shrine and a certain Fujiwara Zanetomo. In the 1152 record, Zanetomo is called jitō, while in the later counterpart he is designated jitō-gesu (*jitō kanete gesu*).[47] The differences between the two titles, their ultimate legitimizing agencies, and the conditions under which the gesu authority was added, have all regretably been lost. Unlike the previous example in which hoshi and jitō came to express a divided superior authority, we gain no sense here of a "public–private" separation. The only obvious point is that upper and lower possessors, Tenmangū Shrine and Zanetomo, were cooperating (perhaps sharing) in a minor appointment function.

The next two examples reveal an entirely different jitō context. In the former case, *jitōnin* (jitō persons), among others, were accused of having invaded a certain Kyushu temple's lands.[48] In the latter instance, a governor's decree addressed to the Iga provincial office demanded an end to violations of Kuroda Estate by unauthorized "provincial agents" and "jitō." The jitō are identified as priest-invaders from a rival central proprietor.[49] What is intriguing in both these cases is that the denomination jitō is not used in a strictly shiki framework; instead, jitō is a collective term implying encroachers upon land. The significance of this can only be appreciated from the perspective of the 1180s. As we shall see presently, warriors during the Gempei fighting began consciously to affect a jitō labeling as part of their justification for lawlessness. It cannot be proved, but it is possible that this kind of "antiestablishment" connotation for jitō traces back in part even before the war.

To complete what is known of the pre-1180 jitō, it is necessary to turn to the Taira's use of that title. For several generations of scholars an unsubstantiated *Azuma kagami* entry of late 1185 stood as proof that the Heishi had made extensive appointments to that post (*AK* 1185/12/21). But this may be a classic example of exaggeration by a chronicle known for such distortions.[50] Fully contem-

47. The term *kanete* is equivalent to "plus" or "and." It is used to imply a dual shiki possession.

48. *Tōdaiji Monjo*, 1144/1/11 Chikuzen no kuni Kanzeonji ryō shōshi ge an, in *HI*, 6:2130, doc. 2523.

49. Ibid., 1175/11/20 Iga kokushi chōsen an, 7:2880, doc. 3716.

50. If Heishi-assigned jitō were as prominent as suggested in this 12/21 entry, why does *AK* fail to mention them earlier? Why wait until nine months after the Taira demise—to the very month, indeed, in which Kamakura secured its own

poraneous records tell a much different story: Heishi-related jitō are found in only one region of a single province, Aki, where the Taira were long dominant. What is more, we see no evidence in post-1185 appointment decrees that any of the figures dispossessed to make room for Kamakura replacements had been holders of jitō shiki. Such Heishi warriors were gesu or the possessors of other traditional titles. Indeed even the known Aki examples give little hint of jitō as part of a Heishi effort to win supporters and extend local influence. The recipient of all but one of these titles was the Taira's oldest adherent in that province, a man already in possession of the land units now confirmed.[51]

In order to grapple with these Aki jitō we need to know something first of Kiyomori's relationship with that province. Heishi influence began there in 1146/2 with Kiyomori's appointment as governor. The Taira leader remained in that post for a full decade and was succeeded by two kinsmen until 1158/8. After that, the Taira's formal control over the Aki governorship became sporadic, yet with no apparent diminution in power.[52] The explanation for this has already been hinted at. During Kiyomori's 1140s tenure as governor, he had forged an alliance with Saeki Kagehiro, a major "resident officer" in Aki and the chief administrator of Itsukushima Shrine.[53] This relationship was carefully nourished over the years and led to a rise in the local fortunes of both men: in 1155 we see a Saeki promotion under Kiyomori as governor, while in 1182 Kagehiro himself was governor and the Taira were now Aki proprietors.[54] This was precisely the kind of correlation of interests that the Taira

countrywide jitō authority? Can this reference to Heishi jitō not be interpreted, therefore, as an effort to cite an immediate precedent by *AK*'s thirteenth-century compilers? For doubt concerning the reliability of the 12/21 *AK* account, see Ōae, "Jitō shiki," p. 25, n. 6.

51. Uwayokote, "Jitō genryū kō," pp. 24–25.

52. Conditions in Aki during the early 1160s are not clear. Then from c. 1165–71 an administrative chief in Kiyomori's house office became governor. After that, and until c. 1180, the legal situation again becomes cloudy (Ishii S., "Aki," pp. 7–8).

53. Itsukushima was both Aki "state shrine" (*ichinomiya*) and the Taira's family shrine—a powerful combination.

54. *Itsukushima Jinja Monjo*, 1155/10/5 Aki kokushi chōsen an, in *HI*, 6:2335–36, doc. 2818; ibid., 1182/3 Aki no kami Saeki Kagehiro yuzurijō, 8:3064, doc. 4026.

program rarely exhibited. At all events the jitō title played no part in this until the 1170s.

The story of these jitō is exceedingly complex, even in outline.[55] Our major concern is with the seven gō-level jitō shiki received by Saeki Kagehiro in 1176. In 1139 the "local owner" of the seven gō, one Fujiwara Naritaka, commended Mita Gō (with provincial approval) to an officer in the Aki headquarters; the donor became gesu-holder over Mita. Nearly thirty years later, in 1167, the donor's heir passed his Mita "public authorization decree" (*kugen*) to the Saeki, thereby enabling that gō to become an Itsukushima Shrine holding. At some point before 1173 Saeki Kagehiro assumed a jitō title over a component village within Mita Gō. This was followed by an equally puzzling development. In 1174, a descendant of the 1139 *recipient* of Fujiwara's Mita commendation acted to convert the remaining six gō into Itsukushima holdings. We do not know what gave this man the right to do so, nor do we know whether this transaction was with the Fujiwara gesu's blessing. Only the outcome is certain: in 1176, Saeki Kagehiro was invested (really confirmed) as jitō over the entire group of seven units.[56]

Of interest to us is the fact that the 1176 appointments did not come from Itsukushima Shrine as the ostensible proprietor. Nor were they assigned personally by Taira Kiyomori. Instead, the entire series of grants was made bureaucratically by decree of the provincial governor.[57] In trying to explain this our clearest line of approach stems from the fact that the seven units had not become shōen, They remained gō, thus suggesting a continued public-sector identification and governor's jurisdiction. We note further that the seven gō were cited as owing payments to the provincial storehouse.[58] However, we still do not know who the governor was, or to what extent he was acting at Kiyomori's behest.[59] We

---

55. The most ambitious effort to unravel the confusion of tenures, commendations, and confirmations is Uwayokote, "Jitō genryū kō," pp. 25–30. See also Yasuda, *Jitō oyobi*, pp. 34–36, 67–74. The two scholars are often in disagreement.

56. The chronology offered here is adapted from Uwayokote, "Jitō genryū kō," pp. 25–26.

57. *Itsukushima Jinja Monjo*, 1176/7 Aki kokushi chōsen, in *HI*, 7:2905, doc. 3771.

58. Ibid.

59. He is referred to merely as "Dai no suke Fujiwara ason." Ibid.

cannot *directly* link the Taira leader with his vassal's jitō investiture, though this connection is assumed.

A related question now arises. Why use the jitō title at all when investiture as a gō headman (*gōshi shiki*) was the standard procedure for such an appointment?[60] In fact, both titles were used in Aki. For at least two of the seven gō—and probably all—Saeki became gōshi and jitō. Successive governor decrees of 1180/8 and 1180/10 illustrate this: the first confirms Saeki as jitō shiki over Kuriya Gō,[61] the next as gōshi shiki over the same unit.[62] Or again, jitō shiki over Mita Gō,[63] and then gōshi shiki over that unit.[64] There is even a confirmation of both titles for Mita Gō—a "gōshi–jitō" investiture.[65] How then are these two shiki distinguished? The documents just cited indicate that contemporaries were indeed aware of differences: while jitō shiki decrees emphasized the hereditary quality of the tenure, based on possession of all past ownership records (see notes 61 and 63), gōshi shiki edicts stressed the holder's administrative responsibility (*gōmu*), including all "public" payments (see notes 62 and 64). The two titles were in this sense complementary, though it is hard to imagine the jitō and gōshi offices in different hands. It would be hazardous to venture too much farther here: inasmuch as both titles were authorized by provincial fiat, clearly no absolute dichotomy into "public" (gōshi) and "private" (jitō) dimensions ever prevailed.

In the end, then, the Saeki and their seven jitō titles tell us very little of the Heishi's usage of that shiki; we can only infer (as mentioned above) that Kiyomori was ultimately responsible for their authorization by the Aki governor. Fortunately, one other record

60. Hereditary holders of gō had been receiving such authorizations for more than a century (Uwayokote, "Jitō genryū kō," p. 27).

61. *Itsukushima Jinja Monjo*, 1180/8/27 Aki kokushi chōsen, in *HI*, 8:2999, doc. 3920.

62. Ibid., 1180/10 Aki kokushi chōsen, doc. 3927, pp. 3001–02. The original gōshi appointment may have come the previous year (ibid., 1179/11/2 Aki no kuni rusudokoro kudashibumi, doc. 3888, p. 2984). This, too, of course may have been just another confirmation.

63. Ibid., 1180/9/6 Aki no kuni rusudokoro kudashibumi, doc. 3923, p. 3000.

64. Ibid., 1180/10 Aki kokushi chōsen, doc. 3928, p. 3002.

65. Ibid., 1179/11 Aki kokushi chōsen, and Aki rusudokoro kudashibumi, docs. 3889–90, pp. 2984–85.

survives that does seem to establish the direct link we have been seeking. In a Kiyomori decree of 1179/11, the Taira leader ordered cancellation of the jitō(s) of Mibu Gō.[66] The implication of this personal dismissal is that Kiyomori had also made the appointments. Specifically, the document tells the story of Mibu Gō's incorporation as shōen,[67] with subsequent jitō encroachments and loss of revenues for the proprietor. What is interesting is that at one point the jitō-holder(s) seem to be referred to as *myōshu*; this would make them local figures on a level quite different from that of Saeki Kagehiro and would suggest, perhaps, that Kiyomori had invested them with jitō shiki in return for pledges of loyalty. It is the *only* hint of a Kamakura-type usage of the jitō title, and yet it remains difficult to square with the Saeki cluster of governor-authorized jitō in the same province.

Our knowledge of jitō shiki in eastern Japan before 1180 is limited to a single example—the 1175 cancellation of a gō-level jitō title by order of the Hitachi Province governor.[68] This almost total absence of data may be significant: to the extent that it reflects an actual condition in the Kantō before the Gempei outbreak,[69] Yoritomo may have known very little of the post that five years later he would claim exclusive jurisdiction over. Of one thing we can be certain: the Genji movement in its first years was not built around any single office title. The stress, as we noted in chapter 3, was on land confirmations using the full range of traditional shiki nomenclature.[70]

66. *Itsukushima Jinja Monjo*, 1179/11 saki no dajōdaijin ke mandokoro kudashibumi, in *HI*, 8:2985, doc. 3891.

67. This occurred in 1170, by dint of retired emperor and Aki governor decrees. A provincial agent had been sent to strike the boundary markers, and the new shōen now became an Itsukushima estate. Referred to in ibid., 1171/1 Itsukushima Jinja ryō Mibu-no-shō denpata zaike chūshin, 7:2773–74, doc. 3568. This register is signed by provincial agents plus a gesu and kumon.

68. Referred to in *Kashima Jingū Monjo*, 1205/8/23 Minamoto Sanetomo kudashibumi, in Kashima Jingū shamusho, comp., *Kashima Jingū monjo* (Kashima, 1942), doc. 120, p. 19.

69. It will be recalled that the pre-shiki usage of the term appears in a Chiba-related document of 1161. See p. 104.

70. The absence of any special concern at first with the jitō title is indicated by confirmations under inherited shiki names, followed by reconfirmations some

There do seem to have been, however, at least a scattering of early Kamakura-appointed jitō.[71] The first of these is an 1180/11/27 jitō authorization for an entire district (gun) in Shimotsuke Province.[72] A handful of others followed, all in the Kantō before 1184, and thus all safely within Yoritomo's sphere of power.[73] We may presume that the Genji chief's authorization of a jitō right not only sealed a vassal-type relationship with the recipient, but acknowledged that the latter now possessed a Kamakura-guaranteed jurisdiction and heritability over the land unit in question. We cannot even attempt to guess why the jitō title was used in these few cases; we can only note that jitō shiki were recognized over different kinds of areas: (1) village (mura), (2) administrative village (gō), (3) provincial district (gun), (4) private estate (shōen), and (5) shrine tribute area (mikuriya).[74] The versatility of the jitō shiki distinguished it from other land offices.

Late in 1183, we have our first indication of a development that would shortly become a countrywide trend. We see a warrior justifying local encroachments and disobedience to retired emperor and proprietor decrees by calling himself a "jitō–gesu."[75] A document of

years later under a jitō right. E.g., a *jinushi* shiki investiture of 1184, followed by a jitō appointment to the same area eight years later: *Ichikawa Monjo*, 1184/3/6 bō kudashibumi, in *Shinano shiryō*, 3:358; and ibid., 1192/12/10 shōgun ke mandokaro kudashibumi, pp. 440–41.

71. Unhappily, not many of these pre-1185 references to Kamakura-assigned jitō come from fully contemporaneous (or reliable) sources. Much as with the war-period shugo, we cannot be certain how much of our story is factual.

72. Referred to in *Shimotsuke Mogi Monjo*, 1192/8/22 shōgun ke mandokoro kudashibumi, in *KI*, 2:23–24, doc. 608.

73. See this list of seven or eight in Uchida Minoru, "Jitō ryōshusei to Kamakura bakufu," *Rekishi kyōiku* 8.7 (1960): 16.

74. (1) *AK* 1182/3/5; (2) The gō referred to here is the same Hitachi Province unit whose jitō shiki was abolished in the 1170s. Perhaps Yoritomo had simply revived the post. In the present record, the Genji leader is seen condemning the lawless excesses of this Tachibana Gō jitō: *Kashima Ōnegi Ke Monjo*, 1184/12/25, Minamoto Yoritomo kudashibumi, in *Kashima Jingū monjo*, doc. 2, pp. 669–70; (3) *AK* 1184/4/23. This may be the most reliable of our pre-1185 Kamakura jitō cases. A document of 1185/8 refers to the appointment having been made earlier to the southern districts of Hitachi Province: *Kashima Jingū Monjo*, 1185/8/21 Minamoto Yoritomo kudashibumi, in *Kashima Jingū monjo*, doc. 123, p. 96; (4) *AK* 1181/int.2/7; and (5) *AK* 1184/1/3.

75. *Ninnaji Monjo*, 1183/9/27 Go-Shirakawa In-no-chō kudashibumi, in *HI*, 8:3102, doc. 4107. An 1184 successor to this lawless figure would omit the term

several months later describes the sequel to this incident, and reveals the jitō title's emergence as the country's first "illegitimate" land office.[76] So far our references to the jitō in a context of "tension" have not been entirely compelling. As the following discussion will illustrate, the claiming of a jitō right now became preeminently an "anti-Kyoto" act.

The sequel document, one of the most important of the war period, deals with the recent ravagings of Kawada Estate, an In-related proprietorship in Echizen Province.[77] The edict begins by accusing the jitō deputy, Jōza, of lawless acts against an imperial temple land whose managership had been passed in heredity to the present complainant. The form of that managership, according to the original investiture, was to be a "jitō-azukari dokoro shiki." Then, during the latter months of 1183, an agent of Kiso Yoshinaka (Yoritomo's cousin) had committed outrages, followed by Jōza, "who claimed himself to be jitō, by order of the Kamakura lord's 'special deputy' (kannōshi)." The estate was entirely devastated by this man, and this led the In's office to pose the following question: "Who would dare call himself jitō or gesu without an order from the proprietor (ryōke)?" The present directive, an In's office prohibitory decree, was in response to the manager's plea for redress.

Some fascinating things are brought out in this record. We have, first, the allegation of a "jitō-azukari dokoro shiki" dating back to 1134. The original of that document, however, shows only an azukari dokoro post; the term "jitō" does not appear.[78] Then why the combined shiki claim of half a century later?[79] Jōza's self-styled

---

"gesu," calling himself only "jitō." See n. 77.

76. I.e., a land office whose greatest attraction was its *lack* of central legitimation.

77. *Ninnaji Monjo*, 1184/5 Go-Shirakawa In-no-chō kudashibumi, in Tanaka, "Ninnaji monjo," p. 75.

78. *Ninnaji Monjo*, 1134/int.12/15 Taikenmon In-no-chō kudashibumi, in *HI*, 5:1956, doc. 2310.

79. It is possible to argue that "jitō" is not in fact being used here in a shiki context; rather, it is a modifying term for azukari dokoro. The proper reading, according to this view, is "jitō *no* azukari dokoro shiki," or "local manager," not "jitō manager." Such a theory, however, does nothing to explain the discrepancy in language between 1134 and 1184. And it does not take into account the court's admission that Jōza was jitō deputy. Conversation with Professor Toyoda Takeshi.

possession of the jitō post is at the heart of this issue. From the outset, the manager's local authority was intended to be inclusive; this had required holding an azukari dokoro post. Fifty years later, however, this was no longer sufficient. To *remain* inclusive, such authority now had to embrace jitō. Confronted by Jōza's claim to this "autonomous" managerial title, the estate manager simply appropriated the jitō name for himself. Our document's reference to Jōza as jitō deputy (*jitōdai*) seems to confirm this: in Kyoto's eyes, the estate manager was now jitō, with Jōza as the subordinate.

The rhetorical question concerning shiki held without central legitimation is the most revealing point of all. What more graphic way to register the shock and disbelief in the capital over this new state of affairs? Warriors claiming land titles in defiance of central authority represented a head-on clash with an aristocratic mentality never before challenged. And this was only the beginning.

The manager in Kawada Estate had taken his grievance to the court. To that extent, thinking was still along traditional lines. During the same month, however, we see an important new development. A Yoritomo decree of 1184/5 shows that in a similar incident it was the bakufu being called on to suppress would-be jitō. Initial recourse, as of old, had been to the court, but the latter's issuance of a prohibitory decree had brought no results. The proprietary agents delivering this edict to the troubled area had simply been rebuffed. Under these circumstances, the estate owner (an unidentified shrine) abandoned primary dependence on the In and turned to the only available alternative: an appeal for assistance was directed to Kamakura, leading to the present Yoritomo order.[80]

Petitions of this kind represent an extremely important new stage. Kamakura's association with "jitō," almost in spite of itself, was being solidified by the old polity's inability to maintain the substance of its central and western province jurisdiction. In the councils of both capitals, and in the hearts and minds of warriors everywhere, "jitō" seemed increasingly to signal a Kamakura institution even before one formally existed. A Tamba Province incident of 1184/9 clearly illustrates this. Responding to an anti-jitō request of the

80. *Ōmori Shi Monjo*, 1184/5/8 Minamoto Yoritomo kudashibumi an, in *HI*, 8:3129, doc. 4156

In's, Yoritomo rejoined in part as follows: "Why are there persons claiming to be jitō? . . . Asserting possession of a Kamakura edict [appointing him jitō], Tamai Shirō Sukeshige has unceasingly committed outrages . . . (*AK* 1184/9/20).

By the spring of 1185 after the Gempei War had ended, the jitō scourge had now spread as far as Kyushu. A record of the fourth month carefully spotlights the means by which local warriors in that distant island were now challenging central authority:

. . . In recent years leading Kyushu residents are becoming influential vassals of Kamakura (*buke rōjū*) and are claiming to hold temple administrator investitures; thus there are persons calling themselves jitō and gesu respectively, who violate shōen and withhold taxes. . . . [81]

How remarkable that in spite of poorly developed communications between east and west, local warriors in Kyushu should already have made the beginnings of a connection between the jitō concept and Kamakura. But warriors were not the only ones to make this connection. The In's concluding remarks in this document reveal how the capital had come to understand the country's ongoing woes:

. . . The majority of complaints concern jitō and gesu. If such persons are not done away with, there can never be a return to former ways. . . . If jitō and gesu are destroyed, we can expect a revival of shōen and a triumphant temple prosperity. . . .

To the extent that such reasoning prevailed, it would certainly have strengthened the bakufu's argument at the end of the year that if Kamakura were effectively to control jitō, it would have to monopolize jitō.[82]

There can be no doubt that by the middle of 1185 Yoritomo had

81. *Itōzu Monjo*, 1185/4/22 Go-Shirakawa In-no-chō kudashibumi an, in *HI*, 8:3172–73, doc. 4241.

82. It will have been noted that some materials cited in this section do not carefully distinguish between jitō and gesu. Others, however, specifically single out jitō. E.g., *Kamowake Ikazuchi Jinja Monjo*, 1185/4/29 Go-Shirakawa In-no-chō, in *HI*, 8:3174, doc. 4244. In the end, of course, it was the jitō shiki that Kamakura asserted exclusive jurisdiction over. See chap. 5.

already begun to move in this direction, in other words, toward a
seizure of jurisdiction over both "lawful" and "unlawful" jitō.[83]
Such jitō control—meaning the exclusive authority to appoint,
discipline, and dismiss—stood to serve bakufu interests in several
ways. It would provide Yoritomo with a means of rewarding and
punishing vassals and simultaneously aid in making his regime
indispensable as a national policing authority. We have already
surveyed Kamakura's gradual assumption of responsibility over
those pretending to be jitō. We must now look at the other side of
this policy—an extension of bakufu appointments to that post.

The earliest reference to a Kamakura jitō grant made outside the
Kantō comes in an *Azuma kagami* entry of 1184/5: a Heishi turncoat,
now in the bakufu fold, was assigned the jitō right over a gō in Iga
Province (*AK* 1184/5/24). Here we see the first sign of a practice
soon to become standard. The award appears to have been non-
confirmatory in nature and was made to the confiscated holding of a
defeated Taira partisan. Our next reference to a Kamakura-appointed jitō does not come until a year later, but it survives in document
form and is much more explicit. In 1185/6, a pair of jitō rights was
granted in Ise Province to bakufu vassal Koremune Tadahisa.[84]
What distinguished these awards is (1) their assignment to shōen
whose central proprietorship the bakufu wished to maintain, and
(2) their adoption of a new concept of jitō duties. These were both
major advances, induced by a desire to stabilize the countryside.
Land rights would be protected on two levels, privileges balanced
with obligations. Jitō (as in the present case) would be made responsible for services owed the proprietor, but proprietors would
be denied a direct dismissal right over jitō. In this duality we see
the essence of the Kamakura jitō.

To the extent, then, that Yoritomo was now beginning to assign
housemen to confiscated areas beyond the east, he was creating the
conditions and establishing the model for the famous 1185/11 court
recognition decree. This argument is central to any understanding

83. As late as 1184/4 we see a jitō shiki being granted by a central owner in
return for commended land. *Tōji Hyakugō Monjo*, 1184/4/16 Taira Tatsukiyo
shoryō kishinjō an, in *HI*, 8:3127–28, doc. 4154. We find no jitō shiki of this type
during 1185.

84. *Shimazu Ke Monjo*, Minamoto Yoritomo buninjō, in *HI*, 8:3179, docs.
4259–60. This is the same Tadahisa who would shortly become first scion of the
great Shimazu house, of later daimyo fame.

of the postwar court–bakufu settlement: Kamakura's acquisition of its monopoly over jitō was not the starting point it is often claimed to be. Rather, it was the product of a combination of war-inspired developments and an adroit reading of the most current trends of the day. Yoritomo seized on the jitō shiki because he saw in it both a reward and compensation device and a technique of control. He did not invent this title; he merely appropriated it and recast it to meet his own needs. On the other hand, we cannot be certain just how widespread this process had become before 1185/11. The appointment of Koremune Tadahisa to a pair of "Taira confiscated lands" (Heike *mokkanryō*) in mid-1185 suggests by inference that other such placements were being made. What else would the bakufu have been doing with its many Taira-seized lands?[85] The sources *Azuma kagami* and *Gyokuyō* provide our only information. In an entry of 1185/7, *Azuma kagami* cites a Yoritomo order to his brother Noriyori in Kyushu, directing that jitō be assigned to certain Heishi confiscated areas (*AK* 1185/7/12). The reference in *Gyokuyō* was noted in the previous chapter. This is an account of 1185/10 describing Yoritomo's assignment of jitō in Iyo as part of a program to check the ambitions of another brother, Yoshitsune. We surmised that lands (shiki) seized from the Taira partisan Nii were granted under jitō title to the Genji vassal Kōno house and the latter's subordinates.

What makes the year 1185 unusually difficult to assess is that Yoritomo's search for a jitō policy tells, in fact, only part of the story. Conditions were too unsettled for Kamakura to limit its thinking to a single track. The Gempei War had ended in 1185/3, but little else was resolved. Armed units were roaming the country-side and using a variety of pretexts to commit lawless acts. The claim of a jitō shiki was certainly the most historically significant of these justifications, but as we have seen, the gesu title was also being used.[86] Beyond that, there were undoubtedly countless outrage-committing warriors who simply allowed the exercise of force to act

85. There is much that we do not understand about these lands. The traditional figure of 500 (chap. 1, n.18) tells us nothing of their shiki level and does not take into account the many proprietary rights returned to central owners. See chap. 5.

86. It is most noteworthy that the azukari dokoro title is not found in this context. This post had increasingly come to be identified with central authority. For details, see my "Jitō Land Possession in the Thirteenth Century," in Hall and Mass, *Medieval Japan*, chap. 7.

as its own explanation. The confusion that prevailed during the summer months of 1185 was capped, finally, by fence-sitting warriors hurrying to style themselves as Minamoto, and then proceeding to move directly counter to stated Kamakura objectives for moderation and peace. How, under conditions such as these, was Yoritomo to undertake the task of restoring the country to stability?

Once again, as in 1183, it was the threat from a Genji rival for power that prompted Yoritomo to act. In the fall of 1185 the defection and rebellion of Yoritomo's kinsmen, Yoshitsune and Yukiie, crystallized the need for new policies and renewed energy. The lord of Kamakura, it was now made clear, possessed a vast number of vassals but lacked the machinery to give them cohesion. To make matters worse, Yoritomo's two clansmen successfully eluded capture and extracted from the court investiture as jitō over the main islands of Kyushu (Yoshitsune) and Shikoku (Yukiie).[87] For Yoritomo, this was the final humiliation. He dispatched an armed mission to Kyoto, whose accomplishments, partly because we read of them in conflicting versions, have fascinated historians ever since. In the traditional view, it was this mission that secured for the bakufu its countrywide appointment right for shugo and jitō.[88]

We get a somewhat more complicated picture, however, by

87. Referred to in *AK* 1185/11/7. Pre-dating this investiture was an anti-Kamakura charge from the In (*AK* 1185/10/18), marking the third time in five years that Yoritomo had been branded as a rebel. It is noteworthy that on the second occasion, in 1183, Yoshinaka was granted title as shogun. Now, two years later, the desired office was jitō. While some scholars have questioned the 11/7 *AK* account, they neglect *Gyokuyō*, 1185/12/27, 3:125, which explicitly cites these island-wide jitō assignments.

88. An excellent account of this mission, based on *AK's* description, appears in Shinoda, *Founding of the Kamakura Shogunate*, pp. 125 ff. The basic sources are *AK* 1185/11/28, 29 and 12/6, which refer directly to shugo and jitō, and *Gyokuyō* 1185/11/28, 3:119, which makes no mention of either figure. The *Gyokuyō* entry states merely that Yoritomo's vassals would assume possession of undefined lands in western Japan and would levy there a general commissariat tax. This seeming inconsistency has led to greater speculation, perhaps, than for any other point in Japan's entire medieval age. For a sample of the writings on this subject, see Ishii Susumu, "Bunji shugo jitō shiki ron," *Shigaku zasshi* 77.3 (1968): 1–37; and Tomoda Kichinosuke, "Bunji gannen shugo jitō setchi ni tsuite no saikentō, *Nihon rekishi* 133 (1959): 11–29.

looking at events over the next several years. While little evidence can be adduced for a beginning network of shugo (see chapter 8), we do note a conspicuous rise in jitō appointments. Yoritomo had clearly become "jitō-in-chief" for the entire country. The point, however, is that Yoritomo's powers were not suddenly limited to this jitō competence; jitō were integral but not yet everything. This is illustrated by data such as the following: (1) a suggestion in 1187 of bakufu authority over several categories of nonvassal warriors— constables (ōryōshi), local land managers (gesu), and resident public officers (zaichō) (*AK* 1187/9/13); and (2) Kamakura jurisdiction over lawless acts, no matter who the wrongdoer or what the category of land. Taking only a single day in 1186, we find bakufu desist orders against warrior outrages in (a) six gō units in Yamashiro, home province of Kyoto, (b) three shōen units in Harima Province, (c) various sites in Suō Province, (d) a Tamba Province estate, and (e) several parts of a Kaga Province domain. The guilty parties in (a) and (b) were only unnamed warriors, but in (c) we find that the miscreant was ranking vassal Doi Sanehira, in (d) Yoritomo's own brother-in-law Hōjō Yoshitoki (!), and in (e) a self-styled jitō.[89] With the country in a condition of such clear unrest, Yoritomo appears to have extracted from the court late in 1185 a virtually unlimited "enforcement authority." The jitō monopoly was merely the central hub in a considerably larger policy.

The significance of 1185 should thus be sharply etched. Kamakura had now enlarged—and gained legal recognition for—a right of interference in local affairs everywhere. It would only be as the country restabilized, and as bakufu needs changed, that a pullback from this advanced posture would come to develop. What remained, as we will be noting in succeeding chapters, was of course the shugo and jitō. From the early 1190s on, it is these two figures who become virtually synonomous with the bakufu itself.

89. *Kamo chūshin Zakki* (a); *Torii Ōji Monjo* (b); *Kamowake Ikazuchi Jinja Monjo* (c) and (d); and *Hiramatsu Monjo* (e); all from 1186/9/5 Minamoto Yoritomo kudashibumi, in *KI*, 1:106–7, docs. 167–71.

PART 3:
THE DUAL
COURT–BAKUFU
POLITY

5 KAMAKURA–KYOTO RELATIONS AND THE JITŌ SHIKI

The unrestrained violence of the war period had served the bakufu well. Kamakura owed its spectacular growth to its own energy and adroitness and to a climate of upheaval that had largely paralyzed central governance. By the end of 1185, Kamakura stood supreme within Japan. Its men and decrees loomed as a permanent wedge between estate proprietors and their domains, and its leader had emerged as the new guarantor of last resort over the countryside.

And yet, as we know, this one-sided dominance of provincial types over courtiers did not become total. To the contrary, the period after 1185 witnessed a resurgence of central authority. What needs to be recognized is that the bakufu played a direct role in this; it actively sought and was largely responsible for the well-known "dual polity" of Kamakura times. The emergence of this dyarchy, and the particular shape it assumed, will be our main topics here.

The difficulty of identifying consistent policies for the bakufu during the later 1180s has already been alluded to. Emergency conditions in the wake of the Yoshitsune affair had demanded powers neither subject to arbitrary veto or delay from the court, nor limited in any way locally. Gradually, however, a move in the direction of a more rational program began to take shape. This trend cannot be dated precisely, and it clearly overlapped with older thinking and ambitions, but the development itself is unmistakable. The basic motivation was a beginning awareness that Kamakura's reach had in fact exceeded its grasp. Complaints continued to pour in from central owners seeking redress against warrior violence, and many of the country's greatest disrupters were proving to be Kamakura-appointed jitō. This latter condition underlined the need for a streamlining of the houseman system. But even more fundamental was that Kamakura's own involvement in diverse governances was shown to be a source of confusion within the land system.[1] To restore stability locally Kamakura needed not greater authority, but rather an authority more rationally distributed. The bakufu did not have the means, it discovered, to govern—or even police effectively—the entire country.

Seen in this light, much of the history of the post-1185 period appears as the chronicle of a new government largely at cross purposes with itself. Kamakura wished to guarantee its stake in the future by expanding its interests and range of contacts, but simultaneously found that retrenchment and a more restrained exercise of power were often more feasible. The policies and decisions of this period reflect this paradox. For example, fewer than six months after assuming full power of local intervention, we find the bakufu forfeiting a countrywide commissariat levy privilege in clear contravention of its followers' interests.[2] The thinking behind this action was less to assuage Kyoto sensibilities than to deny warriors (vassal and nonvassal) an obvious pretext for abuses. This same concern for unstable conditions led to an announcement in mid-1186 that valid jitō would be limited to former Heike and "rebel" areas (*AK* 1186/6/21, 7/7). Here was a policy that augured well for the bakufu, especially in an age of self-appointed jitō.[3] Not only did the Heike and rebel designations remain Kamakura's alone to apply, but they could justify either appointments or dismissals, as the case might demand. Most important, the bakufu was taking a major step toward restricting its national presence to jitō.

1. Emergency resolutions between disputing proprietors are a case in point, e.g., an 1188 decree of Kajiwara Kagetoki (a Yoritomo surrogate) settling an owner-level disagreement over land in central Japan's Settsu Province. *Katsuodera Monjo*, 1188/9/6 Kajiwara Kagetoki kudashibumi, in Ōsaka fu, comp., *Katsuodera monjo* (Osaka, 1931), doc. 216, p. 171. Before very long the bakufu would be refusing such suits.

2. *AK* 1186/3/21. The right to exact *hyōrōmai*, as these war taxes were called, goes back to the famous court edict of late 1185. See *AK* 1185/11/29.

3. Self-styled jitō continued beyond 1185. For example, *Hiramatsu Monjo*, 1186/9/5 Minamoto Yoritomo kudashibumi an, in *KI*, doc. 171, p. 107; and *Iwashimizu Monjo*, 1191/2/10 Iwashimizu Hachiman gūji bettō gechijō, ibid., doc. 508, p. 386.

The other side of this growing interest in jitō was an increasing effort to shed most non-jitō authority. That this aspiration proved difficult to achieve tells us much about the condition of the country during this watershed decade. Kamakura's struggle to shape the contours of a stable court–bakufu polity was largely undermined by Kyoto itself. We see this most vividly in the growing burden of litigation stemming from proprietor appeals to Kamakura.[4] In 1186/7, for example, several dozen *maki* (literally, "books") were delivered from the capital; this led to Yoritomo's issuance of some 252 edicts.[5] To reduce some of this volume Yoritomo adopted a novel and highly revealing approach. Early in 1187 he urged the court to revive a defunct imperial investigative office, the *kirokujo*.[6] This agency, dating back to the eleventh century, had traditionally been associated with examining shōen charters and passing judgment on their validity. Now, however, the kirokujo was to function as a central board for suits arising from the new conditions of lawlessness. Documents of 1188 and 1189 indicate that the office did survive its inception and that it did come to participate in the adjudication process.[7] But it is equally clear that the expectations of the two capitals regarding the kirokujo were doomed to failure. Centrally administered justice in a period of advanced local disorders simply would not work; petitions to the bakufu continued unabated. It was this circumstance that led Yoritomo to seek a further understanding with the court. On 1188/2/2 (*AK*), he announced that he would accept only those suits forwarded by the court. In the face of failure to curb the flow of appeals, Yoritomo sought at least to streamline that flow. An inability to keep pace with the demands made upon it is the lot of many new regimes; Kamakura's response was to share its burden with the "old regime."

4. The picture we get of estate-owners during this period is one of pride mixed with fear and suspicion. There was thus great eagerness to use bakufu influence locally, but little inclination to recognize Kamakura as an equal. Police action and prohibitory decrees were much in demand, but permanent bakufu agents were not.

5. Cited by Iida Hisao, "Kamakura jidai," pp. 43–44, n. 11.

6. *Gyokuyō*, 1187/2/4 and 2/28, 3:322, 336–37.

7. 1188/9/3 Minamoto Yoritomo shojō, in *KI*, 1:195, doc. 341 (from *AK*); and *Tōnan'in Monjo*, 1189/4/16 sesshō Kujō Kanezane migyōsho, ibid., doc. 382, p. 323. Both documents refer to the kirokujo.

On the estate-owner side, it was the unprecedented devastation of their domains that led to dependence on Kamakura. Numerous records reveal this condition, but none in starker terms than a Saidaiji temple register of proprietary holdings: "The above nine [domains] are shōen in name but no longer in fact. In some cases they are public lands or the possessions of others; or perhaps only one-half or one-third ours. . . . " The record concludes with a listing of some twenty-seven additional holdings that had ceased entirely to be shōen. While we find no appeal here for aid from Kamakura, it was precisely this kind of bleak picture that led to bakufu entanglement in so many other cases.[8] One such incident, occurring during the same year, will suffice to describe this process. In an 1191 decree from the Hachiman Shrine in Kyoto we see how central owners, in their search for a permanent deterrent against warrior encroachments, were now anticipating an open-ended bakufu commitment to intervene. As described in this document, a certain local figure had been calling himself jitō and seizing the income shares of the proprietor (ryōke) and his agent (azukari dokoro). The bakufu had once before issued an edict on behalf of the affected Suō Province domain, and (according to our document) was to be informed of any future trouble there. Kamakura, the edict concludes, would mete out punishments in the event of such difficulties.[9] If we multiply expectations such as these by the number of centrally owned estates experiencing warrior violence, the bakufu's "unusual" behavior—seeking voluntarily to return jurisdiction to those formerly holding it—can be better understood.

An explicit attempt to restore a proprietor's control is recorded in a document of 1205.[10] We read first that at some unspecified earlier date Kii Province's Kogawa Temple, proprietor (ryōke) of Kurusu

8. *Saidaiji Monjo,* 1191/5/19 Saidaiji shoryō chūshinjō, in Nagashima Fukutarō, comp., *Yamato komonjo juei* (Nara, 1943), pp. 67–71. The wording of this document suggests that Saidaiji may have suffered as much from the maneuvering of rival proprietors as from warrior despoilment. But bakufu assistance could be of use on both counts. See n. 1.

9. *Iwashimizu Monjo,* 1191/2/10 Iwashimizu Hachiman gūji bettō gechijō, in *KI,* 1:384, doc. 508.

10. *Kōyasan Ikenobō Monjo,* 1205/5/27 Kantō gechijō, in Kōyasan monjo kankōkai, comp., *Kōyasan monjo: kyū Koya ryōnai monjo* (Kyoto, 1936), 9:93–94, doc. 49.

Estate, had had its ownership papers stolen by one of its own members. The temple had appealed to Kamakura for lack of a more effective enforcement agency, and the bakufu had seemingly responded as desired. Kamakura's willingness to assume jurisdiction in this matter suggests that the incident probably occurred during the 1180s.[11] However, when the temple proprietor once again (in 1205) petitioned the bakufu for assistance in a criminal matter, Kamakura demurred. It prohibited the alleged outrages, but took pains to stipulate that this was the last time it would ever do so. Any further trouble in Kurusu Estate was to be referred to the court and resolved there. In Kyoto's eyes, the bakufu's obligation was ongoing, but Kamakura had now declared that it no longer wanted the responsibility of keeping peace in a domain in which it held no interest.

Here, then, is the final outcome of the bakufu's overzealous posture of 1185: a retreat from authority and an effort to restore traditional hierarchies as a counterweight to continued warrior violence. The exception, of course, was the jitō shiki, for which Kamakura asserted absolute authority.[12] The bakufu would limit both its advantage and problems to this single post. One expression of this was the unfolding pattern of jitō appointments and dismissals.

Scholarly disputation has been voluminous on the questions of breadth and comprehensiveness of placement of post-1185 jitō.[13] While it is plain that jitō could not have been assigned to all domains —this would have required literally thousands of appointments— it is equally clear that the bakufu did not show proper caution at first in the jitō disbursements it did make. This meant a long and tedious winnowing process as Kamakura sought to unify its vassal corps, retaining those whose loyalty and duty performance were

11. See *On Ikenobō Monjo*, in *HI*, 8:3180–82, docs. 4263–67, for data on the suffering of Kurusu-no-shō during 1185. It is possible that the theft incident described in our present document was part of this sequence, though no direct connection can be made.

12. A document of 1186 expresses very forcefully that all jitō were to be under Kamakura's jurisdiction, with no interference by estate-owners. *Shimazu Ke Monjo*, 1186/4/3 Minamoto Yoritomo kudashibumi, in Tōkyō Daigaku shiryō hensanjo, comp., *Dai Nihon komonjo, iewake 16*, (Tokyo, 1901–), 1:4, doc. 5. (Hereafter cited as *DNK, iewake*)

13. A good survey is Ōae, "Jitō shiki," pp. 12–26.

sincere and correct, while purging or punishing less reliable elements. However, even this scaled-down competence—the jitō monopoly— would be more than the bakufu could easily handle.

The initial wave of jitō appointments divide into several rather loose categories. Probably the largest group consisted of native warriors receiving bakufu confirmation over native lands, now in the form of jitō shiki. Easterners predominated here, and the receipt of such an investiture often went far toward detaching one's home area from higher authority. This was especially true in the case of Kantō shōen: while the bakufu revived an unknown number of these proprietorships, their central owners had now lost most leverage over them. In many instances, absentee holders were compelled to acknowledge jitō autonomy.[14] In the public sector the issue is more confused. Over many eastern provinces the bakufu itself emerged as the new "superior authority." Presumably this meant that financial and service obligations were now owed to Kamakura, though few details of this relationship are known.[15] Away from the east, only Kyushu experienced a sizable number of confirmatory jitō, and special conditions prevailed there (see chapter 6). Indigenous housemen in much of the rest of central and western Japan were denied jitō shiki as part of a conscious "eastern first" bakufu policy.

Historically more interesting than confirmatory jitō were the many easterners granted that title in areas beyond the capital. Included here were appointments into (1) estates containing rebels and criminals, (2) domains whose proprietors had given support to bakufu enemies, and (3) areas whose officer-level warriors had lost out during the war. Conspicuously absent are documented cases of jitō

14. This is the origin of a practice called *jitō ukesho* that later would spread to most parts of the country. Jitō assumed total rights of estate administration, owing only the delivery of an annual tax to the proprietor. See chap. 7.

15. This new authority was seemingly often only de facto. In the third month of 1186 Yoritomo was "proprietor" (*chigyōkokushu*) over eight scattered provinces in the east (*AK* 1186/3/13). But later, even after having returned several of these, we see little indication of a fully revived central control over provincial headquarters and public land. The bakufu's financial base has been little studied. It is interesting, however, that rather numerous disputes took place involving jitō residing in Kantō public lands. Whether (or the extent to which) this pitted such jitō against the bakufu is not clear.

posted in response to proprietary requests. As we will note shortly, central owners petitioned for jitō dismissals, not appointments.[16] Of the three external jitō types, easily the most important was the third group—easterners appointed to the home areas of those labeled as Heishi. This suggests that the great majority of "Heike confiscated lands" (Heike *mokkanryō*) were management-level tenures rather than proprietorships. To a certain extent this eased the transition process over the 1185 watershed; warriors had only to replace other warriors. But the bakufu's jitō network still experienced an unstable, lurching advance.

One of the major sources of trouble was Kamakura's lack of detailed knowledge concerning the lands to which it was making appointments. Investiture documents tell this story, largely by what they omit. These records contain little or no information on either the background events leading to appointments, or on traditional perquisites and duties.[17] With past and future seemingly moot for many in this first generation of appointees, it is small wonder that neglect of "precedents" became a common occurrence. It was jitō lawlessness, and problems attendant on the appointment process, that served as the basis for much of the period's litigation.

Probably a majority of the suits brought after 1185 were proprietor requests for jitō cancellation or punishment. The bakufu responded to these in a variety of ways. For example, it dismissed jitō in Ise and Nagato provinces in 1187 and 1189 for the crime of shōen encroachment, but it refused to take such action in a similar incident of 1190, issuing a warning instead. Two years later it replaced a lawless jitō with a different Kamakura houseman. Finally, in 1199 Kamakura

16. The view that estate-owners wished at first to have jitō placed in their domains appears in many surveys. The sources do not reflect this, however.

17. A typical example would be one of the first: *Shimizu Ke Monjo*, 1186/1/8 Minamoto Yoritomo kudashibumi, in *Shinano shiryō*, 3:37-38. Shōen administration was ordered discharged pursuant to precedent. But those precedents are not itemized. Nor is there any mention of what induced the posting of this jitō in the first place. Exceptions, of course, do exist, e.g., a record in which ousted native warriors are cited as having constructed a fortification for the Taira: (Yoritomo edict of 1186/10, quoted in *Kushibe Monjo*, 1192/6/3 saki no utaishō ke mandokoro kudashibumi, in Shimizu Masatake, ed. *Shōen shiryō*, (Tokyo) 1933), 2:1996.

rejected outright a proprietor's allegation of jitō encroachment, electing instead to reconfirm that holder in his office.[18] In all these cases—parallel examples with differing outcomes—we note Kamakura's utter control over the fate of jitō shiki. But equally striking is the individualized attention given each judgment. Kamakura was taking the consolidation of its jitō network seriously.

Crimes of violence were not the only kind of jitō-related suits coming before the bakufu. There were also cases turning on whether a jitō had been "lawfully" appointed in the first place. The issue here was usually whether the domain in question had ever actually been associated with the Taira. Why Kamakura would have bothered with such unrewarding appeals is puzzling at first. It was certainly not to oversee the partial dismantling of its own jitō system, when the persons dismissed were both guiltless and unwitting. Part of the answer seems to lie in the identity of the central owners who would benefit from this largesse. Invariably, they were specially patronized religious institutions, with Ise Shrine heading the list. An incident of 1205 is typical. Ise argued that the dispossessed warrior–officer of Ōhashi Estate (Ise Province) was not the true local holder of that domain. The wrong man had been labeled Taira, and a jitō appointed. The bakufu agreed that the latter's tenure should be canceled.[19]

Despite these various instances of bakufu forbearance on behalf of selected temples and shrines,[20] much the greater advantage accrued to Kamakura as interpreter and enforcer of the system. It is interesting, for example, that "Heike confiscated lands" were not determined strictly from wartime events. No final categorizing ever took place, as the following data will reveal. In 1191 Yoritomo sent a pair of agents to Ise and Shima provinces in order to survey Heike-seized areas that had not yet received jitō (*AK* 1191/1/7). In

18. *AK* 1187/6/20, 1189/2/30, and 1190/5/13; *Dazai Kannaishi Usa Gūki*, 1192/11/11 shōgun ke mandokoro kudashibumi an, in *KI*, 2:53, doc. 637; *Kōyasan Monjo*, 1199/9/8 Kantō migyōsho, in *KI*, 2:360, doc. 1078.

19. *Daigoji Monjo*, 1205/3/13 Kantō gechijō, in *KBSS*, 1:7, doc. 9.

20. Professor Yasuda has asserted that the bakufu made a less than total effort to appoint jitō to the lands of powerful sectarian institutions. Yasuda, *Jitō oyobi*, p. 199. But the evidence seems to suggest that the appointments were made and then subsequently cut back, e.g., the early 1186 jitō cancellations on Kōyasan estates in Kii. See n. 24.

view of the known land hunger of eastern vassals, a more likely interpretation was reconnaissance in search of "new" Heishi domains. A second incident shows success in such a quest. In 1205, Kamakura appointed a jitō to what was now, apparently for the first time, designated a "Heike-seized area."[21] A document of some years later provides a third perspective on the bakufu's control of the Heike definition. Looking back on events during the 1180s, the observation appears that a certain local warrior had been divested of his holding and replaced by a jitō because of the Heike leanings of *his brother*.[22]

The central polity's ultimate weakness before the bakufu in jitō matters lay in Kamakura's unrestricted freedom to change its mind on an issue. The experiences of two western province shōen reveal how this might work. In the wake of the Gempei fighting, Ōta Estate in Bingo Province was confiscated from the Heishi on the managerial level.[23] Appointment of a jitō, Doi Sanehira, routinely followed. This development led the retired emperor, who was patron (honke) of Ōta, to counter by establishing Kōyasan Temple as "proprietor" (ryōke): at this very moment, the latter was receiving preferred treatment from Kamakura concerning jitō cancellations. This condition, combined with Doi's well-known encroachments in Ōta, induced the bakufu to dismiss its man in that estate.[24]

But Kamakura, as it turned out, was not prepared to abandon permanently an interest in one of western Japan's largest shōen. A new jitō was appointed in 1196,[25] and all further attempts to gain

21. *Sagara Ke Monjo*, 1205/7/25 shōgun ke kudashibumi, in *DNK, iewake 5*, 1:5–6, doc. 3.

22. *Kasuga Jinja Monjo*, 1258/12/25 Kantō gechijō, in Kasuga Jinja shamusho, comp., *Kasuga Jinja monjo* (Nara, 1928), 1:278–79, doc. 223.

23. Incorporation of Ōta as shōen came in 1166, with one of Kiyomori's sons as azukari dokoro and the In as honke. *Nibu Jinja Monjo*, 1166/1/10 Go Shirakawa In-no-chō kudashibumi an, in *HI*, 7:2664–65, doc. 3375.

24. Early in 1186 Yoritomo's closest adviser, Hōjō Tokimasa, had taken note of jitō ravagings in Kōyasan Temple lands in Kii and ordered all jitō abolished there. *Negoro Yōsho*, 1186/1/29 Hōjō Tokimasa kudashibumi, in *KI*, 1:17, doc. 42. This directive, assuming it was carried out, did not long remain in force. For Doi's dismissal, see *Kōyasan Monjo*, 1186/7/24 Minamoto Yoritomo shojō in *KI*, 1:87, doc. 131.

25. *Kōyasan Monjo*, 1196/10/22 saki no utaishō ke mandokoro kudashibumi an, in *KI*, 2:198, doc. 867.

repeal were rebuffed. On each of the latter occasions Kamakura justified its jitō placement by asserting a Heike and "rebel" lineage for Ōta (see notes 18 and 60).

The second estate, Sasakibe of Tamba Province, exhibits an even bolder disregard of a religious proprietor's wishes. During the war the head priest of a ranking Tamba shrine said prayers for Kamakura and was duly granted a jitō title in 1186 over a domain long held in proprietorship by his shrine. Simultaneously, however, Kajiwara Kagetoki, a Yoritomo confidant, was made jitō deputy, thus paving the way some years later for the expulsion of the priest and the appointment of a Kantō-sent jitō.[26] In matters such as these central owners had no recourse beyond the bakufu's own sense of fair play.

Thus far we have portrayed Kamakura's handling of appeals concerning jitō with only minimal reference to the larger political environment. The effect of the relations between the two capitals on the progress of jitō requires a summary of events to 1200.[27] One of the key postwar developments was the In's resurgence to traditional paramountcy at court. Yoritomo himself played a role in this by failing to maintain an army of occupation in Kyoto and failing to uphold his recent purge of Go-Shirakawa's advisers. The results were generally unfavorable to the bakufu. For example, Yoritomo's chief ally in Kyoto, Fujiwara Kanezane, was promoted to imperial regent (sesshō) at Kamakura's urging but nevertheless denied a major voice at court. Not long afterward the In was obstructive in another way. During the period 1188–89 he refused to grant court approval for a Kamakura military venture in the north. Yoritomo wished to mount such a campaign as part of a bakufu consolidation effort (see chapter 6). Given setbacks such as these we may wonder why Yoritomo would have been promoting the kirokujo and urging central owners to channel Kamakura-bound petitions through the In. But the logic was much the same as that dictating "equity" in the

26. Described in *Higashi Monjo*, 1238/10/19 Kantō gechijō, in *KBSS*, 2:9, doc. 7.

27. There are several excellent handlings of the political history to 1200. Perhaps the best is Tanaka Minoru, "Kamakura shoki no seiji katei—Kenkyū nenkan o chūshin ni shite," *Rekishi kyōiku* 11.6 (1963): 19–26.

disposal of many jitō suits. The search for stability on the land required these policies.

The year 1192 was an eventful one in court–bakufu relations. Go-Shirakawa's death removed a major irritant and sparked a more active involvement by Yoritomo in the politics of the court. This was the year also of Yoritomo's celebrated accession to the post of shogun. By 1196, however, the climate had changed again. The shogunal post was abandoned due to its low prestige,[28] and Yoritomo's influence within the capital was tangibly reduced. Concerning the latter, the Kamakura chief's ill-conceived plan to replace Kanezane's daughter, who was imperial consort, with his own daughter had created a wedge that ambitious court nobles were able to exploit. The regent and his faction were dismissed from their posts, and Yoritomo's wish to become grandfather to an emperor was cut short. From that juncture until 1221 the bakufu did not exercise much leverage over dealings within the capital.[29]

The year 1196 was thus an important turning point in Kamakura political history. Yet it was not accompanied by any alteration in the basic power balance. A somewhat more resistant line on jitō dismissals seems possible,[30] and the bakufu did move to strengthen its grip over native housemen in several western provinces (see chapter 6). But in the key areas of judicial ascendancy and revitalization of traditional hierarchies we encounter no change at all. Yoritomo's

28. The final known shogunal documents date from 1195/5. See *KI*, 2:142–43, docs. 791–92. All historical records after that date identify the bakufu founder as a "former imperial guard's captain," a title standing higher than shogun in the traditional hierarchy. On the other hand, this does not mean that the shogunal title never became important. It did, but only after Yoritomo's line had failed in 1219 and a succession of court figures were installed as nominal lords in Kamakura. Shogun were now essential as objects of a Hōjō regency, and the title itself— *sei i tai shōgun*, "barbarian subduing great general"—served as a useful camouflage. For further details, see Jeffrey P. Mass, "The Jōkyū War—Origins and Aftermath," mimeographed (New Haven, Yale University, 1971).

29. Mass, "The Jōkyu War."

30. E.g., in 1196 Yoritomo wondered aloud why a jitō cancellation petition had been filed when the jitō in question had not been neglectful of his duties. *Yamashiro Matsuo Jinja Monjo*, 1196/6/17 Minamoto Yoritomo shojō, in *KI*, 2:189–90, doc. 849. To the extent that a harder line was taken, it did not continue much beyond Yoritomo's death several years later. The problem arose again in 1205–06. See n. 32.

1196 defeat at court did not cause central owners to turn suddenly away from bakufu justice, and it did not induce Kamakura to relax its program of trying to bolster the "dual polity." Relations between the two governments could apparently be strained in the political realm, yet continue in reasonable tandem on the common issue of local peace.

The conclusion to emerge from this is that internal bakufu needs continued to outweigh in importance the state of Kyoto–Kamakura relations. As we will see in chapter 6, the desire to achieve greater vassal cohesion led to a variety of programs individually adjusted to the different parts of Japan. Here we have concerned ourselves only with the bakufu's willingness to dismiss its own jitō.

While Yoritomo lived, the resulting inconstancy in the defense of vassal aspirations did not lead to major displays of discontent. But after his death in 1199, a power struggle broke out within Kamakura's top echelons, from which the Hōjō emerged by 1205 as the bakufu's leading family.[31] This only increased the tempo of criticism and led in 1206 to an important policy change.[32] As announced in that year, all grants awarded by Yoritomo and his heir, Yoriie (r. 1199–1203) would be permanently secure; no dismissals would take place, save in instances where the gravest crimes had been committed.[33] In this way Kamakura publicly committed itself to the status quo. Kyoto appeals for jitō cancellations would no longer be welcome.

The new policy seemed to work. Containment of jitō crimes, rather than repeal of jitō shiki, became the new order of the day.[34]

31. *AK* is the major source here. For scholarly comment, see Yawata Yoshinobu, "Kamakura bakusei ni okeru Hōjō Tokimasa no shiteki hyōka," *Rekishi kyōiku* 11.6 (1963): 30–32; Kamei Hideo, "Kennin sannen Kamakura seiken o meguru ni san no mondai," *Seiji keizai shigaku* 11 (1963): 31–35; and Yasuda, *Chūsei*, pp. 120–26.

32. The year 1205 seems to have witnessed an unusually large number of jitō cancellations, e.g., *Daigoji Monjo*, 1205/3/13 Kantō kudashibumi, in *DNK*, *iewake 19*, 1:172–73, doc. 188; *Kashima Jingū Monjo*, 1205/8/23 Minamoto Sanetomo kudashibumi, in *Ibaragi ken shiryō, chūsei hen 1*, doc. 121, p. 167; and *Chūin Monjo*, 1205/5/28 Kantō kudashibumi, in Kanazawa bunka kyōkai, comp., *Kano komonjo* (Kanazawa, 1944), doc. 62, p. 40.

33. *AK* 1206/1/27. It is assumed that rights awarded by both Yoritomo and Yoriie were now guaranteed. *AK*'s retrospective reference is to "deceased shogun."

34. Surviving judicial settlement decrees from 1206–21 reveal only admonish-

Similarly, the burden of litigation, so onerous earlier, was now appreciably reduced. But tensions did not dissipate. Go-Toba, the new In, eagerly exploited houseman grievances where possible and in 1221 engineered one of the period's most dramatic events. Acting under the misapprehension that warriors throughout the country were ready to take up arms against the bakufu, the ex-sovereign mounted a short-lived campaign designed to restore unitary imperial government. This was the ill-starred Jōkyū War. Of the war's many consequences none was more important than a new wave of eastern jitō posted into western lands. Henceforth, warriors from the Kantō could be found almost everywhere.[35] At the same time, the uneasy court–bakufu equilibrium of the first two decades of the thirteenth century was severely upset. The "dual polity" was tilted permanently in favor of Kamakura.[36]

Yet even now the two capitals continued to share certain interests. An ominous development was a rise in warrior encroachments to a level unseen since the 1180s.[37] A joint effort, as before, would thus be required to restore the country to peace. Likewise, there was an inevitable confusion of jurisdictions and the added burden of containing a vassal corps now even more widely dispersed. A series of jitō "adjustments" was one obvious counter to this.[38] A second effort was a new program of categorizing jitō by the status of the land

ings, not cancellations. *KBSS*, 1: 10–20.

35. A magistral piece of research on the new jitō-holders is Tanaka Minoru, "Jōkyū kyō-gata bushi no ichi kōsatsu—rango no shin jitō bunin chi o chūshin to shite," pts. 1 and 2, *Shigaku zasshi* 65.4 (1956): 21–28, and ibid., 79.12 (1970): 38–53.

36. Kamakura's authority now came to touch the inner workings of the court. Not only imperial successions but other high courtier promotions were made subject to bakufu approval. Further, a branch office of the bakufu was established in Kyoto, with two deputies (the Rokuhara *tandai*) in permanent residence.

37. The years 1221–23 (especially) show a huge upsurge in complaints submitted to the bakufu. See *DNS*, 5, vols. 1 and 2, and *KBSS*, 1:21–30.

38. We note the following examples: (1) A bakufu refusal to cancel a jitō in Sanuki Province until 1293, despite the fact that the posting had been made in error; the temple estate-owner had not joined the court side in 1221, but was made to suffer a jitō placement anyway. Tanaka, "Sanuki," p. 360. (2) A bakufu acceptance of an appeal for cancellation under much the same argument: the residents of a domain in Suō Province had not fought for the court, but a jitō had been posted. *Tōdaiji Yōroku*, 1233/7/9, Kantō gechijō, in *Zoku zoku gunsho ruijū, shūkyō bu* (Tokyo, 1908), 11:27. The bakufu's freedom to dispense justice as it pleased was now of course even more pronounced than in Yoritomo's day.

units receiving the appointments. We can go no farther here than to outline the basic intent of this new classification system.[39] In the event that a domain had possessed a jitō (or jitō-level figure, i.e., gesu) prior to Jōkyū, the new appointee was called "originally appointed jitō" (*hompo jitō*) and expected to carry on all privilege and income precedents. Otherwise, the appointee was called "newly appointed jitō" (*shimpo jitō*) and ordered to adhere to a uniform set of low perquisite levels. The way was thus prepared, ironically enough, for court battles on which of two unequal jitō classifications should be applied in individual cases. Proprietor and jitō habitually diverged on this question, with the result that alongside requests for punishment and dismissal of jitō, there now were added owner attempts to gain a shimpo labeling for those who were demonstrably hompo.[40]

We have referred repeatedly to the jitō as the only exclusive Kamakura possession on the land. Another way to represent this is to note that the gesu and all other indigenous shōen posts, even when held by bakufu housemen, came to be acknowledged by both capitals as under the estate-owner. Much effort was expended to establish the jitō–gesu distinction as the basis for coexistence between the two great power centers.

The jitō–gesu story, a critical one for understanding the origins and nature of the "dual polity," begins in late Heian, when the two titles came to denote roughly parallel management rights over land. Gesu, however, had a longer history and were normally associated with shōen. Jitō could be found in equal numbers in both land sectors.[41] Then, during the war years, the two titles largely merged, uniting in a lawless challenge to central proprietorship. But the jitō

39. For details, see Mass, "The Jōkyū War."
40. Western writers have misunderstood these categories on two essential points, namely, the assumption that (1) hompo simply meant pre-1221 and shimpo post-1221 and (2) shimpo jitō, because of their regulated perquisites, were normally better off than those of hompo standing. The outstanding scholarly treatment is Yasuda, *Jitō oyobi*, pp. 197–226.
41. The historical distinction between jitō and gesu is drawn more sharply by Professor Uwayokote. For him, jitō have an unmistakable public land lineage, while gesu belonged to shōen (Uwayokote, "Jitō genryū ko"). But in chap. 4 we saw that late Heian jitō appeared in more than just a "public" context.

post retained its greater versatility and emerged from the fighting as the more important of the two shiki; it was this title that Yoritomo seized in its entirety in 1185. At the same time, full gesu jurisdiction did not revert immediately to the center. Only after several years did Yoritomo apparently decide to abandon all claim to that office. Part of the rationale was to simplify the lines of authority and to facilitate an end to the period of crisis. Yet consistently, as we shall see, Kamakura held the major responsibility for keeping the jitō and gesu jurisdictions separate.

The exclusiveness of these posts is revealed in many ways. First, regarding appointments, estate deputies or their agents enjoyed the sole privilege over gesu shiki.[42] Kamakura appointed gesu only very rarely.[43] Moreover, to keep the jurisdictions distinct, jitō and gesu were not normally assigned to the same shōen; appointment to one generally involved absorption of the other.[44] This point is made explicit in a bakufu judgment edict of 1240: a gesu's authority had ceased in a certain Aki Province domain, coincident with the investiture of a jitō.[45] Combined "jitō-gesu" assignments tell essentially the same story. Since all of these appear to have been bequests from Kamakura, jitō-gesu meant jitō embracing gesu, or, more specifically, jitō acceding to the latter's bundle of rights.[46]

42. E.g., during the Yoritomo period—*Yoshii Yoshinao Shi Shozō Monjo*, 1189/1/22 Ninnaji gū-no-chō kudashibumi, in *KI*, 1:204, doc. 361. This is a Ninnaji gesu appointment to a domain in Mimasaka Province.

43. E.g., the bakufu's appointment of a houseman to a gesu shiki in Suō Province in 1193: *Nagato Mori Ke Monjo*, 1193/4/16 shōgun ke mandokoro kudashibumi, in *KI*, 2:73, doc. 668. The format of this document is exactly the same as that for jitō appointment decrees; only the term "gesu" is different. In another case, a testamentary document, we see the passage of a gesu shiki in Kii Province that previously had been awarded by Yoritomo: *Kōyasan Monjo*, 1197/10/13 Mongaku yuzurijō an, in *KI*, 2:259, doc. 939.

44. Observation first made by Yasuda, *Jitō oyobi*, pp. 40–51.

45. *Kobayagawa Ke Monjo*, 1240/int.10/11 Kantō gechijō, in *DNK, iewake 11*, 1:549.

46. E.g., "jitō-gesu" appointments by Kamakura to shōen in Settsu Province near the capital and Higo Province in Kyushu (unnamed document collection, 1204/7/26 Kantō kudashibumi, in Kimura Tokue, comp., *Tosa monjo kaisetsu* (Tokyo, 1935), doc. 1, p. 1; and *Takuma Monjo*, 1209/12/11 shōgun ke mandokoro kudashibumi, in Teramoto Hirosaku, comp., *Kumamoto ken shiryō, chūsei hen 5* (Kumamoto, 1966), p. 607. One exception—a "gesu-jitō shiki" (note in-

While exceptions exist to the mutually exclusive pattern regarding these posts, they do not show jitō and gesu coexisting as rivals. For example, a document of 1195 refers to separate jitō and gesu shiki (*jitō narabi ni gesu shiki*), but the holder in this case was a single person.[47] In another instance, a jitō moved to confirm a hereditary gesu, thereby suggesting separate holders. But here, clearly, the jitō possessed jurisdiction over the gesu.[48] A third example shows an important variation: a dispute between a jitō and proprietary deputy over control of a gesu. The one title was obviously superior to the other.[49] In all these cases, then, we see essentially the same thing. Jitō and gesu did not exist as competitors.[50] The importance of each office lay in the authority system it represented.

Beyond the estate-owner's appointment authority over gesu, there are ample records to show his final jurisdiction in justice and enforcement matters. The only time this was not true was during the crisis period of the mid-1180s. We can trace the restoration of this authority to proprietors by examining several examples. In 1186, in the midst of martial law, Yoritomo assumed responsibility for rescuing a beleaguered local gesu. The latter was reconfirmed not by

version) from 1186—seems to be a carry-over from before the bakufu. There is no indication that the land rights referred to in this testamentary document were in any way Kamakura-related. See *Sakuyō Shi*, 1186/8 Yama shi onna yuzurijō, in *KI*, 1:104, doc. 163.

47. *Kawachi Kongōji Monjo*, 1195/6/14 Minamoto Yoshikane kishōmon an, in *KI*, 2:147, doc. 799. Jitō were sometimes combined with other titles, e.g., with gōshi (*Shiga Monjo*,1240/4/6 Ama Shinmyō shoryō haibunjō, in Takita Manabu, comp., *Hennen Ōtomo shiryō* [Kyoto, 1942], 1:361, doc. 416), and with azukari dokoro (*Engakuji Monjo*, 1229/11/26 shōgun ke mandokoro kudashibumi, in *Kamakura shishi*, 2:5, doc. 2, p. 5).

48. *Noda Monjo*, 1231/11/14 jitō kudashibumi, in *DNS* 5, 7:215 A slightly earlier document suggests that the jitō probably shared this authority with the estate proprietor. Ibid., 1229/9/11 jitō-otsukai buninjō, in *DNS* 5, 5:505.

49. *Shimazu Ke Monjo*, 1293/1/13 Kantō gechijō, in *DNK, iewake 16*, 1:192.

50. The closest we can come to coexistence is an ousted gesu and newly appointed jitō at loggerheads. In 1227, a post-Jōkyū jitō appealed the violations of his predecessor, the former gesu of Toyokuni Estate, Yamato Province. According to this petition, the dispossessed gesu had fought on the court side in 1221, while the suitor had been loyal to Kamakura Nevertheless, the gesu resisted his dismissal and teamed with the estate manager and other persons to ally against the jitō and his deputy. *Kasuga Jinja Monjo*, 1227/8 Taira Shigeyasu gejō, in *Kasuga Jinja monjo*, 1:539–42, doc. 448.

the domain proprietor but by the bakufu.[51] By 1193 we see a change: a gesu cancellation case showing Yoritomo's involvement but not his final judgment. In this incident, the gesu-holder in a court proprietorship was dismissed and banished by order of the estate-owner.[52] In 1206, we find a gesu case, which, from beginning to end, was handled by the proprietor. A certain local officer had complained of depravations by the gesu, who was ordered to send a proxy to the capital to present his side of the case. In the meantime, the seized lands and expelled persons were to be restored.[53] A final sequence shows that the bakufu was now positively eschewing jurisdiction over gesu. During the period 1210–13 a local dispute arose over which of two persons was the lawful posses or of a gesu post in Mino Province's Ōi Estate. An affidavit from the bakufu stated that although details of the trouble had been sent to Kamakura, the latter would not handle the case: Kamakura's authority had lapsed upon its cancellation of the Ōi jitō shiki sometime earlier.[54] The proprietor (Tōdaiji) responded to this by reconfirming its own man as gesu, adding also that Kamakura's own inquiry had settled the question of jurisdiction. This authority lay properly with the estate-owner.[55]

The outbreak of the Jōkyū War upset the jitō–gesu balance in much the same way that it had led to a dramatic rise in jitō "adjustments." Thus we find Kamakura joining disputes that it normally would have avoided. In late 1221, for example, a gesu was expelled from a certain Tamba Province domain under proprietorship of the Gion Shrine. The province's shugo had first been called in but had

51. *Harima Ebina Monjo*, 1186/6/25 Minamoto Yoritomo kudashibumi, in *KI*, 1:81–82, doc. 118. *AK* 1189/7/19 reveals that the guilty warrior was a Kamakura houseman. Thus we have the bakufu lining up with one local figure, a non-vassal gesu, against another local figure who happened to be a houseman.

52. *Negoro Yōsho*, 1193/9/23 Hachijō-In-no-chō kudashibumi, in *KI*, 2:88–89, doc. 687.

53. *Aoki Monjo*, 1206/8 azukari dokoro kudashibumi, in *Shinshū Shimane kenshi, shiryō hen 1*, p. 374.

54. *Tōdaiji Yōroku*, 1211 Ōe Hiromoto shojō, in Gifu ken, *Gifu kenshi, shiryō hen, kodai-chūsei 3* (Gifu, 1971), doc. 181, p. 529.

55. *Tōdaiji Monjo*, 1212/1 Tōdaiji bettō mandokoro Ōi-no-shō gesu shiki buninjō, ibid., doc. 182, p. 529, and undated Tōdaiji kumonjo kudashibumi an, doc. 183, pp. 529–30.

not been able to settle the affair. Thereupon a direct appeal was made to Kamakura, which ordered its newly established branch in Kyoto (Rokuhara) to secure both the shrine and the gesu in their traditional rights. Rokuhara complied by issuing an edict of guarantee.[56] But incidents such as these were clearly the product of special times. More commonly, the jitō–gesu axis remained entirely viable. Indeed, the separation itself, reminiscent of hompo and shimpo disputes, sometimes became the object of contention. Whether a person was jitō or gesu now emerged as an issue.

For obvious reasons, central owners stood to gain by ridding their lands of jitō when a gesu under their own authority might perform the same services. Once this truth was perceived by Kyoto's proprietors, the practice ensued of refusing to recognize a jitō, or rather of treating a jitō as if he were a gesu. An example of 1232 is explicit on this point. A proprietor had brought suit to Rokuhara alleging violations of an interior portion of an Iyo Province domain by "gesu Kunishige." The accused houseman responded by turning the charge back on the proprietor's deputy, who, he claimed, had actually seized the disputed area. Documentation was presented, proving that Kunishige was indeed jitō over the entire estate. The bakufu dismissed the proprietor's suit and reaffirmed its vassal's jitō shiki.[57]

The domain-owner's subterfuge in this case is worth underlining. It consisted of two elements: a claim that Kunishige was actually a gesu, his probable status before upgrading to jitō; and submission of a complaint concerning an interior unit of land. The complexities of this effort are treated in chapter 7. Here we need only remark on the obvious significance to all parties of an accurate shiki designation. Had Kunishige's family not been able to show possession of a valid jitō title, or to prove inclusion of the disputed area under that title,[58] the very essence of their tenure's relationship to higher authority would have been altered. Kunishige would have been

56. *Yasaka Jinja Monjo*, 1221/int.10/14 Kantō migyōsho, in Yasaka Jinja shamusho, comp., *Yasaka Jinja monjo*, (Kyoto, 1940), 2:461–62, doc. 1688, and 1221/12/29 Rokuhara shigyōjō, doc. 1689, p. 462.

57. *Chōryūji Monjo*, 1232/7/27 Rokuhara gechijō, in *Ehima ken hennen shi*, 2:259–60.

58. The holding of a jitō shiki did not imply full or equal authority over all component parts of the appointment area.

denoted gesu and recognized as directly subject to proprietary control.

If a proprietor could go to such lengths to convert a jitō into a gesu, we should not be surprised to find gesu calling themselves jitō. A proprietor's decree of 1234 reveals just such a case.[59] In Tannowa Estate in Kii Province, the resident gesu began impounding taxes and committing other lawless acts, all under the claim that he was a jitō. The domain-owner appealed to Kamakura, which immediately subpoenaed the culprit's documentary proof. The latter, as it happened, did possess bakufu records, indicating that at least he was a Kamakura houseman. But the records also proved that he was decidedly not a jitō. After issuing a stern warning to its man, Kamakura passed further disposition in the matter back to the domain-holder. It was for this reason that the present document, a final prohibitory decree, originated from Kyoto, rather than from Kamakura.

In other instances the disagreement was between Kamakura itself and a proprietor. In a pair of documents relating to Ōta Estate, we find conflicting designations for two Kamakura houseman brothers. A record of 1190 from the proprietor's side calls them gesu, while a bakufu document of 1205 cites them as jitō.[60] The explanation for this discrepancy lies in events during the intervening period. In 1196, after eliminating the two brothers,[61] the bakufu appointed one of its own leading members as Ōta jitō. This led to a series of proprietor appeals for cancellation, all summarily denied by the bakufu. The document of 1205 belongs in this latter group. As argued by Kamakura, Ōta was not only a former Heike land and therefore deserving of a jitō, but the appointment of such an officer was not an innovative act. In advance of the present holder, there had been the two brothers (see note 60). All indications are that these brothers had in fact been only gesu.[62] However, it was now to the bakufu's advantage to remember them as jitō.

59. *Asahina Ennosuke Shi Shozō Monjo*, 1234/5/20 saki no udaijin ke mandokoro kudashibumi, in *DNS* 5, 9:551–52.

60. *Kōyasan Monjo*, 1190/11 Kongobuji daitō gusō gejō an, in *DNK, iewake 1*, doc. 52, p. 48, and 1205/int.7/12 Kantō migyōsho, doc. 107, p. 112.

61. The ouster is described in chap. 6.

62. E.g , a bakufu document of 1195 refers to them as "shōen officials" (*shōkan*). *Kōyasan Monjo*, 1195/6/5 Kanto gechijō, *DNK, iewake 1*, doc. 85, pp. 79–80.

In ways such as this the jitō–gesu principle had woven itself into the national fabric.

We have followed in this chapter the emergence of a civil–military division of authority in the era after Gempei. The major innovation was Kamakura's unfettered jurisdiction over jitō and its accompanying decision to abandon all else. This development, however, did not come in the first days after 1185. As long as the crisis continued, the bakufu could not help but function as the mainstay of national governance. However this proved to be a heavy burden, and before long Yoritomo began seeking ways of extrication. The technique eventually settled on was to limit involvement in local matters to supervision of jitō.

The power configuration that emerged not only forced Kamakura into constant contact with Kyoto, but placed the bakufu on a treacherous course. Since proprietors were denied a direct right of dismissal over unruly jitō, Kamakura had to be prepared to deal harshly with its own men. At the same time, it had clear obligations to those men, especially in view of the absence of sanctions against domain-holders bringing false suits. A further complication was Kamakura's desire to patronize certain temples and shrines. When favored religious institutions opposed even law-abiding jitō—as they often seemed to do—how was the bakufu to react? The result was a jitō network in perpetual motion.

A corollary to Kamakura's total responsibility for jitō was its promotion of the separation with gesu. This widening of an almost indistinguishable gulf (by 1185) between two middle-level managerial posts became the jurisdictional fulcrum of a new age. To the bakufu was left the task of keeping this gulf—and the whole structure of law—viable.

6 THE EXTENSION OF KAMAKURA AUTHORITY AFTER 1185: THE BAKUFU'S CONTROL OVER ITS MEN

In chapter 5 we were concerned with court–bakufu relations and the effort to promote a jitō system that would be of maximal benefit to Kamakura, and yet of minimal harm to Kyoto and the traditional land system. In this chapter we will see that more was required to achieve this than just the working out of stable lines of authority between the two capitals. The bakufu was confronted with the need to seek greater consolidation of its own countrywide network of vassals. The various policies devised as part of this program will be our main topic here, and we begin with the region of greatest bakufu influence, eastern Japan.

In late 1183, preparatory to expanding Kamakura power into the west, Yoritomo undertook to establish personal relations with many eastern warriors not yet under his sway. Most of these men appear to have been either middle-level warriors making up the bands of Yoritomo's great vassals, or warriors owing primary loyalty to Yoshinaka and Yukiie. Our information is very limited here, but the few cases for which we have data indicate that reaching such persons often required elimination of their leaders. The outstanding example of this is, of course, Yoshinaka, though in his case a desire to be rid of a rival for chieftainship over the Minamoto was the paramount concern. Second in importance was Kazusa Hirotsune, leader of a provincewide military band (Kazusa Province) in the Kantō. Hirotsune, who in 1180 had delivered to Yoritomo the latter's largest contingent of troops to that point, was accused of complicity in a plot, hunted down, and then killed. Yoritomo's motivation became clear several months later. In return for reassignment of rights confiscated at the time of Hirotsune's death, the latter's private retainers elected to become vassals of Yoritomo rather than their late lord's avengers (*AK* 1184/2/14). In another case we see the destruction in mid-1184 of Ichijō Tadayori, a major force within Kai and Suruga provinces.[1] But in all of these instances the objective appears the same: to obliterate a major vassal in the hope of gaining greater influence over the warriors in his area.

How far this effort had gone in individual provinces by war's end is not clear. We may assume that Yoritomo's power now spread more or less comprehensively across the Kantō. But this was not true for the Chūbu region just to the west. Subsequent events would show that by 1185 the bakufu had not yet achieved a satisfactory control over many of these eastern housemen. Kamakura's command structure during the war had never been unified, and this allowed many warriors to fight under traditional chiefs. Local relationships were thus reinforced at the expense of the nominal lord, Yoritomo, who remained an absentee figure in distant Kamakura.

How to make these Chūbu houses more responsive to Kamakura's rule was thus a problem high on the list of priorities after the war. This was not merely out of a natural desire to control warrior families throughout the east. Failure to achieve such dominance meant added difficulties in trying to sustain meaningful relationships beyond the east. What Yoritomo devised was something both novel and ingenious. He determined to go to war again, though not against the recalcitrants themselves. The Kamakura lord would seek an "external" adventure in which warriors across the country, but especially those from the Chūbu, would be compelled to fight under direct Kantō command. The 1189 Ōshū campaign in northern Japan was the eventual result.

Kamakura's relations with the northern region must be summarized first. For almost a century this area, consisting of the two huge provinces of Mutsu and Dewa, had been under semi-independent control of a local family called Fujiwara.[2] By 1180, the

---

1. *AK* 1184/6/16. For a discussion of this stage in Kamakura's consolidation effort, see Okutomi Takayuki, "Kamakura bakufu kuni goke'ninsei no kenkyū," in *Mejiro gakuen joshi tanki daigaku kenkyū kiyō*, 5 (1968), pp. 22–23.

2. This northern hegemony dates from the end of the Later Three Years War

head of this territorial enclave was ensconced in a splendorous private capital, Hiraizumi, and was well-placed to pose a threat to Yoritomo's fledgling movement to the south. The Taira in Kyoto were alert to this possibility and took steps to win the support (or at least prevent the enmity) of Fujiwara Hidehira, the northern scion. As a clear counterweight to Yoritomo in the Kantō, they arranged to have Hidehira elevated in the eighth month of 1181 to the governorship of Mutsu Province.[3] The Genji chieftain thus found himself flanked by a real enemy, the Heishi, and a potential enemy, the northern Fujiwara, both of whom had received investitures from the court. The events of 1183–85 saw the elimination of the Heishi, but did nothing to alter the status of Hidehira, who had refrained from joining the Gempei War. Then, in 1185, the Yoshitsune rebellion began. The hero of the anti-Taira fighting was forced to become a fugitive during the next year and a half, taking refuge finally in the northern capital of Hiraizumi (*AK* 1187/2/10).

From this point, according to the official *Azuma kagami* account, events began to move inexorably toward a confrontation. Despite opposition from the In, who vainly hoped to retain the Fujiwara in their counterweight position, Yoritomo was already laying initial plans for battle. Wearying finally of the court's delaying tactics, and without waiting for the latter's proclamation of war, the bakufu chieftain left Kamakura in the seventh month of 1189 at the head of a great army.[4] Yoritomo was fully aware that Yoshitsune was already dead at the hands of his guardians, who hoped thereby to stave off an invasion, but higher stakes were now being played for. After a series of brief military encounters in which the opposition seemed almost to melt away, the north lay prone before the bakufu's

in the 1080s and constitutes the only exception to the active dominance throughout Heian of the court-centered polity. Extant source materials on the northern Fujiwara (mostly chronicle and diary entries) have been collected in Tōhoku daigaku tōhoku bunka kenkyūkai, comp., *Ōshu Fujiwara shiryō* (Tokyo, 1969).

3. *Gyokuyō*, 1181/8/6, 2:520–21, describes the recommendation that led to Hidehira's appointment: "Given the problems of the Kyoto army [*kampei*] in putting down the Kantō traitors [*zokuto*], would it not be wise policy for Mutsu local notable [*jūnin*], Hidehira, to be appointed governor of that province?" The appointment was made on 1181/8/15 (ibid., p. 523).

4. *AK* 1187/7/19. Unbeknown to Yoritomo, the court had acquiesced finally and issued its war declaration against the north on the very same day.

armies. Hiraizumi was entered on 8/22, and Kamakura power now extended the entire length of the country.

This, in short compass, represents the main thread of events relating to the Fujiwara defeat.[5] Certainly Yoritomo was eager to destroy his neighbor to the north, and he clearly coveted the vast lands in this region.[6] But as we have also noted, Yoritomo recognized the organizational advantage to be gained from mounting a unified military campaign against a vulnerable enemy. Loyalty and bravery on behalf of the lord of Kamakura could be tested under actual battlefield conditions. The bakufu chief could add or subtract vassals based on performance. It is this aspect of the Ōshū campaign that will concern us.[7]

Looking first at the overall size and composition of the 1189 army, there is no doubt that it was the greatest fighting force yet seen in Japan.[8] It was also the first military effort that was truly a national campaign; virtually all provinces were represented. This force, however, was commanded by men exclusively from the Kantō. A Tōkaidō division was jointly led by Hatta Tomoie (Hitachi Province) and Chiba Tsunetane (Shimōsa). Hokurikudō was under Usami Sanemasa (Izu) and Hiki Yoshikazu (Musashi). And Tōsandō, the central division, was led by Yoritomo, with Hatakeyama Shigetada (Musashi) as head of an advance guard. The subcom-

5. An excellent survey of the Hidehira–Yoritomo–Go-Shirakawa relationship during the 1180s is Ōtsuka Tokurō, "Kamakura bakufu no seiritsu to Ōshū Fujiwara shi no dōkō," in *Rekishi kyōiku* 8.7 (1960): 23–29.

6. On 1189/2/30, e.g., we see a bakufu entreaty for jitō to open new lands in Awa, Kazusa, and Shimōsa provinces (*AK*). These jitō were to collect unattached persons (*rōnin*) for the task of clearing and working these lands. No doubt such implorings were designed to undercut the demands issuing from jitō desirous of new bakufu grants. The broad lands of sparsely settled northern Japan must have loomed as a considerable incentive in 1189.

7. It is interesting that the operations of 1180–85 and 1189 find a ready parallel in the two stages required to establish virtually all of Japan's successive governments. Thus the creation of the Tokugawa bakufu required military action in 1600 and 1614, while the establishment of its successor in Meiji involved fighting in 1868 and 1877. Here, then, is an illustration of what Professor Hall has called the "incompleteness" of civil war in Japan (*Government and Local Power*, pp. 12–13).

8. *AK*'s figure of 280,000 is obviously an exaggeration (1189/9/4), though we can certainly imagine several tens of thousands.

manders were also men from the bakufu's home area, e.g., Doi
Sanehira, Shimokabe Yukihira, Miura Yoshizumi, and Kajiwara
Kagetoki.[9] The latter, for example, is known to have been active in
western Japan where he drew up an Ōshū-related "armed unit
register" (gumpei chūmon) for Mimasaka Province.[10] Even as
far away as southern Kyushu it was an easterner charged with
recruiting and leading troops all the way across Japan. Early in
1189, Koremune Tadahisa, jitō-in-chief of the huge Shimazu Estate,
was ordered to gather up officers (shōkan) possessing sufficient
weapons and to proced forthwith to the Kantō. Those showing
loyalty would be permitted to swear homage (kenzan) before
Yoritomo.[11]

Concerning Chūbu, a disproportionately large share of the names
appearing in Azuma kagami's 1189 entries belong to housemen from
the non-Kantō east. This suggests a conscious effort by Yoritomo
to call these recalcitrants to battle.[12] Apparently most responded
to this call, even while aware that they were sacrificing their autonomy within the Genji movement. To have refused meant almost
certain dispossession. Thus, a vassal who changed his mind while
on his way to join the Ōshū army suffered immediate confiscation
of his homelands (AK 1189/10/28). But Yoritomo had more in mind
than merely winning new vassals and trying to subordinate old
ones. He had already determined to launch a new stage in his
ongoing Chūbu purge.

Even before the move north we see the first signs of what was
about to befall unwanted housemen. In 1189/5, we note an elabora-
tion on the usual pattern regarding jitō cancellations: Yoritomo
urged the court to request dismissal of a certain jitō in Suruga Province.[13] This jitō happened to be a member of the "opposition"
Genji. The episode takes on added meaning in light of its sequel
some months after the Ōshū campaign. In mid-1190, Yoritomo

9. Kawanishi Sachiko, "Bunji gonen Ōshū seibatsu ni tsuite no ichi shōsatsu,"
Seiji keizai shigaku 11 (1963): 26.

10. Ishii S., "Bunji shugo jitō," p. 37, n.28.

11. Shimazu Ke Monjo, 1189/2/9 Minamoto Yoritomo kudashibumi, in DNK,
iewake 16, 1:7-8, doc. 9.

12. Kawanishi Sachiko, "Ōshū heiran to tōgoku bushidan," Rekishi kyōiku
16.12 (1968): 38.

13. Ibid., p. 35, citing AK 1189/5/22.

exiled this Suruga vassal to distant Oki Island (*AK* 1190/8/13). On the same day, moreover, he took similar steps against two other leading Chūbu figures. Owari chieftain Yamada Shigetaka was sent to Hitachi, and his counterpart in Shinano, Takeda Shigeie, was dispatched to Tosa.[14] Having thus destroyed the Ōshū bloc on his eastern flank, Yoritomo commenced to dismantle the Chūbu group on his western side.

As we saw in the case of Kazusa Hirotsune in 1184, elimination of a major houseman could lead to enrollment of a province's lesser warriors as full vassals. This is apparently what happened in Chūbu from 1190. Our information is limited to the just-exiled Yamada Shigetaka of Owari, but soon after his departure his one-time retainers elected to unite with Yoritomo. Because these fighting men wielded a considerable influence in Owari and Mino, it was probably only now that the bakufu gained hegemony over those two provinces.[15] The importance of this can be linked to Yoritomo's failure to visit Kyoto until the end of 1190—instead of soon after Ōshū. Consolidation of the east was more obligatory than dominance of the north.

Actually, even now Yoritomo fell somewhat short of his goal. For example, in 1193 the Kamakura lord felt the need to dispose of his last remaining brother, Noriyori, who had served for some years as Suruga governor (*AK* 1193/8/17); while in 1194, he moved against old-line vassal Yasuda Yoshisada of Tōtomi (*AK* 1194/8/19). In Hokurikudō such problems were never in fact resolved, at least not during Yoritomo's lifetime. The Jō family of Echigo, for instance, continued to resist full assimilation even though it did acknowledge Yoritomo's lordship. In this case, the Jō scion's participation in the Ōshū campaign had not led to any lasting bakufu influence over his family. Instead, the Jō leader, Nagashige, continued to harbor a strong antipathy for the Minamoto that dated all the way back to the Gempei War. Biding his time until after Yoritomo's death, he appealed to the court in 1201 for an anti-Kamakura charge, only to be embarrassed by the latter's refusal. The bakufu now decided

14. Cited by Kawanishi, "Bunji gonen," p. 29.
15. Ishii S., "Bunji shugo jitō," p. 29. Also *AK* 1192/6/20, which states that the retainers (*rōtō*) of Shigetaka were to be recruited for imperial guard duty by the new Mino shugo.

to move, and Nagashige was soon captured and executed. But even at that, his followers continued to assert their traditional power in Echigo, and actually expanded their influence for a time into Shinano and Sado.[16]

Notwithstanding exceptional cases such as the Jō of Echigo, it is evident that the Ōshū campaign had played a significant part in the organization of the bakufu's houseman system. In addition to the role played in opening the Chūbu region to extensive Kamakura power, Yoritomo now had the opportunity, alluded to above, to draw up a "balance sheet" on general vassal performance. Even for regions as far away as southern Kyushu we find documents that illustrate a very simple loyal–disloyal criterion. An 1189/11/24 confirmation decree shows a Satsuma warrior, Tōnai Yasutomo, being rewarded for his valiant Ōshū service. A second Yoritomo decree shows a jitō cancellation deriving from a vassal's refusal to answer the Ōshū conscription order.[17]

Unfortunately, not more than a handful of these Ōshū-related records remain extant. We can only presume that rewards and punishments on a large scale were a natural outgrowth of the war in northern Japan. But whatever the actual volume, the Ōshū campaign had been important to the bakufu: it had provided Kamakura with an opportunity to recruit new housemen, test the loyalty of old housemen, establish lines of command under eastern warrior supervision, and create a local administrative base in the north.

A brief description should be added of this new northern outpost. One of the first steps taken by Yoritomo after defeating the Ōshū Fujiwara was to guarantee the security of the great landholding temples of Hiraizumi.[18] In this way, the Kamakura lord moved to establish himself as ultimate protector over estates in the northern region. Just before leaving the Ōshū capital, Yoritomo appointed

16. *AK* 1201/2/3, 3/4, 3/12, 4/2, 4/3, and 5/14. Also *Hyakurenshō*, 1201/1/23 and 2/25, p. 172.

17. *Kokubunji Monjo*, 1189/11/24 Kantō migyōsho, in Kyūshū shiryō kankō-kai, comp., *Sappan kyūki zatsuroku, zempen* (Fukuoka, 1955), 1:107–08, doc. 72. The object of the confirmation was the district chieftainship (*gunji shiki*) for Satsuma's Kagoshima Gun. *Sata Monjo*, 1192/2/29 Minaraoto Yoritomo kuda-shibumi, in *Hennen Ōtomo shiryō*, 1:213–14, doc. 220.

18. *Chūsonji Monjo*, 1189/9/10 Kantō migyōsho, in Iwate ken kyōiku iinkai, comp., *Ōshū Hiraizumi monjo* (Morioka, 1958), doc. 41, p. 15.

the leader of a minor Musashi Province band, Kasai Kiyoshige, to
the post of police commander (*kebiishi*) of Hiraizumi Gun (*AK*
1189/9/24). That the Kasai were a family of undistinguished lineage
is significant. We will see shortly that Yoritomo, as a defense measure against great vassal autonomy, regularly entrusted obscure
military figures with important responsibilities. The next stage in
the bakufu leader's northern program took place in Taga, on Yoritomo's way home.[19] There he directed the provincial officers of
Mutsu to continue the "precedents" laid down by the Ōshū Fujiwara (*AK* 1189/10/1). This typifies another feature of the Kamakura
lord's strategy: his attempt to establish control by superimposing his
own authority over existing administrative apparatuses.

Yoritomo arrived back in Kamakura on 10/24, after an absence
of about three months. On the very same day, he ordered commence-
ment of an extensive land survey in Dewa Province, directing that
the provincial office not disturb jitō private fields (*AK* 1189/10/24).
Obviously the Kamakura lord had made a number of appointments
to this post before returning home. Two weeks later, Yoritomo
dispatched Ōe Hiromoto, a ranking aide and high bakufu officer,
to the central capital in order to "negotiate" the Ōshū region's
future; all rewards proffered by the court were to be declined (*AK*
1189/11/7). On 12/6, Yoritomo received full authority over the two
northern provinces (*AK*), in effect a recognition of an already pre-
vailing condition. After several additional months the bakufu moved
to finalize its control over the north. On the occasion of a rebellion
by personnel within the Mutsu provincial office, Yoritomo deposed
them and sent as a replacement Izawa Iekage (*AK* 1190/3/15).
Once again the Kamakura lord used a minor figure for a major task.
Izawa was not even a landed warrior; he was a private servant
(*zōshiki*) of Yoritomo, a mere petty bureaucrat who received a
monthly stipend (*geppō*).[20] From 1190, however, Izawa belonged
among the mighty, with duties embracing a control over provincial
administration, the hearing of public suits, the overseeing of grain
production, and the receipt from jitō of public services and tributes
(*AK* 1190/10/5). At the same time, Kasai, who had been left in com-

19. Taga was the provincial capital of Mutsu Province.

20. Fukuda Toyohiko, "Yoritomo no zōshiki ni tsuite," in *Shigaku zasshi*
78.3 (1969): 16, citing *AK* 1187/2/28.

mand of Hiraizumi, was now given permanent control over police enforcement and houseman command for the northern region. Both families came to hold their posts in heredity and later were designated "northern province supervisors" (Ōshū *sōbugyō*).[21] The Izawa even went so far as to adopt their formal title of *rusu* (proxy governor) as a new surname.[22] But long before that, the bakufu was exercising full governance over the north through its two supervisors. A document of 1193 shows Yoritomo disposing freely of public land in Mutsu in a way wholly reminiscent of his activities in the Kantō from 1180.[23]

A converse to the Yoritomo policy of elevating low-ranking families to positions of great authority was the elimination of prestigious houses native to an area. We have already seen this in the Ōshū region (the northern Fujiwara), Kantō (Kazusa Hirotsune), and Chūbu (Ichijō Tadayori). Such efforts in areas beyond the east, however, were deferred until the mid-1190s. In the provinces of central and western Japan the bakufu was forced to operate under certain disadvantages. One of these was largely of Kamakura's own making: its program of dividing a jurisdiction over jitō and gesu with Kyoto inhibited its freedom of action concerning many native housemen. This condition was then compounded by the bakufu's attitude in general toward noneastern vassals. As part of a "Kantō first" mentality, it normally refused jitō titles to such housemen, even though this meant surrendering jurisdiction over them.

An additional problem derived from the fact that some provinces possessed two levels of Kamakura vassals, the great public officer chieftains and their traditional subordinates. This meant that families such as the Inaba of Wakasa and the Kōno of Iyo entered the 1190s as unofficial commanders over their province's Kamakura housemen: a barrier had been placed between the bakufu and those who were nominally its vassals. For reasons not entirely clear, the Ōshū campaign had done little to reduce these western magnate

21. Ōtsuka, "Kamakura bakufu," p. 29.
22. The Rusu documents appear in Miyagi kenshi hensan iinkai, comp., *Miyagi kenshi, shiryōshū 1*, (Sendai, 1965), 30:49 ff.
23. *Shiogama Jinja Monjo*, 1193/3/7 shōgun ke mandokoro kudashibumi, in ibid., p. 144.

houses to subservience, and this led to an effort after 1190 to devise new control policies. Thinking proceeded along several lines. The deployment of a uniform network of shugo was the most innovative program and will be treated in chapter 8. At the same time, an attempt was begun to place a lid on the size of the houseman corps. Finally, purges were launched against great vassal houses now in all parts of the country.

The decision to limit the size of the houseman rolls was a marked departure from policy during the 1180s. As we have seen, even as late as the northern campaign, submission to Minamoto lordship was often the major requirement for becoming a Kamakura houseman. Thus the distinction between houseman and nonhouseman was not always clear in advance of the final compiling of vassal lists. This condition was especially severe in areas beyond the capital where relatively few warriors possessed jitō shiki; by definition that office presupposed bakufu affiliation. The result was a decision in the 1190s to seek a vassal tabulation in the separate provinces, followed by a drafting of authoritative registers. Not only would a final itemization of duly recognized housemen and their titles impose a certain cohesion on the bakufu's vassal system, but Kamakura would be aided in its effort to distinguish between its own jurisdiction and that of Kyoto's.

Unfortunately, evidence survives for only a few of these registers: Tamba (1192), Wakasa (1196), Tajima (1197), Satsuma (1197), Ōsumi (1198), and Izumi (indeterminate).[24] But we can glean several interesting points even from this slim data. For example, the average number of houseman families per province was between 30 and 40, although we know from other information that larger totals were possible. Hizen, for instance, had some 140 Kamakura vassals, almost all of very small size.[25] It also seems clear that the preparation of these registers was designed less as an aid to housemen than as a means of institutionalizing Kamakura's countrywide band. Individual vassals did not, as a result of inclusion on a list, improve their chances of being issued a bakufu confirmatory document. We know this because occasionally a vassal persevered to the extent of taking

24. Tanaka, "Kamakura shoki," p. 23, for citations.

25. Seno Seiichirō, "Hizen no kuni ni okeru Kamakura goke'nin," *Nihon rekishi* 117 (1958): 34.

his case personally to Kamakura. One such instance is that of Nejime Kiyoshige from remote Ōsumi in southern Kyushu. Despite Kamakura's stern discouragement of personally delivered appeals from its western housemen, Kiyoshige's son, some years later, succeeded in achieving his father's goal—receipt of a Kamakura investiture decree. But cases such as this were clearly exceptional.[26] The fate of most western province housemen is recorded matter-of-factly in an official bakufu statement of the 1230s: "Western province vassals [Saigoku goke'nin] were reported in registers by shugo during the time of Yoritomo. Even though the imperial guard and other [houseman] services were discharged, persons possessing shiki and granted bakufu decrees [Kantō kudashibumi] were very few. . . ."[27]

Without entering into a lengthy discussion of the causes of the Jōkyu War, many of the warriors joining the court side in 1221 were these same unrewarded housemen from western Japan. The bakufu, of course, branded such opponents as traitors, even though, as gesu-types, few in this group had ever left central jurisdiction. Here at any rate was the basis of the new wave of jitō in the period after 1221. As noted in the last chapter, the confiscated holdings of westerners were parceled out to men almost exclusively from the Kantō.

In fact, however, this story of purge and dispossession of central and western province vassals traces all the way back to the mid-1190s. The special object of Yoritomo's attention during this period were the great chieftains whose support he had so eagerly sought late in the Gempei War. By examining several of these purge incidents we can gain an additional insight into the bakufu's eastern partisanship.

The basic character of Inaba power in Wakasa Province was described in chapter 3. Centered in the public land sector and in the provincial office, it was the authority of a dominant resident officer.

---

26. Okutomi, "Kuni goke'nin," p. 22. Another example is the investiture in 1216 of Saeki Tamehiro of Aki as a gō-level jitō. This is the same Saeki family that had figured so prominently under the Taira. Obviously, they had made good their conversion to the Minamoto standard. Kawai Masaharu, "Kamakura bakufu no seiritsu to saigoku no dōkō," *Rekishi kyōiku* 8.7 (1960): 35.

27. *Shimpen Tsuika*, no. 68, 1234/5/1, in Satō Shinichi and Ikeuchi Yoshisuke, eds., *Chūsei hōsei shiryōshū* (Tokyo, 1969), 1:91. (Hereafter cited as *CHS*.)

By the end of the Gempei fighting this dominance, if anything, had
been strengthened: Tokisada, the scion, retained his hold over
traditional subordinates even while the latter were now nominally
the vassals of Yoritomo. The Kamakura chief was clearly aware of
this, which explains his refusal to grant Tokisada rewards. None of
the latter's many gōshi and gesu (public and private) titles was elevated to jitō rank.[28] Nevertheless, for more than a decade Yoritomo
undertook no overt act against the Inaba. Only in 1196 did conditions change. In the ninth month of that year, Tokisada was divested
of his entire portfolio of land and office rights—a vast shiki complex
to which Kamakura possessed no legal claim.[29] We can only guess
at the pretext offered for such a massive confiscation. Presumably
Tokisada was accused of rebellious intentions, for this would have
allowed Yoritomo to convert the latter's land rights into jitō shiki.
But there is no escaping the conclusion that Yoritomo had acted
largely to rid himself of an unwanted vassal.

What happened next is even more interesting. Into the vacuum
left by the departed Inaba, Yoritomo raised up one of his own
servant–followers and installed him as the new power within Wakasa.
He did this by restructuring the diverse inheritance seized from
Tokisada into an updated shiki combination. Tsutsumi Tadasue, son
of Yoritomo's own wet nurse, was now made shugo and jitō-in-chief
(sōjitō) within Wakasa Province.[30]

Actually, it is not entirely certain whether Wakasa Tadasue (for
that is the surname his family later took) became sōjitō immediately
upon his or his deputy's arrival in Wakasa. If he did not, a suspected
delay of three or four years is attributable to opposition both locally
and in Kyoto. On the other hand, it is equally possible that successive investiture decrees of 1199 and 1200 were merely "reappoint-
ments" designed to underscore Kamakura's determination to have
its man take control in Wakasa. Whatever the facts in the matter,

28. See Tanaka, "Wakasa," pp. 253 ff. for much of the narrative content presented here.
29. The confiscation is recorded in *Wakasa no kuni shugo shiki shidai*, 1196/9/1
entry, *DNS* 4, 5:267.
30. Ishii Susumu, "Kamakura jidai 'shugoryō' kenkyū josetsu," in Hōgetsu
Keigo sensei kanreki kinenkai, comp., *Nihon shakai keizai shi kenkyū, kodai-
chūsei hen*, p. 328. (Hereafter cited as Ishii S., "Kamakura 'shugoryō.' ")

the complicated power transfer was certainly consummated by 1200. Tadasue now came to enjoy a full combination of old and new, including the provincial tax office (*saisho*), shugo title, sōjitō posts over Onyū and Mikata districts, and some twenty-five individual jitō shiki. He was at once holder of the highest titles that Kamakura could normally bestow—as well as holder of the key post within Wakasa's provincial headquarters. Such indeed was the encompassing nature of the bakufu's power in Wakasa that for 150 years— the entire life-span of the eastern regime—no evidence has turned up of even one native jitō investee. From the time of the Inaba ouster the province was simply dominated from the Kantō. Indicative of this is what happened in the late 1220s: the Wakasa family, at the height of its powers, was itself divested of most of its holdings, this time in favor of the bakufu's leading house, the Hōjō. For a full century thereafter successive Hōjō scions held the public sector of Wakasa largely as a private possession.[31]

The Inaba's downfall in 1196 was not an isolated incident. The bakufu was responsible for a major dispossession in Bingo Province during the same year. This involved Ōta Estate, described in some detail in the previous chapter. This unusually rich shōen (600 chō) possessed a pair of native gesu brothers whom the bakufu wished to replace. At the same time, the domain proprietor, Kōyasan Temple, had its own reasons to wish the departure of these two brothers. A document of 1190 describes their many acts of violence within Ōta.[32] But Kōyasan, despite its jurisdiction over gesu, was apparently unable to discipline this unruly pair; it turned for help (as had so many other proprietors) to the bakufu.

Events came to a head in 1196. The two brothers were accused suddenly of unnamed rebellious offenses (*muhon no toga*) and divested of both their land rights and status as housemen.[33] Kamakura,

31. Material in this paragraph is drawn from Tanaka, "Wakasa," pp. 254–63.
32. *Kōyasan Monjo*, 1190/11 Kongobuji gusō gejō an, in *DNK, iewake 1*, 1:48–51, doc. 52.
33. At least we believe this is what happened. The reference to "rebellious offenses" comes in a 1206 document quoted within a later record of 1223 (ibid., 1223/11 Ōta-no-shō jitō chinjō an, 8:598, doc. 1949). For a discussion, see Egashira Tsuneharu, *Kōyasan ryō shōen no kenkyū* (Tokyo, 1938), p. 264, and Hattori Kentarō, *Hōken shakai seiritsu shiron* (Tokyo, 1958), p. 28, p. 30, n. 8.

however, was not acting merely on behalf of a beleaguered proprietor. For much against Kōyasan's wishes it proceeded to appoint a jitō to Ōta Estate.[34] The recipient, significantly, was Miyoshi Yasunobu, a onetime court noble who had abandoned the capital during the war and entered bakufu service. Once again, therefore, Yoritomo conferred a rich reward on a personal aide lacking a private territorial base.

Our final example, concerning the Kōno of Iyo, shows a somewhat different result.[35] Here we find the bakufu failing at an attempt to utilize a shugo to gain leverage over Iyo's housemen. Admission of this failure came in 1205 when Kamakura withdrew its shugo and authorized the Kōno chief, Michinobu, to assume the substance of that authority but not its accompanying title (*AK* 1205/7/29). The bakufu was thus continuing to adhere to its old policy of denying westerners full equality with housemen from the Kantō. To make matters worse, fewer than four months later Kamakura broke usual practice by appointing a Kōno rival, the native family of Kutsuna, to an independent Iyo jitō shiki.[36] The final chapter came in 1221 when Michinobu gave vent to long years of resentment by joining the court side in the Jōkyū War. However, this played right into Kamakura's hands. Michinobu was divested of all his holdings and summarily exiled to a distant province.[37] By contrast, the Kutsuna remained loyal and were granted a confirmation of their original 1205 jitō award.[38]

Kamakura's expansion into Kyushu shows some of the same patterns that we saw in other parts of Japan. The advancement of low-ranking easterners and the elimination of native houses of prominence are both in evidence. But Kyushu also provided unusual

---

34. *Kōyasan Monjo*, 1196/10/22 saki no utaishō ke mandokoro kudashibumi, in *DNK, iewake 1*, 8:586–87, doc. 1942.

35. For the Kōno during the Gempei War, see chap. 3.

36. *Chōryūji Monjo*, 1205/11/12 shōgun ke kudashibumi, in *Ehime ken hennen shi*, 2:206.

37. *Inaba Shi Shozō Monjo*, 1224/1/29 Kantō gechijō, in ibid., p. 250. A Michinobu son who had sided against his father was permitted to continue the family name, with only a fraction of the Kōno inheritance.

38. *Chōryūji Monjo*, 1221/int.10/12 Kantō gechijō, in ibid., p. 245.

problems and special opportunities. In the end, this most distant of all regions was made subject to bakufu direction at a level probably higher than most other parts of the west.

Our account of Kyushu begins toward the end of the Gempei War. In 1184 and then again early in 1185 Yoritomo made overtures to the warriors of Kyushu, though the initial response was not encouraging (*AK* 1184/3/1 and 1185/1/6). Not only was Yoritomo's brother, Noriyori, delayed from crossing over from the western tip of Honshu (*AK* 1185/1/26), but Kyushu provided much of the leadership for the fateful last Taira defense at Dannoura (*AK* 1185/3/24). Equally troublesome was a rise during 1185 in the number of warrior outrages against Kyushu estates. Noriyori, in command of the Kyushu armies of occupation, proved unable to stem this tide and was replaced in 1185/7 by the bakufu's two troubleshooters for central Japan, Kondō and Nakahara.[39] Scholars have long debated the significance of this development. For one group, the court's request of this action was tantamount to a complete surrender of its Kyushu jurisdiction: the government–general (dazaifu) and indirectly the separate provincial offices of Kyushu now fell under bakufu supervision.[40] A second group has viewed events much more cautiously: Kamakura's power over Kyushu developed only gradually, as indicated, for example, by the court's continued issuance of decrees to dazaifu as if nothing fundamental had changed.[41] The weight of evidence, as we shall see, clearly favors this latter position.

One measure of proof that Kyushu was still largely free from bakufu power was Yoshitsune's appeal to the court late in 1185 for a Kyushu-wide jitō shiki (see p. 118). It was seemingly only at this juncture that Yoritomo took his first positive step toward winning a real control there. He dispatched as his personal deputy a minor vassal from Izu, one Amano Tōkage. Neither Amano's arrival date in Kyushu, nor the precise limits or title of his assignment is known

---

39. *AK* 1185/7/12. See chap. 3 for the activities of these two men in central Japan.

40. Ishii Susumu is the leading spokesman: "Kamakura bakufu ron," pp. 110, 122. The contention here is a legal one—that the court's authorization was similar to its authorization for the east in 1183/10. See chap. 3.

41. Seno Seiichirō, "Chinzei bugyō kō," pp. 38 ff.

for sure.[42] But we do have sufficient materials to show his general activities. The following is a brief summary: Amano was bakufu military commander in Kyushu and led forays against uncooperative warrior groupings (*AK* 1187/9/22). He personally granted confirmations of bakufu-authorized land rights, co-signed dazaifu decrees giving validity to jitō appointments, participated in the cancellation of jitō, and carried out levy exemptions on behalf of Kamakura-related religious institutions.[43] He was in short the bakufu's chief spokesman in Kyushu, a responsibility much different from the full powers of governance traditionally suggested by scholars. In fact, we know that not all of Amano's works were either good or effectual. Amano was guilty on more than one occasion of self-aggrandizing deeds,[44] and his difficulties in gathering up warriors for a local militia effort reflect (to paraphrase *AK* 1188/2/21) an actual Kamakura weakness in Kyushu at this time. It would be several years before the bakufu could qualify as the preeminent governing force on that island.

Kamakura met its various challenges in Kyushu with a diversified, though slowly evolving, program. At the center of this effort was a tendency to be even less discriminating than elsewhere about whom it accepted into vassalage. The larger local powers, who had generally opposed the Minamoto, were mostly destroyed during 1185–86,

42. At the latest the arrival date was 1186/2, but there are many theories: see, e.g., Satō, *Soshō seido*, p. 259, and Ishii Susumu, "Dazaifu kikō no henshitsu to Chinzei bugyō no seiritsu," *Shigaku zasshi* 68.1 (1959): 32. The standard theory is that Amano was the first in a succession of so-called "Kyushu administrators" (Chinzei *bugyō*), and that he immediately came to dominate the dazaifu. However, as Seno has pointed out, these are only assumptions. E.g., we have only *AK*'s word that Amano was called Chinzei bugyō (e.g., 1186/12/10); contemporaneous documents do not refer to him by this title.

43. An Amano confirmatory edict of 1189/7/19 is quoted in *Shimazu Ke Monjo*, 1329/10/5 Kantō gechijō, in *Dazaifu*, 7:196–97. Also see *AK* 1187/2/20. For the other activities (in order) see *Kokubunji Monjo*, 1188/3/13 Dazaifu shugosho kudashibumi, in *Dazaifu*, 7:191. *Munakata Jinja Monjo*, 1191/8/1 Taira Moritoki hōsho, in ibid., p. 203; and *Munakata Jinja Monjo*, 1188(?)/4/10 Minamoto Yoritomo migyōsho, ibid., pp. 191–92.

44. In documents of 1187 and 1189 we find Yoritomo condemning the excesses of Amano agents in Shimazu Estate: *Shimazu Ke Monjo*, 1187/9/9 Minamoto Yoritomo kudashibumi, in *Dazaifu*, 7:188, and ibid., 1189(?)/5/14 Taira Moritoshi hōsho, p. 196.

thereby leaving northern Kyushu almost barren of major native houses.[45] But numerous smaller families still remained, and these had to be won over. To accomplish this, Kamakura adopted an unusually liberal program of jitō shiki confirmatory grants. This meant both more native jitō in Kyushu than any other western region and a vassal corps too large for one man to manage single-handedly.[46]

Amano was replaced around 1195, and his authority was parceled among three eastern families destined for a long and prosperous association with Kyushu. We have already encountered Koremune Tadahisa, an early jitō recipient in Ise Province. In 1185 and 1186 Tadahisa was granted successive gesu and jitō rights over the vast Shimazu Estate of southern Kyushu.[47] This authority was progressively expanded until it reached its final form around 1197 with the addition of shugo titles for the three provinces of that region.[48] Yet typically, Koremune house origins are obscure.[49] As elsewhere, Tadahisa's lack of prestigious roots, combined with his personal loyalty to Yoritomo, were apparently what commended him for promotion.

The second family was the Ōtomo, a minor (gō-level) house from the Kantō's Sagami Province. So unheralded was this family that

45. The few larger houses that had aided the bakufu were disposed of along with the Heike partisans. The justification given was their favorable reception to Yoshitsune. Sotoyama Mikio, "Kamakura ki ni okeru Ōtomo shi no dōkō," *Rekishi kyōiku* 16.12 (1968), p. 63. (Hereafter cited as Sotoyama, "Ōtomo.")

46. Indeed, as Seno Seiichirō notes, there was constant disorder and rivalry among these small-sized jitō who were neighbors ("Kamakura bakufu no seiritsu to Kyūshū chihō no dōkō," *Rekishi kyōiku* 8.7 [1960]; 42 [Hereafter cited as Seno, "Kyūshū chihō"]).

47. *Shimazu Ke Monjo*, 1185/8/15 Minamoto Yoritomo kudashibumi, in *DNK, iewake 16*, 1:2–3, doc. 3. This gesu assignment by Yoritomo was in accord with a decree from the estate proprietor. And ibid., 1186/4/3 Minamoto Yoritomo kudashibumi, doc. 5, p. 4, which refers to Tadahisa's jitō appointment. The original jitō investiture document, coming during the interim, has evidently been lost.

48. Actually, two of these titles (Hyūga and Ōsumi) were taken from Tadahisa early in the thirteenth century, but his family's power was not adversely affected. For the next seven centuries, the family of Tadahisa, now surnamed Shimazu, would wholly dominate southern Kyushu.

49. For a discussion, see Asakawa, *Iriki*, p. 100.

Yoshinao, its head, is recorded as having gone to battle in Ōshū followed by only a single retainer (*AK* 1189/8/9). Yet here too this obviously low-ranking figure was made shugo in perhaps two Kyushu provinces during the 1190s, became holder of voluminous jitō shiki, and is thought by some to have shared with the Mutō the exalted title of Kyushu administrator (Chinzei bugyō).[50]

The third family was the Mutō, the most influential among the triumvirate during Kamakura times. Once again, Mutō Sukeyori's origins are obscure; we have no information at all concerning his place of birth or eastern holdings.[51] During the 1190s, however, he was dispatched to Kyushu by Yoritomo, and he assumed, in addition to several shugo titles, a major authority within the dazaifu. Recent scholarship has tended to discount the view that he instantly came to control that agency; his powers, like those of Amano before him, remained limited, at least at first. But it is worth noting that he alone among his eastern compatriots decided to settle permanently in Kyushu.[52] The Shimazu and Ōtomo, by contrast, continued to work through private deputies until the Mongol invasions of 1274 and 1281 forced both families to shift their bases westward.

Perhaps the most novel device with special application in Kyushu was a bakufu office called sōjitō, or jitō-in-chief. The remaining pages of this chapter will examine this institution. The condition giving rise to sōjitō in Kyushu was the presence there of an unusually large number of jitō holders. The post was permitted only to easterners, who were placed in a supralocal position over one or more of these indigenous jitō. Unfortunately, we cannot assert positively that sōjitō appointments were made only for purposes of control. Among the small number of sōjitō coming down to us, at least several appear more as honorariums than as mechanisms of con-

50. The older view that the Shimazu, Ōtomo, and Mutō divided all nine Kyushu shugo posts is now discredited. See chap. 8, n. 21. For the Ōtomo jitō shiki see the testamentary documents of Yoshinao's widow: *Shiga Monjo*, 1240/ 4/6 Ama Shinmyō shoryō haibunjō, Ama Shinmyō yuzurijō, and Ama Shinmyō shobunjō, in *Hennen Ōtomo shiryō*, 1:361–66, docs. 416–18.

51. Seno Seiichirō, "Chinzei ni okeru tōgoku goke'nin," pt. 1, *Nihon rekishi* 167 (1962): 17–18.

52. Ibid., pt. 2, *Nihon rekishi* 168 (1962): 41–42. It was not until the 1220s that the Mutō came to dominate the dazaifu completely.

trol.[53] But the scholarly consensus continues to support a primary emphasis on the post's administrative content. During the Yoritomo period when sōjitō were first implemented, most of the evidence seems to bear this out.[54]

Before looking at sōjitō in Kyushu, we should note a few instances of this institution elsewhere. All show easterners in control of regions in which a native magnate had just been deposed. The objective here was clearly to fill a vacuum of at least the dimensions of a district (gun). Most conspicuous is the case of Tsutsumi (Wakasa) Tadasue's placement over two of the three districts in Wakasa Province. This appointment, as noted earlier, came in the wake of the 1196 ouster of the native Inaba. The titles seem clearly administrative and were probably in lieu of regular district officers (gunji). A second case in point is Shimokabe Yukihira's posting as sōjitō to the southern districts of Hitachi Province. This came soon after the 1181 elimination of the Shida, a Minamoto collateral (AK 1184/4/21). Our final example is Hatakeyama Shigetada's placement over a district in Mutsu Province after destruction of the Ōshū Fujiwara and their allies.[55] This sōjitō is of special interest because it permits insight into the nature of the holder's authority. Apparently, Hatakeyama possessed a judicial competence, as indicated by a petition that he resolve a boundary dispute affecting a ranking shrine's lands. But the incident was too important to be judged by himself. As Hatakeyama himself asserted, the matter would be passed to Kamakura for settlement.[56]

In none of these non-Kyushu sōjitō cases, however, do we find

53. Yasuda has taken this fact and argued that sōjitō was not for control at all, but rather merely a supplemental awards program for easterners (Jitō oyobi, pp. 405–25).

54. Representative of the concensus view is Yamakuma Korezane, "Sōjitō ni tsuite," Nihon rekishi 170 (1962): 56–62. What we will see actually is a transition: during the thirteenth century sōjitō tended to evolve into little more than absentee titles yielding income.

55. When this placement was made is not clear, though it probably came soon after the 1189 campaign. Hatakeyama, a gō-level warrior from Musashi, was one of Yoritomo's trusted lieutenants in the Ōshū episode. His sōjitō post is referred to in AK 1200/5/28.

56. Ibid.

evidence of local jitō.[57] The concentric placement of jitō appears to be unique to that island, which helps to explain the association of sōjitō with Kyushu.[58] The outstanding example in Kyushu is that of Koremune (Shimazu) Tadahisa of Shimazu Estate. We have already noted Tadahisa's appointment in 1186 as jitō proper. His position was then elevated to sōjitō at some point before 1187/5.[59] Two years later we see an expression of this new authority: on the occasion of the recruitment order to Tadahisa in advance of the Ōshū campaign (p. 147), the latter set about conscripting both "small jitō" and nonhousemen alike. A document of 1192 shows another side to Tadahisa's competence. This is a bakufu order directing that he expedite the transfer of lands from a former Heike follower to a certain designated houseman. The latter was to hold this unit as a jitō shiki within the larger estate.[60] The edict referred to here, it is evident, is the only one extant among an obviously larger group. Each of the itemized holdings of the dispossessed Taira partisan was slated for distribution as a jitō shiki. Tadahisa was to be sōjitō over many smaller native jitō.

Actually, the condition of jitō assignments to Shimazu Estate is more complex than indicated so far. For example, there is evidence to show that Chiba Tsunetane, a revered bakufu elder, held a sōjitō title over a portion of the same domain. This was Iriki District, the site of Dr. Asakawa's classic study.[61] Such an appointment, however,

57. The year 1200 yields another sōjitō, this one in the Chūbu province of Tōtomi. What is curious, at first glance, is that the holder, unlike others in the east, was sōjitō over only a single shōen. Why, then, use that title? The answer seems to lie in the sōjitō's concurrent possession of the estate managership—the azukari dokoro title. Perhaps the prefix "sō" was added merely for emphasis. *Nakayama Monjo*, 1200/6 sōjitō kanete azukari dokoro kishinjō, in Shizuoka ken, comp., *Shizuoka ken shiryō* (Shizuoka, 1938), 4:339–40. A similar sōjitō–azukari dokoro combination appears in a shōen of Kyushu's Chikuzen Province: *Munakata Jinja Monjo*, 1212/10/26 sōjitō kanete azukari kudashibumi, in Itō Shirō, comp., *Munakata gunshi*, (1932), 2:147.

58. A document of 1248 explicitly makes this association. See p. 165.

59. First mentioned in *Shimazu Ke Monjo*, 1187/5/3 Minamoto Yoritomo kudashibumi, in *DNK, iewake 16*, 1:6, doc. 7.

60. *Shimazu Ke Monjo*, 1192/10/22 Kantō migyōsho an, in *DNK, iewake 16*, 1:257–58, doc. 298.

61. See *Shimazu Ke Monjo*, 1186/8/3 Minamoto Yoritomo kudashibumi, in *DNK, iewake 16*, 1:5, doc. 6, for Tsunetane's assignment as district chief (*gunji*) over five "public–private" (*yose-gōri*) areas within Shimazu. One of these was

is not that remarkable. The bakufu enjoyed a broad authority over this largest of all Heike confiscated lands, and the sheer enormity of the domain (covering the better part of three provinces) made multiple sōjitō desirable. On the other hand, Chiba Tsunetane seems a curious choice for such an appointment. He was both a ranking eastern warrior and a very old man by the 1190s.[62] At all events, we know only that he became sōjitō over Iriki between the time of his regular jitō investiture in 1197 and his death four years later.[63]

A small area in northern Kyushu provides the most intimate picture of a sōjitō interacting with a native "small jitō" (shōjitō). During the course of more than sixty years we are able to follow the vicissitudes of this relationship by drawing on a single record—an unusually detailed bakufu judgment decree of 1248. The account that follows is based on this chronicle.[64]

On 1186/5/6 a certain Yoshida Ieshiki, a minor (myōshu-level) vassal, was granted a normal jitō shiki over his traditional homelands in Chikugo Province. At some point before 1197, the bakufu's special deputy for Kyushu, Amano Tōkage, was appointed sōjitō over these same units.[65] While the motivation behind this investiture is not explained, we may presume that it involved a combination of administrative control and private reward.[66] For Ieshiki, however, the dispensation was clearly ominous: it was apparently to allay his fears that the bakufu granted him a confirmatory edict in 1197. In this way, Kamakura was giving formal recognition to two levels of jitō shiki over the same area.

Iriki, to which a later document refers as having been under a Tsunetane sōjitō shiki. This later record of 1250 is translated in Asakawa, *Iriki*, pp. 132–33.

62. This is the same Tsunetane (1118–1201) of Shimōsa Province who suffered confiscation of his homelands in the 1130s (see pp. 48–50). Now, at the end of his life, he held land rights in remote southern Kyushu.

63. Asakawa, *Iriki*, p. 134, n. 13. Actually, Shimazu received neither of its two (or more) sōjitō as permanent residents; duty performance was by deputy, as both Tadahisa (except for occasional visits) and Tsunetane remained in the east.

64. *Murozono Monjo*, 1248/9/13 Kantō gechijō, in *KBSS*, 1:84–87, doc. 81.

65. Actually before 1195, since Amano was ordered to return to Kamakura prior to that date. Seno, "Kyushu chihō," p. 40.

66. There is simply no way to determine the background for the selection of these two myō as a sōjitō assignment area. If they comprised only a reward, we are left with the dilemma of why the bakufu did not assign to its chief officer for Kyushu parcels that would not have to be shared with a native jitō.

During the generation that Ieshiki was jitō and Amano's successor, Nakahara Chikayoshi, was sōjitō, a clear superior–subordinate relationship developed.[67] The primary reason for this, however, is not what we might have presumed: Ieshiki's own weakness on the land induced him to seek a confirmatory decree from his sōjitō superior. At the same time, Chikayoshi decided to utilize this opportunity to gain an added leverage over his local counterpart. Despite Ieshiki's clear possession of a Kamakura jitō shiki, in 1201 Chikayoshi deliberately confirmed the latter as a mere jitō deputy (*jitōdai*). The distinction between deputy and regular title-holder is crucial here. The former was a post that only the bakufu could grant, the latter an office thoroughly under jitō control. The jitō was a vassal of the Kamakura lord, the jitō deputy a vassal of the jitō.

Ieshiki's acquiescence in this 1201 scheme requires clarification. In the first place, Ieshiki was a jitō and had the documentation to prove it. Only the bakufu could alter that condition. Thus, the price for sōjitō assistance—diminished pride—was probably viewed as bearable, especially in view of Ieshiki's local troubles. In 1215, for example, when one of Ieshiki's own retainers rebelled and demanded his myōshu titles, he was forced to turn for help to the new sōjitō, Nakahara Suetoki, who happily complied. The latter issued a document confirming Ieshiki's lowly myōshu posts.

A pattern was thereby set. Ieshiki and his son Sokua continued to assert a valid "small jitō title [*shōjitō shiki*] . . . as per the western province custom," while the successive sōjitō continued to emphasize either the myōshu or jitō deputy status of their resident subordinates. This relationship, however, could not go on indefinitely. A conflict broke out soon after the accession of a new sōjitō in 1244. The latter brought suit, using a most interesting argument. He asserted that the 1186 and 1197 edicts to Ieshiki had preceded the original sōjitō appointment. By this he obviously meant to claim that the sōjitō assignment, when it came, had *superseded* Ieshiki's earlier appointment; this was the reason for Ieshiki's jitō deputy designation by successive sōjitō. Sokua, however, mounted a winning defense. As the records clearly proved, the 1197 bakufu decree had come

67. Nakahara, by birth a court noble, was another close confidant of Yoritomo. See Seno Seiichirō, "Nakahara Chikayoshi to Chinzei to no kankei," *Kyūshū shigaku*, special issue 37–39 (1967): 29–40.

after the initial sōjitō appointment. It had been Kamakura's intention, "as per the western province custom," to authorize both jitō.

The judgment portion of the document is a highly explicit statement of Kamakura's reasoning in such matters. In sum, Sokua was to retain both his local authority and his subordinate status since, from the time of Yoritomo, it had been the practice *in Kyushu* that myōshu-level jitō be called "small jitō" after appointment of a sōjitō. For the bakufu, then, the original decision to establish two jitō levels—one resident, the other absentee—still stood. The only unclear point concerns a final admonition that Sokua obey sōjitō directives. What this might have involved, in view of the shōjitō's reconfirmed local authority, remains uncertain. But perhaps it was enough merely to have reminded Sokua that, despite his victory, sōjitō interests were not to be violated.

The foregoing was a suit brought by a sōjitō against a shōjitō. The opposite could also occur, showing that absentee authority might still transcend on-the-land power. In a record of 1227, for instance, we find a shōjitō seeking redress against a prestigious sōjitō overlord. According to this document, the residents of the disputed domain had traditionally paid an annual tax (*nengu*) to the proprietor, and a rental fee (*kajishi*) to the two jitō. In the past, this last sum had been divided evenly; now it was being commandeered in full by the sōjitō. This act led to the present suit. To determine the validity of this claim Kamakura made a number of inquiries. Among those interrogated was a former sōjitō for the contested area. Although this person was unable to resolve the issue at hand, he did make clear that the sōjitō shiki in this case was a nonheritable honorarium. His deposition expressed total ignorance of conditions in that far-off estate. The dispute was ultimately judged in favor of the shōjitō.[68]

It is interesting that sōjitō, admitted by the sources to be a Kyushu institution, never came close to dominating in that island. The basic reason for this was probably the unwieldiness of overloading a domain hierarchy (except a very large one such as Shimazu) with

68. *Ryūzōji Monjo*, 1227/3/19 Kantō gechijō, in Saga kenritsu toshokan, comp., *Saga ken shiryō shūsei* (Saga, 1958), 3:7–8.

multiple jitō. After the initial period of expansion, the instability of having concentric jitō must have mitigated against the nondiscriminatory use of this institution.[69] But even during the Yoritomo period alternative policies often promised better results. One such instance was the bakufu's handling of the Matsuura warrior league (*tō*), whose members had fought on the Heishi side at Dannoura (*AK* 1185/3/24). Rather than attempt to destroy this extensive group of fighting men, based largely in Hizen Province, Yoritomo elected to enroll them as separate Kamakura housemen and even to grant them individual jitō shiki. Careful strategy was involved here. Because of the nature of tō organization in the Matsuura case, Kamakura was actually working to promote an already advanced state of internal disunity. The chieftain's line did not have to be destroyed and replaced, for example, by a sōjitō because it was known to be feeble anyway. Conversely, to make contact with component Matsuura branches, individual collaterals had only to be made equal before the bakufu.[70]

The sōjitō, then, was only one of several programs that the bakufu developed in order to expand its interests across the land. It found expression in the appointment of types such as Amano Tōkage, Shimazu Tadahisa, and their first generation equivalents in Mutsu, Wakasa, and Hitachi provinces. With the possible exception of Amano, whose command authority rested more on his Kyushu "deputyship" than on his sōjitō titles, the four other figures were given assignments that were demonstrably political in content. Their appointments, in other words, were designed to promote bakufu regional strength. By contrast, later sōjitō were often little more than income-producing titles possessing but a slender memory of direct local superintendence.

Concerning, finally, the overall direction and extent of the baku-

69. Note the unusual case of the eastern Fukabori house as *shōjitō* in Kyushu under another eastern house as sōjitō. Trouble began right from the start. For details, see Jeffrey P. Mass, "The Early Development of the Kamakura Bakufu" (Ph.D. diss., Yale University, 1971), pp. 226–31.

70. Seno seiichirō, "Chūsei ni okeru tō—Matsuura tō no baai," *Rekishi kyōiku* 7.8 (1959). Elsewhere Seno notes that within a single shōen some twenty or more Matsuura families were eventually recognized as individual jitō ("Hizen," p. 39, n. 11).

fu's efforts in Kyushu, statistics tell the story in vivid detail. During the Kamakura period nearly ninety easterners, many of humble origin, received land rights of some kind in Kyushu. Of these, only *one* came from a province west of Owari in the Chūbu.[71] On the other hand, not a single case has been found of a Kyushu vassal receiving any kind of bakufu award outside Kyushu.[72] Superior and inferior, as reflected in sōjitō and shōjitō, were clearly etched.

A cursory examination of bakufu growth into all parts of Japan has shown a tendency to turn existing conditions to advantage by intruding easterners as administrative superiors. The thirteenth century was thus a period of warrior hegemony by men whose base areas were in the Kantō. The special edge enjoyed by these easterners was the grip they held over a preponderance of the country's jitō and shugo posts. This not only placed the power of the bakufu behind them, but allowed also for a condition of immunity from central interference. Warriors from a half dozen provinces, in other words, became a new national elite. This was to prove one of Kamakura's major legacies.

71. Seno, "Chinzei ni okeru tōgoku goke'nin," pt. 2, pp. 38–40. Naturally, many of the same family names appear several times.
72. Seno, "Kyūshū chihō," p. 44.

PART 4:
THE GROWTH OF
THE SHUGO AND
JITŌ SYSTEMS

7 THE JITŌ ON THE LAND

In this chapter we will undertake to answer the question of what a jitō shiki meant to those who received this office. What were the special qualities of the post that made it desirable, and why do we consider jitō-holders symbolic of a new level of warrior activity on the land? Our subject ultimately is the jitō appointee as an incipient local magnate—the most innovative and dynamic figure of his age. Yet to appreciate what made the jitō different, we must be aware that there was much he had in common with other land officers of his day; belying his reputation in history, the jitō was not a catalyst or opposition figure in every respect. Not only were there many jitō activities that were regular and routine, but there were many jitō who were neither strong nor ambitious. It is this kind of composite picture that we seek.

The physical diversity among jitō shiki was unlimited. Jitō appointment areas could be of any size, whether a full province,[1] a myō unit, a village, an island, a shōen, a public district or gō unit, or whatever.[2] Indeed, there was nothing mandating that a jitō grant

1. *AK* 1193/12/20 records Sasaki Sadatsuna's appointment as jitō shiki over the island province of Oki. See also the phrase "*kuni gun jitō*" (provincial and district-level jitō) in *Itōzu Monjo*, 1192/9/18 shōgun ke mandokoro kudashibumi, in *Ōita ken shiryo*, 1:63–64, doc. 24. References such as this, however, do not appear after the initial consolidation phase of Kamakura history. By the early years of the thirteenth century, phraseology such as the following is more representative: "*shokoku no shōen gō ho no jitō*," or jitō countrywide in shōen, gō, and ho (*AK* 1204/10/18). With shugo in place by this time, the need for "provincial jitō" had disappeared. The only close study of this institution—Ishimoda, "Ikkoku jitō"—is an attempt to develop around provincial jitō an entirely new framework for understanding the 1180s. But Ishimoda's effort has drawn extensive criticism.

2. E.g. (in order), *Sonezaki Monjo*, 1187/5/9 Minamoto Yoritomo kudashibumi, in *Ōita ken shiryō*, 9:425–26, doc. 501 (myō jitō); *Nitobe Monjo*, 1219/4/27

even be over a unit of territory; an appointment could, for example, be over a religious institution.[3] Nor did the jitō recipient necessarily have to be either a warrior or a duly registered houseman: a grantee might be a temple or shrine,[4] a court noble by birth,[5] or, at the other end of the social scale, a male or female attendant at the shogunal court (*AK* 1204/12/22). If only theoretically, the prospect of receiving a jitō benefice was open to any person or institution that might perform services on behalf of the bakufu.[6]

Appointment to a jitō shiki, as to any other local officership, carried with it certain rights to income. These were as varied as the land units themselves. Precedent and the type of arrangement at time of first appointment were the chief determinants of a jitō-holder's lawful perquisites. We are thus able to speak only of categories of income; the combinations in individual cases were without limitation. These categories can be summarized as follows:

(1) *Kyūdenpata*, or salary land (rice and dry) from which the jitō as an estate or public-sector official drew his remuneration. These fields, worked by local residents, were totally exempt from tax or service payments (*shotō*).[7]

Hōjō Yoshitoki kudashibumi, in *Iwate ken chūsei monjo*, 1:1, doc. 1 (mura jitō); *Aokata Monjo*, 1196/7/12 utaishō ke mandokoro kudashibumi, in Seno Seiichirō, ed., *Aokata monjo* (Fukuoka, 1957), 1:1, doc. 1 (shima jitō); *Chūjo Ke Monjo*, 1192/10/21 shōgun ke mandokoro kudashibumi, in Niigata ken kyōiku iinkai, comp., *Okuyama-no-shō shiryōshū* (Niigata, 1965), doc. 2, p. 97 (shōen jitō); *Minagawa Monjo*, 1187/12/1 Minamoto Yoritomo kudashibumi, in Kanagawa ken, comp., *Kanagawa kenshi, shiryō hen 1, kodai-chūsei 1* (Yokohama, 1971), doc. 161, p. 474 (gun and gō jitō).

3. E.g., a jitō shiki appointment to Kei Shrine, Bungo Province. *Hirabayashi Shi Monjo*, 1236/7/28 shōgun ke mandokoro kudashibumi, in *Shinano shiryō*, 4:53–54.

4. Normally taking the form of bakufu commendations, these nonetheless were awards of jitō shiki. E.g., a pair of shōen-sized jitō titles to Usa Shrine in 1275: *Itōzu Monjo*, 1275/10/21 Kantō kishinjō an, in *Ōita ken shiryō*, 1:105, doc. 71–1.

5. Ōe Hiromoto received a number of jitō shiki, e.g., one over Yashiro Estate in Suō Province. See *Kushibe Monjo*, 1191/3/22 jitō Nakahara (Ōe) kudashibumi, in *Shōen shiryō*, 2:1996.

6. In practice, of course, the scramble for rewards beyond an initial confirmatory grant over one's home region remained almost wholly an eastern warrior luxury.

7. Yasuda argues that *kyūdenpata* were totally possessed by jitō (Yasuda, *Jitō*

(2) *Jitō myō*, or lands directly administered by a jitō from which only the annual rice levy (*nengu*) was due the estate-holder.

(3) *Jitō tsukuda* and *hori no uchi*, or demesne lands held in full "ownership" by a jitō. No payments of any kind were due from these. Such fields were generally small and located in the immediate vicinity of the jitō's residence. Unlike other land categories, which were cultivated by farmer families of long residence (*hyakushō*), these demesne units were worked either by a jitō's personal house membership or by service families (*zaike*) attached to his family.

(4) *Kachōmai*, or a special surtax that gained regular and continuous usage from the 1220s.[8] Kachōmai was levied on designated land of varying size but at a uniform rate. It therefore represented a departure from earlier practice that had left the matter of jitō income to a combination of local custom and negotiation between the principals themselves.

(5) Profits derived from performance of police (*kendan*) services.

(6) Receipt of a share of taxes collected by a jitō on behalf of a proprietor.

(7) *Hyōrōmai*, or commissariat tax. Such income was authorized only during military emergencies, such as during the Gempei and Jōkyū periods.

(8) An appointment right for lower shōen officers and the opportunity to control their functions and exact fees.

(9) Special levies on nonagricultural enterprises and percentage shares of miscellaneous local products.

We may take as a sample income register a record of 1223 for the jitō of Takahara Estate in Aki Province. The more important entries are as follows: (a) kachōmai of five shō of rice (nine liters) per *tan* (.1 chō, or .294 acre) to be drawn from a two-tan area (hence a ten-shō income level); (b) a two shō per tan rental fee (*chishi*) levied on a salt farm; (c) a one-third share of receipts from various itemized products (cotton, mulberry, etc.); (d) total authority over the estate's constable (*sōtsuibushi*); (e) salary rice land (*kyūden*) of five chō

---

oyobi, pp. 304–06). However, a question exists concerning the "proprietor-employer's" residual authority over such lands.

8. *Kachōmai* was known earlier, but it became an integral part of the income regulations for shimpo jitō in the years after Jōkyū. See p. 136.

(14.70 acres); and (f) salary dry land (*kyūhata*) of five chō.[9] No jitō myō or personalized demesne areas are listed, and we find nothing explicit regarding criminal confiscation profits.

Applying the formula of specificity to jitō functions, there is ample evidence to show that while almost all jitō were active at some level in the fiscal and police branches of local administration, in individual instances a jitō might be an estate's top tax collector, its chief of police, its judicial officer in minor criminal cases, its personnel director for sub-gesu appointments, and its chief promoter of agricultural productivity and "public works" projects. Such preponderance of power, however, was not the norm. Much more common, as we will see, was a condition in which jitō were forced to share this authority with the estate proprietor's direct representative, the azukari dokoro.[10] The nature of the relationship between these two figures went far in determining the health or efficiency of any Kamakura-period domain. Should there be serious rivalry or tension, the shōen in question would likely be subjected to major dislocations. But if, by contrast, the azukari dokoro and jitō were able to cooperate in the day-to-day administration of a shōen, then that estate probably prospered. Power and privilege would be in proper tandem, with the various shiki-holders each standing a good chance to receive his appropriate due. Thirteenth-century jitō-related documents generally incline toward descriptions of trouble on the land. But enough materials survive to show that there were many occasions in which a spirit of collaboration, if not confraternity, prevailed.

Areas of possible cooperation between jitō and proprietors (or proprietary deputies) were spread over the full range of estate administration. Naturally, this relationship was most effective when the interests of both sides were being served. One of the best ex-

9. *Kobayagawa Ke Monjo*, 1223/6 Aki Takahara-no-shō jitō tokubun chūmon, in *DNK, iewake 11*, 1:543–44.

10. Sometimes a shōen had more than one azukari dokoro (e.g., Ōta Estate), and sometimes an azukari dokoro held jurisdiction over more than one shōen. On still other occasions there was one azukari dokoro in residence and another in Kyoto (Yasuda Genkyū, *Nihon shōen shi gaisetsu* (Tokyo, 1966), pp. 155–56). A second office name—*zasshō*—was sometimes used as an alternative to azukari dokoro.

amples relates to the opening of new land. In 1229, for instance, an estate proprietor responded favorably to a jitō petition regarding such a project. In the estate-owner's own words, "The restoration of smoke from every house means prosperity in the village and is the basis for peace. The petition to open new land is therefore accepted." Closer to the proprietor's interest were the taxes he could expect to receive from the new fields. For the first year these were to be waived. In the second year the amount due was to be one *to* (eighteen liters) of rice per tan, with an annual increment thereafter of one *to*, up to a three-*to* total. All taxes were to be deposited in the shōen warehouse, and each year a list of the persons engaged in cultivation was to be submitted to an agent of the proprietor.[11] It is obvious that here was an arrangement of distinct advantage to both estate-owner and jitō. The former could look forward to increased revenues, while the latter would enjoy the responsibility of overseeing the entire project. An absentee proprietor's interests would thereby be sustained, as would the local management rights of a jitō-in-residence.[12]

Common action revealed itself in other ways, such as in matters requiring an administrative or judicial-type settlement. A 1248 document cosigned by a proprietor (ryōke) and a jitō illustrates this. The issue was a dispute over which of two estate officials would exercise ultimate responsibility for the promotion of agriculture and replacement of farmers who had fled.[13] That the matter was resolved by a jitō and ryōke acting in concert is the main point. It suggests that the two exercised something akin to a joint "superior authority."

Sometimes a third party would join a jitō and estate proprietor or deputy in a common action. In a document of 1236, for example, the jitō, azukari dokoro, and kumon collectively exhorted a certain

11. *Isshi Monjo*, 1229/2/21 Matsuura-no-shō ryōke kudashibumi, in Kyōtō daigaku bungaku-bu kenkyūshitsu, comp., *Hirado Matsuura ke shiryō* (Kyoto, 1951), pp. 148–49. For the general tax arrangement of shōen, see pp. 190–91.

12. A comparable example appears in *Kobayagawa Ke Monjo*, 1238/11/11 Ichijō Nyūdo dajōdaijin ke mandokoro kudashibumi an, in *DNK, iewake 11*, 1:547, doc. 4.

13. *Hata Monjo*, 1248/7/16 ryōke-jitō ryōhō rensho gechijō, in Fukui kenritsu toshokan, comp., *Wakasa gyoson shiryō* (Fukui, 1963), pp. 297–98. The kumon was a common estate-officer title, ranked below jitō and azukari dokoro. See Yasuda, *Nihon shōen shi gaisetsu*, p. 158.

village to pay its taxes.[14] A share in dues receipts may have been the main inducement here. A jitō house in Aki, for instance, received percentage interests of the annual tax from adjacent shōen, amounting to a one-third and two-fifths total.[15]

One of the most common areas of shared responsibility between a jitō and azukari dokoro was the realm of policing and its attendant activities. At the beginning of the medieval period no sharp distinction existed to separate police, judicial, and related administrative functions. When the exercise of authority involved any part of the sequence from investigation through pursuit, capture, incarceration, and then confiscation of the property of criminals, it was called *kendan*. Needless to say, this kendan authority (normally rendered simply "police") was a complex of privileges whose possession would be highly prized by a jitō. Not only would it permit a jitō to use force legally, but it would provide him with supplemental income and a means to come into contact with the various levels of shōen personnel.

The assignment of kendan to a resident estate officer was a legacy from the Heian period. So also was the practice of allowing a share of the confiscated wealth to fall to an enforcing official.[16] It was therefore the usual conjunction of local precedent, the category of jitō shiki (confirmatory or external), and the terms of an initial settlement that determined how much of the kendan authority a jitō might receive. In the case of Miri Estate in Aki, for example, the jitō enjoyed a full 100 percent share.[17] How this arrangement came into being is not known, but it is clear from a dispute document of 1223 that both the privilege and its range were now hereditary with the office. Two generations of jitō had already possessed that authority.

14. *Minase Jingū Monjo*, 1236/3 rensho kudashibumi, in Ōsaka fu shiseki meishō tennen kinenbutsu chōsakai, comp., *Minase Jingū monjo* (Osaka, 1939), doc. 176, p. 233.

15. *Kobayagawa Ke Monjo*, 1243 Aki Nuta shin-no-shō kenchū mokuroku; 1252/11 Aki Nuta hon-no-shō kenchū mokuroku, in *DNK, iewake 11*, 1:556–82. The tax-collection operation, and jitō involvement in it, is treated on pp. 000–00.

16. E.g., *Tōdaiji Monjo*, 1174/3 sō Jōshin ge, in *HI*, 7:2835, doc. 3656. In this document we find a gesu and kumon being granted the confiscated lands, residence, etc., of a convicted murderer.

17. *Kumagai Monjo*, 1223/3/18 Taira bō seibaijō, in Saitama kenritsu toshokan, comp., *Kumagai ke monjo* (Urawa, 1970), doc. 9, p. 29.

Thus, when the estate proprietor moved to secure a reversal, claiming that police matters should henceforth be handled by the domain constable (sōtsuibushi), the bakufu rejected this as an attempt to alter an earlier precedent.[18]

This incident in Miri involved a proprietor's seeking to gain approval for a full cancellation of a jitō's kendan authority. In other instances the goals were more modest and the techniques more imaginative. In Ushigahara Estate in Echizen, for example, the proprietor attempted to secure bakufu recognition for a two-thirds to one-third division favoring himself. His argument was that this had long been the regular procedure. The jitō, however, proved that to be untrue. He demonstrated that the jitō-holder over the past three generations had possessed the kendan authority totally. The bakufu accepted this obvious "precedent" and reaffirmed it with a new decree.[19]

In still other cases it was the estate-holder, not the jitō, who evidently began the Kamakura period with the kendan authority securely in his grasp. But the passage of time and the steady pressure of jitō incursions sometimes led to dispensations such as the following. In a suit of 1247, the estate deputy of Tara in Wakasa Province argued that the Tara domain had been converted from public sector to shōen with no change or diminution in the authority of the proprietor. This included the kendan. The jitō rejoined that this was false, that in fact his family had held the kendan privilege since the age of Yoritomo. The bakufu was thus faced with irreconcilable positions. To break the impasse and discover the truth it sought direct testimony from the cultivating peasantry of Tara itself. The story that these farmers told was essentially one of change over time: the kendan had first been exercised by the estate deputy, although from very early the matter of heavy fines was somewhat ambiguous. In the present generation, at any rate, these fines were being paid to the jitō. The bakufu's resolution of the dispute was a compromise: it ordered a fifty–fifty division of the full kendan package.[20]

If it took the jitō of Tara more than half a century to gain a

18. Ibid. Obviously the sōtsuibushi in Miri was an appointee of the proprietor.
19. *Hōon'in Monjo*, 1243/7/19 Kanto gechijō, in *KBSS*, 1:67–68, doc. 72.
20. *Tōji Hyakugō Monjo*, 1247/10/29 Kantō gechijō, in ibid., doc. 79, p. 81.

secure half interest in the kendan, there were other jitō who had a much easier time of it. This was often the result of local disturbances that the proprietary deputy was not able to handle on his own. The jitō, with his strong military lineage, might then be called in. An incident of 1214 shows such a development, though the appeal for assistance in this case went through the bakufu. In Bizen Province, unauthorized persons had been hunting and cutting lumber on lands owned by Kinzanji Temple. In response to a petition, Kamakura ordered the jitō to assume responsibility for prohibiting such actions.[21] Whether this meant that the jitō now emerged as the sole or permanent kendan agent is not clear. Perhaps this was never specified in writing. Nevertheless, it is worth noting that a generation later it was the jitō himself who was accused of committing lawless acts in the same region.[22] An officer initially assigned to guarantee local peace ended by disturbing it.

The jitō's duties as kendan officer varied from case to case. Minimally, however, they must have included, apropos of a local constable, the issuance and posting of regulations and prohibitions. For example, a jitō edict of 1201 for Noto Province's Ōya Estate warns against interference with a temple construction project then underway.[23] An earlier decree by the same jitō provides an example of the function for which the Bizen jitō (just cited) was assigned his kendan powers. Within the confines of a certain Buddhist area there was to be no hunting or lumber cutting. Persons who disobeyed could expect to be fined.[24]

As revealed here, the opportunity to convert the kendan privilege into a lucrative source of revenue was one of its greatest attractions. For many jitō the temptation to abuse this power was very great, and our documents literally abound with such stories. The jitō of Kunitomi Estate in Wakasa Province will serve as an example. By examining the various ways in which this figure overstepped his rights, we

21. *Kinzanji Monjo*, 1214/9/26 shōgun ke mandokoro kudashibumi, in Fujii Shun and Mizuno Kyoichirō, eds., *Okayama ken komonjo shū* (Okayama, 1955), 2:7, doc. 9.

22. Ibid., 1241/6/11 Rokuhara migyōsho, doc. 14, p. 9. The Bizen Province shugo was also accused in this 1241 incident.

23. *Saikōji Monjo*, 1201/8 jitō kudashibumi, in *Kano komonjo*, doc. 61, pp. 39–40.

24. Ibid., 1197/int.6/9 jitō gechijō, doc. 58, p. 38.

are able to gain greater insight into the limits of the kendan package in general. The list of kendan abuses in Kunitomi begins with the jitō's imposition of fines on farmers who were entirely guiltless. To insure that these fines were paid, a second, more severe measure was then adopted: incarceration of peasant relatives in advance of remittance. Beyond that, the jitō used his power of arrest as a lever to convert local officials into personal retainers. Finally, the jitō (by implication) called guiltless men criminals as a means of acquiring their property.[25]

Above all else, this incident reveals the thoroughly blurred stages of the kendan continuum. If the jitō was a policeman, he was also most likely a judge and a jailer. A criminal, once apprehended, would be made to sit out his initial confinement in a jitō-administered prison. If the case were not a serious one, the jitō would then act as "local prosecutor." Judgment and imposition of punishments might also be included as jitō privileges. Finally, any fines exacted or properties confiscated could well find their way into jitō coffers. As we will see in even clearer detail regarding shugo, the distinctions of the age concerned categories of suits, criminal acts, and persons. There was no strict separation between police authority and the dispensing of justice.

The ultimate reach of a jitō's judicial competence varied considerably, though in most instances it did not extend beyond local criminal matters. Occasionally, however, we see evidence, even in early Kamakura, of something more substantive. Probably this was the result of a proprietor defaulting on a privilege that traditionally had been his. Such authority easily redounded to jitō, who could take advantage of their actual presence on the land. An incident of 1205 seems to suggest this. In a matter involving punishment and replacement of a ranking local official, we see a jitō in Iyo Province "holding court" and calling for full particulars to be sent to himself. This action had been requested by the area's proprietor and is directly reminiscent of similar appeals to Kamakura calling for punishment and replacement of jitō.[26]

25. *Mibu Monjo*, 1216/8/17 Kantō gechijō, in Kunaishō toshoryō, comp., *Mibu shinsha komonjo* (Tokyo, 1930), pp. 51–55.

26. *Oyamatsumi Jinja Monjo*, 1205/7/14 jitō Taira bō kudashibumi, in *Ehime ken hennen shi*, 2:202.

In particularly distant provinces the likelihood was even greater that a jitō might soon come to pose, virtually without reference to higher authority, as the final judicial voice. We see this in a decree of 1208 from a "jitō office" (*jitōsho*) in Satsuma. The officials of certain gō units under the latter's jurisdiction were ordered to return a residence area that had been illegally commandeered.[27] In point of practice this unnamed jitō may have come to represent the highest functioning (if not nominal) authority in his administrative region.

Moving from the kendan and its related privileges to the jitō's rights as an estate administrator, we find that jitō were particularly active in the area of local appointments. The level in the shōen (or public-land) hierarchy at which the jitō's appointment–dismissal authority left off and the proprietor's began was determined by the customary practices of the land unit in question. It was a system, in short, in which an estate's officialdom tended to become segmented into dual tracks, each possessing a different focus of loyalty. This does not mean, however, that there could not be cooperation here too. Before examining the much more common occurrence of independent appointments by the two sides, it will be useful to cite one or two examples of joint investitures. In a Sado Province shōen in 1293, we see a local appointment decree cosigned by a jitō and the representative of the shrine proprietor.[28] This kind of joint effort appears also in a post-appointment phase: on the occasion of bequeathal of Tosa Province land rights in 1284, an earlier (1220s) testamentary document approved by a jitō and a kumon was submitted to the present authorizing agency.[29] From these and other examples it is clear that the phenomenon of joint appointments and confirmations, with jitō as one of the parties, was a regular practice during the thirteenth century.

27. *Haseba Monjo*, 1208/3/3 jitōsho kudashibumi an, in *Sappan kyūki zatsuroku, zempen*, 2:15, doc. 113.
28. *Sado Hachimangū Monjo*, 1293/12/7 Wakamiya gon no dai kannushi buninjō, in Shimoide Sekiyo, comp., *Sado Honma ibun Sakurai ke monjo* (Kanazawa 1966), doc. 14, p. 199.
29. *Aki Monjo*, 1284/5 daikan Fujiwara kudashibumi, in *Aki monjo* (Kochi, 1954), unpaginated. See also *Kōchi kenshi, kodai-chūsei hen* (Kochi, 1971), pp. 281–82.

Nevertheless, there are many more instances of jitō either acting alone or contesting with a proprietor over possession of a local appointment right. In 1214, for example, the jitō of Ōya Estate in Noto personally assigned a local priesthood; in 1223, a jitō in Aki is recorded as holding authority over an estate constableship; and in 1274 a Tamba Province jitō made an appointment to a local temple director's post.[30] Not surprisingly, the jitō's (or proprietor's) right to exercise such power was often disputed by the other; the bakufu would then have to be called in. Thus, in 1227, Kamakura awarded victory to the jitō in a conflict over possession of Ōta Estate's kumon post. The result was the same in Aki's Takahara Estate in 1240, and in Wakasa's Tara Domain in 1247.[31] After midcentury, compromise solutions emerged as an alternate possibility, as, for example, in a Satsuma Province case of 1293. In this instance authority over the gesu and a single myōshu post went to the estate deputy; while three other myōshu titles plus the posts of kannushi, kumon, and tadokoro were transferred to the jitō.[32]

A great deal was at stake in these legal battles for control of an area's officer corps because shōen officials possessed many of the same authority and perquisite forms as the jitō himself. A kumon or sōtsuibushi enjoyed personal myō areas, received salary lands and other gratuities, and exercised varying degrees of power over general peasant fields. For the jitō, this meant that control over a major segment of an estate's official class went far in establishing him as de facto hegemon within that domain. Thus in the Satsuma case just cited, when the jitō was awarded authority for the kannushi, kumon, and tadokoro, he also came to control, as noted in the baku-

30. *Saikōji Monjo*, 1214/8 jitō bō kudashibumi, in *Kano komonjo*, doc. 68, pp. 42–43. *Kobayagawa Ke Monjo*, 1223/6 Aki Takahara-no-shō jitō tokubun chūmon, in *DNK, iewake 11*, 1:543–44. *Kan'onji Monjo*, 1274/8 Kan'onji bettō shiki buninjō, in Ayabe shidankai, comp., *Kajika chūsei shiryō* (Kyoto, 1951), p. 39. The jitō in this case, however, also possessed his domain's azukari dokoro post.

31. *Kōyasan Kōzanji Monjo*, 1227/7/7 Kantō gechijō, in *KBSS*, 1:54, doc. 59; *Kobayagawa Ke Monjo*, 1240/int.10/11 Kantō gechijō, in *DNK, iewake 11*, 1:549–50; *Tōji Hyakugō Monjo*, 1247/10/29 Kantō gechijō, in *KBSS*, 1:82, doc. 79.

32. *Shimazu Ke Monjo*, 1293/1/13 Kantō gechijō, in ibid., doc. 193, p. 255.

fu's confirmation decree, their accompanying rice and dry fields, and even their personal residence areas.[33]

But how was such local power achieved in the many cases in which jitō did not begin with this authority? A record of 1232 is very precise on this point, though conditions of course varied widely. On the occasion of a dispute between the jitō and estate deputy of Fukui Domain in Harima Province, the proprietor's side charged that after the jitō was appointed he began to use his influence to win the loyalty of certain shōen officers. These latter, it was alleged, subsequently disobeyed orders handed down by the estate-owner. Even the proprietor's awarding of new salary fields had not brought them back into line. The jitō countered by arguing that an agent of the retired emperor had long before made his way to Fukui and had granted the jitō an income register that specifically included these local officer titles. Subsequent to that the bakufu chieftain, Minamoto Yoriie (r. 1199–1203), gave his own approval to the arrangement while on a private hunting expedition. Thus, the jitō claimed, not only did he possess the shiki in question, but he was eligible as well for an increase in his own salary fields! The bakufu, admitting puzzlement in the case, nevertheless awarded victory to the jitō. It stated that the proprietor had not adequately refuted the jitō's statement concerning the original income register.[34]

Several conclusions emerge from this. As we have seen in other contexts, the jitō's local presence and immunity from direct proprietary action gave him an enormous advantage in contests where the exercise of power was the dominant theme. Second, bakufu justice was never preemptive; it awaited the lodging of actual complaints rather than seeking to quell local difficulties based on reports from its men in the field. And third, the bakufu's failure at first to seek information on jitō perquisites meant that the subject remained hazy until major trouble occurred. This is certainly what happened in the case of Fukui Estate.

Before we leave the jitō's appointment authority, a word should be added about the use and abuse of the deputy, or jitōdai, prerogative. As indicated earlier, the jitō deputy was a creation and vassal

33. Ibid.
34. *Jingoji Monjo*, 1232/9/24 Kantō gechijō, in ibid., doc. 51, pp. 47–48.

of the jitō; under normal circumstances he was not subject to direction or discipline from either the bakufu or a proprietor.[35] This meant, among other things, that the jitō had complete freedom on the question of jitōdai selection. Generally, he chose a member of his own family, either a younger son or the head of a branch line, perhaps an uncle or nephew. In other instances, a member of the local gentry would be called on to perform in this capacity. This was especially true in the rather numerous cases of favored eastern houses possessing multiple jitō shiki, sometimes in the most diverse parts of the country.[36] On those occasions, the scarcity of reliable housemen might dictate such a course; or perhaps the jitō could find no easterner willing to travel halfway across Japan to take up a frontier post. A third possibility was that the jitō shiki involved was simply too small or too distant to warrant sending a permanent deputy. The jitō system was a cumbersome affair in this regard, with deputies—some external, some local— playing an important role.

And yet the system, despite its complexities, seemed to work well enough during the first half or more of the Kamakura period. We noted in the last chapter, for example, that the great Shimazu and Ōtomo houses of Kyushu operated almost entirely through deputies for nearly a hundred years. They were the greatest powers in a remote part of the country while continuing to reside in the Kantō. This suggests something very important about the first century of Japan's "medieval age." Absentee authority, far from being quickly destroyed, had actually expanded in a sense to embrace jitō. Many

35. Thus the bakufu refused to enter a dispute in 1244 between a jitō and his deputy: the former's appeal for assistance against unnamed deeds by the latter elicited only a vague warning to the jitōdai, not positive action. The principle of non-involvement in such matters was explicitly expressed in the bakufu's edict. *Tōfukuji Monjo*, 1244/12/7 Rokuhara shigyōjō, in *Ehime ken hennen shi*, 2:282. Jitōdai appointment decrees took a form exactly the same as the bakufu's jitō investiture documents. E.g., *Kabajimmyōgū Monjo*, 1197/6 jitōdai buninjō, in *Shizuoka ken shiryō*, 2:823–24.

36. E.g., the Naganuma house possessed several holdings in its home province of Shimotsuke, plus land rights in Mutsu, Mino, Mimasaka, Bingo, Musashi, and Awaji. *Naganuma Monjo*, 1230/8/13 Naganuma Munemasa yuzurijō, in *Fukushima ken*, comp., *Fukushima kenshi, kodai-chūsei shiryō* (Fukushima, 1966), 7:776, doc. 105.1.

of the country's estates now became objects of dual (usually rival) forms of legitimation. The clearest expression of this lay in the azukari dokoro–jitōdai tandem: the one was proxy for a central owner, the other deputy for a jitō. During Heian times patronage had extended down from the court to provincial clients who were the country's greatest warriors. Now, during the Kamakura age, many of those warriors were jitō, with their own absentee connections over land.[37]

The power to appoint deputies could readily be exploited. We have seen that the jitō-holder enjoyed a protective insulation from direct disciplinary action by a proprietor. The jitōdai added a second layer of immunity for the jitō bent on local encroachment: only the bakufu could dispossess a jitō, and only the jitō could dispossess a deputy. The consequences of this emerge in a remarkable record of 1222. The proprietor of Ushigahara Estate in Echizen complained of a massive encroachment by a jitō-led group consisting of "nine jitō deputies from various villages within the estate, five sōtsuibushi and kumon, and more than 100 of their followers." Residents of the shōen had been forced to feed these "invaders," and the latter had committed all manner of lawless deeds. The bakufu, which was handling the case, ordered these outrages to cease and stipulated that nine jitōdai was excessive; henceforth, there could be only two deputies, one in the northern part of the domain, the other in the southern.[38]

How are we to interpret this result? In the first place, while the judgment had clearly gone against the jitō, his extensive local network had hardly been dealt a fatal blow. He was to "deactivate" his village-level deputy corps but was allowed to replace this group with a pair of jitōdai of greater authority. In addition, it was the

37. This condition did not survive beyond about 1275. As the thirteenth century wore on there developed a tendency for deputy houses, cut off for several generations from trunk lines, to begin moving toward disengagement. For the Ōtomo's difficulties on this point see Fukuda Toyohiko, "Dainiji hōken kankei no keisei katei—Bungo no kuni Ōtomo shi no shujūsei o chūshin to shite," in Yasuda, *Shoki hōkensei no kenkyū*, pp. 36 ff. This fascinating subject lies beyond our scope.

38. *Sampōin Monjo*, 1222/4/5 Kantō gechijō, in *DNK, iewake 19*, 2:38–39, doc. 302.

jitō himself, not the bakufu or the proprietor, who was to take charge of this rearrangement. Lastly, nothing was said concerning the jitō's obvious conversion of the Ushigahara official class into a band of personal retainers. Indeed, what strikes us most about this episode is the jitō's manifest success at creating an incipient local hierarchy. He had saturated the shōen with men whom he called jitōdai, and he had clearly subordinated Ushigahara's traditional officer corps. The jitō was now local overlord, with vassals and rear-vassals, even while formal authority continued to reside with a central temple.

The Ushigahara jitō case was not necessarily typical, however. There were many jitō during early Kamakura who suffered not from too much adrenalin but from too little. In chapter 6 we read of a shōjitō in Kyushu who was in danger for a time of having his myōshu titles seized by a subordinate. Parallel cases easily come to mind. In an incident of 1207, a jitō complained to Kamakura that a certain officer in a neighboring estate had moved his shōen's boundary markers in order to seize rice. Would the bakufu, he begged, please issue an edict restoring the old frontiers? Or again, we find a Kamakura judgment of 1223 in which a jitō was rescued from the encroachments of one of his own retainers.[39] Most revealing of all, however, is the story of a post-Jōkyū jitō assigned to a domain in Settsu Province. Even in this region of small farmers, the new appointee was totally unable to crack local resistance. As a last resort, he appealed to the bakufu for a change of venue, and some years later this was granted.[40] These episodes, then, are a reminder that the jitō of Kamakura times were not uniformly successful. There were always some who had to struggle merely to survive.[41] In such cases, the use of jitōdai would have been more a risk than a luxury.

39. *Sangun Yōryaku Shō No Ge Shihai Monjo*, 1207/7/4 Kantō gechijō, in *KBSS*, 1:10, doc. 15. *Munakata Jinja Monjo*, 1223/9/13 Kantō gechijō, in *Munakata gunshi*, 2:152.

40. The jitō's petition is noted in a bakufu document of 1232: *Fukabori Monjo*, 1232/12/1 Hōjō Yasutoki shojō, in *Saga ken shiryō shūsei*, 4:28–29, doc. 54. It took eighteen years for the request to be honored. Ibid., 1250/10/23 Kantō kudashibumi, doc. 4, p. 3.

41. This statement takes in a great deal of ground, for instance the fragmenting of jitō shiki under the period's divided inheritance system, and the disposal by sale of jitō shiki shares. These topics cannot be treated here.

Equal in importance to the jitō's relations with officer-level personnel were the controls developed over those actually working the land. Aside from the kendan-related activities already discussed, contacts were most extensive in the areas of labor services and general tax collection. Taking these in order, we note that labor levies were a regular feature of the Japanese estate system. All members of the middle and upper ranks of the shōen hierarchy might benefit from such services at levels determined by the customary practice of individual domains. What is interesting is that all such labor was compensative, at least theoretically. Partly to minimize the unsettling effects of farmers being withdrawn from their traditional fields, strict work schedules were enforced and rations or others forms of payment were established as regular remuneration.[42] As part of the estate apparatus the jitō was naturally expected to conform with this procedure, though, as elsewhere, the temptations to abuse his position were great. Here was an inevitable zone of conflict between jitō on one side and proprietor and peasants on the other. An early incident shows this to have been a problem from the start of the period. In 1186, the public resources of Suō Province were assigned to Tōdaiji for the purpose of defraying that temple's extensive reconstruction costs. However, five newly assigned jitō, utterly neglectful of this worthy cause, proceeded to make a shambles of the effort to collect timber from that richly forested province. A complaint was lodged alleging seizure of some 186 koku of rice earmarked as rations for local laborers.[43]

Within shōen, the basic thrust of jitō energies regarding labor services was to secure greater control over an estate's resources. A record of 1238 affords an intimate view of such a project. Since the

42. It was in the interests of farmers, too, that standards be announced and adhered to. As Professor Southern has remarked apropos of Europe, "What men feared and resented in serfdom was not its subordination, but its arbitrariness. The hatred of that which was governed, not by rule, but by will, went very deep in the Middle Ages. . ." (*The Making of the Middle Ages* [London, 1959], pp. 112–13). In thirteenth-century Japan, where the degree of peasant subordination under a proprietor was certainly less severe than in Europe, we find a number of farmer–estate deputy agreements concerning labor levies. An unusually explicit example is *Matsuodera Monjo*, 1252/5/11 Karakuni Mura tone hyakushō to okibumi, in Osaka fu kyōiku iinkai, comp., *Izumi Matsuodera monjo* (Osaka, 1957), doc. 3, p. 9.

43. *AK* 1187/4/23. For a full examination of this incident, see Ōyama Kyōhei, "Kokugaryō jitō no ichi keitai," *Nihon rekishi* 158 (1961): 58–66.

time of the first jitō in Sasakibe Estate (Tamba Province), shōen residents were drafted into cultivation service for the jitō's own fields. The levy had fallen on each person three times a year and food rations were provided thrice daily. In 1237, however, the jitō suddenly seized two tan of land from each village, divided the commandeered fields among the peasantry, and provided the latter with seeds but no rations. The jitō defended these actions in a highly revealing way: he asserted that the drafting of farmers to work jitō lands was "not the practice [only] of this estate but is common everywhere."[44] We should note in this regard that the estate deputy complained only after the jitō began distributing village land as if it were his own, and after he had ceased providing laborers with daily food allotments. This portended a highly unfavorable chain reaction of events. Cultivators, diverted from an estate's tax-yielding lands and forced to feed themselves, would be less capable of paying the levies owed to the proprietor. At the same time, the fields now seized by the jitō would narrow the estate-holder's tax-producing area.

For the farmers themselves, such labor services fell into two essential categories: those that were seasonal and regular, and those that were arbitrary and erratic. The latter were to be avoided at all costs, since to submit was to allow a jitō virtually to rule by caprice. Peasants confronting such a prospect had two avenues open to them. They could ally with higher authority in an effort to resist a jitō, or they could attempt to negotiate directly with the jitō concerning rates and times. An example of the former came in 1280 in response to a jitō's asserting "emergency need" as justification for labor assignments.[45] A contract of two decades earlier reveals the latter. As described in this record of 1260, one person per household was to serve the jitō twenty-five days per year. In addition, during the busy agricultural periods three persons per household were to serve for three-day stints, with no more than fifteen persons engaged at any one time.[46] Such agreements were no guarantee, of course, that

44. *Higashi Monjo*, 1238/10/19 Rokuhara gechijō, in *KBSS*, 2:14, doc. 7.
45. *Aokata Monjo*, 1280/11/25 hyakushō tō rensho kishōmon, in *Aokata monjo*, 1:27–28, doc. 28.
46. This 1260 document is referred to in *Gakuenji Monjo*, 1263/8/5 Kantō gechijō, in Gakuenji monjo kankōkai, comp., *Gakuenji monjo no kenkyū* (Hirata, 1963), doc. 18, pp. 272–73.

there would not be trouble anyway, but they did provide at least a modicum of security. Peasants so protected could attempt to regulate their lives according to the calendar and now enjoyed the hope of bakufu support in any legal action brought on their behalf.

The particular disposition of the 1260 incident shows that a change in local power relations had now largely obliterated the efficacy of past practice: the 1260 accord was in the form of a fresh "compromise" (wayo). During the earlier part of the Kamakura period the setting of proper levy scales was still a matter of determining an estate's "customs." This could be a very complicated process, especially in domains producing crops and commodities in addition to rice. Each item might well have its own battery of precedents. Our clearest illustration of this comes in a settlement edict of 1207 bearing on Wakasa Province's Kunitomi Estate. Careful examination of this record yields a fascinating portrait of how a jitō might utilize labor services to control both peasants and an estate's economy.[47]

First on the list of disputed points was a trout-catching service. A clear precedent existed here, but performance was causing difficulties for farmers during the harvest season. The bakufu judgment in this case was that while the jitō possessed an undiluted monopoly over estate trout fishing, he was to exercise that privilege with leniency. On this point, then, Kamakura sought to uphold two principles that were often in conflict: the maintenance of a customary service arrangement, now under a jitō, and the desire for smooth efficiency in shōen rice production. The result was an ineffectual call for jitō mildness.[48]

The second item concerned jitō-controlled hunting services during the silkworm culture season. It was a levy that weighed heavily on the peasantry, and its abolition was therefore requested. Only then, it was argued, could the local population dutifully pay its taxes. The jitō rejected this, claiming that the service had been performed without complaint during the previous ten years. Once again, the bakufu found itself caught between two principles. It ordered jitō indulgence in this matter too.

47. *Mibu Monjo*, 1207/12 Kantō gechijō, in *Mibu shinsha komonjo*, pp. 48–50.
48. It was ineffectual because nine years later another suit was required, with many of the same complaints. See n. 51.

Third on the list was a jitō-enforced indigo service, and here the outcome was very different. Years before when Kunitomi was still in the public sector, it had been an important indigo-producing area. However, on the occasion of the region's incorporation as shōen, the proprietor had exempted the local population from paying all indigo dues. This was doubtless by prearrangement: in return for commendations of land the notables of the area gained autonomous control of a local product. But then a jitō was appointed, and this figure resurrected the old indigo service, now under his own authority. The bakufu was thus confronted, as it were, with sequential precedents. It chose the more recent one and ordered abolished all jitō involvement in estate indigo.

Fourth was a bakufu refusal to allow the jitō deputy to have his horses cared for by farmers. Provisions for one or two jitō-owned horses was a reasonable burden when the title-holder himself made trips to Kunitomi, but the privilege was not to extend to the deputy. When trips by the latter or by the jitō's children were involved, the expenses were to be met from the jitō's myō fields.

The fifth item became an issue in many shōen. The jitō was requisitioning horses and human labor to aid in the transport of taxes from neighboring areas to Kyoto. The bakufu outlawed this practice, but did not close the door entirely. Should there be precedents permitting such activity, these, and not the bakufu's blanket prohibition, were to be followed.

Sixth was a complaint from the peasant population that the labor-to-rice commutation rate used by the jitō to offset his own obligations to Kamakura (horses and labor) was much too severe. The bakufu agreed and cut this figure in half.[49]

The final item concerned a variety of services imposed by the jitō's women and deputies. For example, a complaint was lodged over the high costs stemming from the constant "comings and goings" of ladies in the jitō's entourage. Kamakura ordered these burdens ended.

The particular assemblage of jitō rights here relates directly to the backgrounds of both Kunitomi Estate and Wakasa Province.

49. Kamakura housemen owed military and other specially designated services to the bakufu. From estates held by capital proprietors there were no regular rice levies paid to Kamakura.

It will be recalled that the introduction of Kamakura influence into Wakasa had come in 1196 in the wake of the Inaba purge (see p. 154). Two references in our 1207 document link Kunitomi to the chain of events following this ouster: the hunting-service precedent of "ten years," duration and an explicit reference to "practices from the time of [Inaba] Tokisada." In other words, the present jitō-holder was Wakasa Tadasue, heir to the Inaba fortune, and his privileges were an amalgam of pre-1196 precedents and rights established at the time of appointment. In this context, Tadasue was denied an authority over indigo production because of an earlier exemption and granted a fresh hunting service.

It is interesting that the bakufu's settlement of this suit was met by a continuation of jitō and jitōdai excesses in Kunitomi. Most revealing of these was the deputy's incarceration of farmers and the estate's kumon officer in order to extort signed acknowledgments of the jitō's authority. When the matter came to trial in 1216 the bakufu was unable to settle the issue, stating only that if the allegations were true the local affidavits would be invalid.[50] A second item adjudicated at this time—the jitō's use of emergency labor in six construction projects—drew from Kamakura a more direct show of support: "As the jitō, why should he not be able to issue such orders?"[51] Clearly, the right to use local labor adhered to the jitō shiki.

It was mentioned above that the kendan process, labor levies, and tax collection provided the major opportunities for jitō contact with peasants. To understand the third category we must have a clearer picture of the general fiscal composition of shōen. Essentially, a shōen's territory was divided into waste regions, forest areas, dry lands, and wet rice fields. The latter two categories yielded regular income, and were themselves divided into nontaxable and taxable fields. The nontaxable areas were composed of "salary lands" for shōen officers and fields whose produce was otherwise set aside for local consumption. The tax-yielding portions included the estate-

50. Such was the importance of written proof that bogus documents became a common practice on both sides. For the bakufu's dismissal of "compelled records" (atsujō) submitted by an azukari dokoro against a jitō, see Kobayagawa Ke Monjo, 1240/int.10/11 Kanto gechijō, in DNK, iewake 11, 1:548.

51. Mibu Monjo, 1216/8/17 Kantō gechijō, in Mibu shinsha komonjo, pp. 51–54.

holder's demesne areas (*tsukuda*) and the tilled fields of the shōen's regular myō units.[52] The myō areas provided the bulk of the estate's revenues, payable as service or commodity levies (*kuji*) and the regular annual rice tax. *Nengu*, as the latter was called, was calculated as so many *to* per standardized unit area, and the full levy was made on individual myō heads.[53] The latter would then assign payment shares to the cultivators or tenants actually working the land. Finally, the total assessment, after collection by the myōshu himself, would be delivered to a shōen officer, usually the jitō, estate deputy, or someone immediately indebted to them.[54] In the matter of tax collection, as with so much else, domain management tended to polarize on lines of loyalty or command centering on these two figures.[55]

The nature of such a division could directly affect the condition of the peasantry. Much evidence survives to show that jitō used their tax collection rights over myō to penetrate those areas at the expense of myōshu interests. In particular, efforts were made to force persons within the myō complex to work jitō private fields.[56]

52. *Tsukuda* was generally small but had the advantage of being directly administered by agents of the proprietor. In Tomita Estate in Owari, for example, there was proprietary demesne of only three chō: *Engakuji Monjo*, 1327/5/18 Owari no kuni Tomita-no-shō ryōke zasshō keijō, in *Kamakura shishi*, 2:130–31, doc. 74. It was very common also for the proprietor to hold no tsukuda. His leverage, as we have seen, lay elsewhere.

53. A 1218 document relating to Ōta Estate describes this for an interior village: a tax payment of 2 shō per tan was levied on each of that village's 27 myō, with a total paddy area of 32.832 chō (10 tan = 1 chō). *Kōyasan Monjo*, 1218/3/11 Ōta-no-shō Uga mura kumon kyōkyūmai chōfu, in *DNK, iewake 1*, 8:594–95, doc. 1947.

54. E.g., the kumon's involvement in Ōta Estate tax collection. The 1218 document just cited (n. 53) was drafted by the Ōta kumon officer.

55. A number of instances are known of sole jitō authority and at least several of exclusive estate deputy control. Ōta Estate is an example of the latter: Yasuda, *Jitō oyobi*, p. 246, citing a document of 1223. But most often there was a division between the two based on individual myō. Miri Estate in Aki Province serves as a case in point. Out of a paddy-land total of 84 chō, a full 47 were under the jitō's responsibility. Shimada Jirō, "Zaichi ryōshusei no tenkai to Kamakura bakufu hō," in Inagaki Yasuhiko and Nagahara Keiji, eds., *Chūsei no shakai to keizai* (Tokyo, 1962), p. 246.

56. E.g., in Miri Estate (Aki) and Tara Estate (Wakasa). Yasuda, *Jitō oyobi*, pp. 309–10, and Kuroda Toshio, "Wakasa no kuni Tara-no-shō," in Shibata Minoru, ed., *Shōen sonraku no kōzō* (Osaka, 1955), pp. 203 ff.

Beyond that, cultivators under the myōshu's paternalistic rule might be compelled to turn over their receipts without going through their chief. A third technique was to force cultivators off their fields and then to replace them with local persons owing direct services to a jitō. A corollary was to claim that fields had been abandoned when in fact they had not. This could lead either to direct jitō confiscation or to the commandeering of livestock and farm implements.[57] In all these ways, jitō emerged as the most feared and powerful figures on the land. From top to bottom—that is, vis à vis the proprietor, estate officialdom, and peasantry—they were creating the substance of local proprietorship.

Any shōen that failed to produce a steady flow of revenue literally ceased to be of value to its central holder. Due to jitō involvement in the tax-collection process, this problem became acute in estates all across the country. The jitō had many ways to abuse his privilege. Most common of course was a simple refusal to pay. The amounts involved were often very sizable, as taxes in default tended to accumulate over long periods. Thus in Tamba Province a jitō was accused in 1238 of holding back some 300 koku over seventeen years. An Awaji Province case of forty years later saw almost the same figures: 310 koku over eighteen years. And in a second Tamba shōen the totals in 1287 were 560 koku over five years.[58] At other times the devices used by jitō were more artful. A Yoritomo-period jitō, for example, used the claim of a crop failure to justify withholding taxes. And in 1307 a proprietor accused a jitō of surreptitiously changing the size of a domain's rice measuring cup![59]

57. Documents relating to Ategawa Estate in Kii tell this story and more. See especially *Kōyasan Monjo*, 1275/5 Ategawa-no-shō Kamimura hyakushō tō so-jōan, in *DNK, iewake 1*, 5:679–81, doc. 1130; and ibid., 1275/10/28 Ategawa-no-shō Kamimura hyakushō to gonjōjō, 6:486–90, doc. 1423.

58. *Higashi Monjo*, 1238/10/19 Rokuhara gechijō, in *KBSS*, 2:10–12, doc. 7; *Iwashimizu Monjo*, 1278/12/8 Awaji no kuni Ukai betsugū zasshō jitō wayojō, in *DNK, iewake 4*, 1:415, doc. 216; *Tōji Monjo*, 1287/12/10 Kantō gechijō, in *KBSS*, 1:230, doc. 167. This at least was the figure alleged by the estate-owner side.

59. *Suwa Jinja Monjo*, 1191/2/21 saki no utaishō ke mandokoro kudashibumi, in Suwa shiryō sōsho kankōkai, comp., *Suwa komonjo shū* (Nagano, 1931), 15:99, doc. 219; *Saidaji Monjo*, 1307(?)/1/23 Fushimi Jōkō inzen an, in *Yamato komonjo juei*, doc. 95. p. 87.

In an age in which tax payments came increasingly to be paid in coin, problems also developed over shifting exchange rates. In Minabe Estate in Kii, a dispute ensued when the jitō claimed an 80 kan equivalency for 200 koku of rice, and the proprietor, Kōyasan, demanded the present market rate.[60] The same kind of difficulty arose when the issue concerned fluctuating prices for commodities. We see this in a case of 1278 involving cotton and silk values in Akanabe Estate in Mino. The jitō of Akanabe called for a free-floating ratio, while the estate deputy demanded a fixed exchange rate.[61] By the end of the period, even tax defaults were being recorded in terms of cash.[62]

In internment cases reaching a bakufu courtroom, decisions tended to follow a set pattern: immediate repayment when the amounts owed were small, and restitution under a deferred plan for more serious withholdings. However, the time period for the latter seems always to have been three years,[63] and actual punitive judgments—for example, loss of the tax responsibility—are almost nonexistent. The result was that abuses tended to be ongoing, with the amounts owed growing ever larger. In this circumstance, proprietors took to seeking resolutions on their own with jitō. Appeasement rather than confrontation was the main thrust of this effort, and a particular settlement mode called ukesho emerged as its dominant expression. Under this arrangement proprietors would formally surrender all domainial involvement in return for a written promise that the jitō deliver a given tax figure every year. In a legal sense, central owners were merely investing jitō with full plenipotentiary powers over shōen. But actually they were opening the way to jitō rulership over the land. Proprietors withdrew their estate deputies and entered into a relationship of trust with the very figures

60. *Kōyasan Monjo*, 1278/12/27 Kantō gechijō, in *KBSS*, 1:192–93, doc. 144.

61. *Tōdaiji Monjo*, 1278/12/8 Rokuhara gechijō, in *Gifu kenshi, shiryō hen, kodai-chūsei* 3:226–28, doc. 216.

62. The jitō of Yura Estate in Awaji was accused of owing 100 kammon in back taxes. *Jakuōji Jinja Monjo*, 1319/12/27 Kantō gechijō, in *KBSS*, 1:357, doc. 282.

63. This was the bakufu's general regulation (*Goseibai shikimoku*, art. 5, in *CHS*, 1:6). An actual example is Sasakibe Estate in Tamba. See n. 58, Higashi Monjo.

least noted for that virtue.[64] It is hardly surprising, therefore, that ukesho rarely provided satisfactory long-term resolutions. Typical were Minabe and Tomita Estates, in Kii and Owari provinces respectively.

The Minabe account begins in the 1190s when a court personage assigned 100 koku of the annual tax (20 percent of the total) to a temple within the Kōyasan complex.[65] The latter was simultaneously permitted to assume authority over a gesu shiki.[66] Considerable confusion arose in the years following, especially on the question of destination of taxes. Collection and payment was under a series of local ukesho-type arrangements.[67] Then in 1221 the gesu fought on the court side during the Jōkyū War, and a jitō was appointed in his place.[68] The latter clearly regarded his new title as a means of self-aggrandizement, and within a matter of months he had been called before a bakufu tribunal. During this proceeding he cited a jitō ukesho precedent of several generations, and then compounded this falsehood by claiming that the amount stipulated for payment was uncertain. The bakufu's judgment underlined its support of the status quo: the jitō was to deliver the tax according to the original 80–20 proprietary division.[69]

This was only the start of trouble. Before the following year was out a second trial had become necessary, with much the same result: 100 koku was ordered sent to the proprietor in Kii and 400 to the patron in Kyoto, but responsibility for both was placed under the jitō's ukesho.[70] Over the course of the next century we find

64. Trouble with jitō over taxes was not always the inducement behind an ukesho. In Mino's Akanabe Estate, e.g., the proprietor (Tōdaiji) had long required a local representative who could marshal the resources of the domain to control the damage-causing Kiso River. When a jitō was appointed after Jōkyū, Tōdaiji negotiated an ukesho arrangement with him. See Koizumi Senyū, "Jitō uke ni kan suru ichi kōsatsu," *Nihon rekishi* 298 (1973); 16.

65. *Kōyasan Monjo*, 1194/4 saki no Saiin-no-chō kishinjō, in *DNK, iewake 1*, 1:309, doc. 286, and ibid., 1194/4 Rengejōin butsuji yōto chō, 7:522–24, doc. 1663.

66. Ibid., ?/11/3 saki no Saiin ryōji, 1:310, doc. 287.

67. Ibid., 1222/9/13 Kantō gechijō, 7:529–30, doc. 1665, and 1222/7/10 Minabe shōkan nengumai kishōmon an, doc. 1666, pp. 530–31.

68. Referred to in ibid., 1278/12/27 Kantō gechijō, 1:323–25, doc. 307.

69. Ibid., 1221/12/24 Kantō gechijō, 2:428–29, doc. 265.

70. Ibid., 1222/9/13 Kantō gechijō, 7:529–30, doc. 1665.

continuous instances of jitō malfeasance, which even an exchange of jitō holders was not able to halt.[71] Eventually the proprietor resorted to a rather desperate strategy: Kōyasan appealed in 1325 for cancellation of the Minabe jitō shiki itself![72] Before Kamakura could react to this, the contesting parties, however, were able to arrive at a compromise. Its terms suggest that the jitō, as always, was seeking to avoid sanctions by making promises he had no intention of keeping. He thus agreed to the following arrangement: he would repay the amount in arrears, an enormous 1,396 koku over a mere three years. Should he fail to meet that deadline he would surrender his jitō post and all its privileges for five years. And if there were still further defaults, jitō authority would be suspended for three more years.[73] That none of this came to pass seems evident since seventy years later conditions deteriorated to the point that the domain itself was physically divided between the two arch rivals.[74] Perseverance and a series of judgments and agreements that were punitive only in the future ended by earning a jitō a legal proprietorship over a half-sized estate.

The second case is that of Tomita Domain in Owari.[75] Our earliest reference is to an ukesho being established in 1211 under a Hōjō family jitō shiki. Proprietorship was held by the Kon'oe, a branch of the Fujiwara. Over the next several generations taxes were continually withheld, until in 1283, the Hōjō took the unusual step of "commending" their jitō post to Kamakura's own Engakuji Temple.[76] But this did not improve conditions. Finally, in 1327 a revision of the original ukesho was negotiated on terms highly unfavorable to the proprietor. In addition to reducing the annual tax to 110 kammon cash, the Kon'oe agreed to forgo all claims on sums in arrears and to cease sending out its own investigators (*junkenshi*). Should Engakuji fail to heed this agreement, both earlier suits and

71. Referred to in ibid., 1278/12/27 Kantō gechijō, 1:323–25, doc. 307.
72. Ibid., 1325/1 Rengejōin Gakurō sojō kotogaki, 2:445–48, doc. 284.
73. Ibid., 1326/8/21 Minabe-no-shō nengumai wayo ukebumi, 1:319–20, doc. 303.
74. Ibid., 1393/9/8 Ōuchi shi bugyōshū hosho an, 5:499, doc. 986.
75. Unless otherwise indicated all information is drawn from *Engakuji Monjo*, 1327/5/18 Owari no kuni Tomita-no-shō ryōke-zasshō keijō, in *Kamakura shishi, shiryō hen*, 2:130–31, doc. 74.
76. Ibid., 1283/3/25 Hōjō shi shitsuji hosho, doc. 6, p. 7.

the stipulations of the 1211 ukesho would be revived. The footnote to this fatuous effort came several years later when it was the Kon'oe, not Engakuji, whose relationship with Tomita was ended. After the downfall of the bakufu in 1333 a certain court lady emerged as the new recipient of the annual tax, while Engakuji's own position was strengthened.[77]

The cases of Minabe and Tomita show ukesho as an unsuccessful technique designed to guarantee a proprietor a regular annual income from estates. Failure (or the prospect of failure) often led to experimentation with other plans and programs. One of the best known is *shitaji chūbun*, or the division of estates between jitō and proprietor, as for example in Minabe. In such cases proprietors sought to salvage revenues by assuming more, not less, responsibility.[78] In point of fact, however, there was always great diversity in central-owner efforts to save their domains. These range from appointing a lawless jitō to a deputy azukari dokoro post,[79] to extracting an agreement that a jitō transfer lands of his own for a given period in order to make up "back taxes."[80] Sometimes these arrangements worked well enough for a time. But the very fact that they were attempted suggests that the jitō in question were not apt to remain satisfied with them indefinitely. Central–local land disputes during the thirteenth century went through a sequence of stages with very few "final resolutions."

In the period before 1270 or so we find few examples of regional alliances under jitō leadership. The major reasons for this were bakufu opposition and the time and energy required to secure a solid grip even over one's own estate. The pre-Mongol Kamakura period thus emerges as an age of discrete incidences of lawlessness

77. Ibid., 1334/7/11 Go-Daigo tennō rinji an, doc. 83, p. 140.
78. This institution is treated in Mass, "Jitō Land Possession in the Thirteenth Century," *Medieval Japan*, chap. 7.
79. Referred to in *Kōyasan Monjo*, 1275/5 Ategawa-no-shō Kamimura hyaku-shō tō sojōan, in *DNK, iewake 1*, 5:679–81, doc. 1130. This appointment was immediately followed by further outrages.
80. E.g., 4.5 chō of rice land for eleven years to offset 600 koku of unpaid taxes. *Iwashimizu Monjo*, 1281/3/3 Awa no kuni Kushifuchi-no-shō azukari dokoro-jitō wayojō, in *DNK, iewake 4*, 1:395–96, doc. 198.

committed by particular jitō against particular proprietors.[81] Jitō expansion did not take the form of external movements across territory; instead, it saw jitō attempting to "pile up" authority over single-estate hierarchies. In this sense the closest we can come to actual physical growth was where a jitō moved to "round out" his authority over an already existing unit. The import of this is revealed in an incident of 1222. Tajima Province's Nii Estate consisted of three small-sized noncontiguous units located in three separate gō.[82] Each of these gō had a jitō, and in the unstable period soon after Jōkyū the three jitō moved to obliterate the temple-owner's power over its small parcels. They did this by calling these parcels gō territory, which they once had been, and then seizing their income.[83] But such an effort was a far cry from later attempts to create new territorial amalgams.

If the boundaries and symmetry of jitō appointment areas were only occasionally objects of dispute, the size and quality of a jitō's perquisites were a far more common problem. Actually, we have seen this in many contexts already. When proprietors brought suit against jitō it was usually because the latter had taken something that did not belong to them. But jitō in fact had little opportunity to advance a local condition by means other than violence or chicanery: duty performance was admired during these times, but not rewarded. There existed no concept of regular incremental advances of what was under a jitō shiki.[84]

Jitō reacted to this dilemma in various ways. Since an initial rights package held only the promise of permanence, there were some jitō who attempted to characterize their legacies as unworthy of a Kamakura-appointed officer. Such was the case in Tamba

81. For one of the very few examples of jitō invading external lands see *Sampōin Monjo*, 1211/4/6 Kantō migyōsho, in Toyama ken, comp., *Etchū shiryō* (Toyama, 1909), 2:321.

82. Shōen were income-producing areas and thus did not require continguous territory.

83. *Ninnaji Monjo*, 1222/7/7 Kantō gechijō, in *KBSS*, 1:23, doc. 26. The bakufu outlawed this effort by the three jitō.

84. The bakufu was no help here. Its rewards were geared to vassal service, not to exemplary performance as a land manager. Such rewards took the form of confirmations of older posts or grants of wholly new jitō offices.

Province's Sasakibe Estate, where hyperbole and ridicule were the jitō's chief weapons. In a legal action in which the jitō was defendant, he began his rebuttal by calling Sasakibe "a small and distant place." He then went on to describe what his retainer had found on first visiting that estate: extensive fallow lands dotted with ponds and a river region. In the jitō's own words his "income share was only a name not a fact." This, he concluded, should more than offset the estate deputy's charge that he had withheld taxes from his personal fields (myō). To the jitō's grief, however, the bakufu remained unconvinced by this appeal. It awarded victory to the proprietor.[85]

In the same general context were jitō attempts to subsume various types of land under a jitō-controlled category. In Kunitomi Estate in Wakasa, for example, the jitō was accused of absorbing into his own myō area (jitō myō) the fields and service families of absconding and ruined farmers.[86] More ambitious still was a jitō effort of 1209 whose apparent goal was to convert an entire village into a jitō residence area (*hori no uchi*). The plan was defeated, however, by a bakufu judgment ordering that both the tax authority and tax proceeds continue under the shrine proprietor's administration.[87] Had the decision gone the other way, the area would have become unencumbered jitō land since, by definition, hori no uchi was free from all higher claims.

The country's estate-owners were able to use many of the same manipulative tactics *against* jitō. Proprietary efforts to label jitō as gesu have already been discussed. A second method derived from the favoritism shown certain religious institutions. An incident involving estates owned by Ise Shrine illustrates this. In 1194, Yoritomo judged that even jitō salary fields (*kyūden*) and residence lands (hori no uchi), both normally tax-exempt, would be obliged to pay certain tributes to Ise.[88] But the greatest weapon of proprietors

85. *Higashi Monjo*, 1238/10/19 Rokuhara gechijō, in *KBSS*, 2:10, doc. 7.

86. *Mibu Monjo*, 1207/12 Kantō gechijō, in *Mibu shinsha komonjo*, p. 50.

87. *Katori Monjo*, 1209/3/17 Kantō gechijō, in Chiba ken, comp., *Chiba ken shiryō, chūsei hen, Katori monjo* (Chiba, 1968), pp. 68–69. Actually, the ambitions of this jitō extended well beyond this single village. He sought nothing less than to gain leverage over the proprietary institution itself—Shimōsa's Katori Shrine. The technique attempted was to secure control over the "seating arrangement," i.e., the hierarchy of the shrine's officialdom. Ibid.

88. *Saisho Monjo*, 1194/2/15 Minamoto Yoritomo migyōsho, in Miyata Toshi-

lay simply in their freedom to bring suit. Here was a privilege that could easily be exploited. This became especially apparent from 1232 when the bakufu issued its famous Jōei Formulary, a collection of precepts to guide Kamakura houseman behavior.[89] Central owners quickly mastered these and began accusing jitō of having broken bakufu laws. The result was to place Kamakura in a difficult position: either it had to issue adverse judgments against too many of its own men or risk undermining its newly promulgated set of rules.

The bakufu's answer to this dilemma was twofold. In supplementary legislation it took steps to reduce the advantage given to proprietors in 1232.[90] And it sought to reinforce the view that local precedents were to serve as a protection for both sides. A case occurring in 1244 shows how this might work. The matter involved an estate deputy's attempt to compromise a jitō ukesho that the azukari dokoro himself had agreed to just four years earlier. The bakufu rejected this effort as a "false suit" (ranso).[91] But the most illuminating example of this type came several years earlier in Iyo Province. This incident deserves careful study, since it brings together many of the themes treated in this chapter.

The case involved an island domain in Iyo over which Kutsuna Kunishige held the jitō shiki.[92] The specific issue was whether the jitō possessed an interior unit, Matsuyoshi Myō, as part of his privilege, or whether the proprietor enjoyed jurisdiction. During the first stage of the dispute, the estate-owner brought suit to Rokuhara alleging that "the gesu of this island has been violating Matsuyoshi Myō." Rokuhara rejected that claim on grounds that Kunishige was demonstrably jitō.[93] However, this verdict largely bypassed the central point—the nature of the relationship between Matsu-

hiko, comp., *Saisho Monjo, Ibaragi ken komonjo shūsei 2* (Mito, 1962), pp. 23–24.

89. The Formulary (called *Goseibai shikimoku*) appears in *CHS*, 1:3–31.

90. Changes in the direction of bakufu legislation and policy are ably treated in Kano Kayoko, "Shikken ki ni okeru Kamakura bakufu no seikaku," *Nihon rekishi* 239 (1968): 56–75.

91. *Chūjō Ke Monjo*, 1244/7/21 Kantō gechijō, in *Okuyama-no-shō shiryōshū*, p. 100.

92. The family's actual surname was Fujiwara until sometime later. They are known historically, however, as the Kutsuna of Iyo.

93. *Chōryūji Monjo*, 1232/7/27 Rokuhara gechijō, in *Ehime ken hennen shi*, 2:259–60. See p. 000.

yoshi Myō and the jitō post. This gave the proprietor a second chance: a year later he took his complaint directly to Kamakura.[94]

The bakufu's settlement of the matter included a full review of developments to that point. These included the Kutsuna's original jitō investiture of 1205, as well as subsequent bakufu confirmations in 1208 and 1221.[95] The edict also contained a summary of Kunishige's defense argument. From the time of his grandfather's commendation (in 1182) to Chōkōdō Temple, his family had paid an unusually large figure in annual taxes.[96] However no part of that total had been drawn from Matsuyoshi: the latter's 3 chō of rice land and 13 chō of dry land comprised Kunishige's salary fields (kyūden). Kamakura responded favorably to this explanation, and dismissed the proprietor's suit.[97]

What, then, had been accomplished? The successive attempts by Chōkōdō to gain control of Matsuyoshi reveal different strategies. In the Rokuhara phase, the proprietor sought to justify its claim by labeling Kunishige as a gesu. After that failed, it switched to an assertion that Matsuyoshi owed regular taxes, i.e., that it was not jitō kyūden. The results in this second instance were much more momentous: the disputed myō, whose status had never been clarified,[98] was now established as integral to the Kutsuna's jitō post. It was placed under a permanent jitō shiki shelter.[99]

The weight of evidence in this chapter has suggested that for jitō bent on establishing local control, the essential problem was one of

94. Evidently, Rokuhara judgments were not considered final; they could be appealed to Kamakura.

95. *Chōryūji Monjo*, 1205/11/12 shōgun ke kudashibumi, in *Ehime ken hennen shi*, 2:206; *Kutsuna Ke Monjo*, 1208/int.4/27 Kantō kudashibumi, in ibid., p. 214, and *Chōryūji Monjo*, 1221/int.10/12 Kantō gechijō, in ibid., p. 245.

96. This tax figure and the year 1182 are both cited in the Kutsuna house genealogy. See Kageura Tsutomu, comp., *Kutsuna ke monjo, Iyo shiryō shūsei 1* (Matsuyama, 1964), p. 22.

97. *Chōryūji Monjo*, 1233/12/10 Kantō gechijō, in *Ehime ken hennen shi*, 2:263.

98. As indicated earlier (p. 129), such failures by the bakufu were standard. In none of Kamakura's earlier decrees (1205, 1207, 1208, 1221, and 1232) was Matsuyoshi's exact relationship to the Kutsuna specified.

99. In a document of 1302, Matsuyoshi is referred to simply as the "jitō's share" (*jitō bun*). *Chōryūji Monjo*, 1302/7/7 Kantō gechijō, in *Ehime ken hennen shi*, 2:441–42.

consummating in law a series of de facto local successes. For much of the Kamakura period, Japan retained its earlier litigiousness. This meant that resourceful jitō developed mixed programs of co-operation on some issues and the measured placement of obstacles in others. They sought out areas of vulnerability in a proprietor's legal armor and went to work there.

The jitō was assisted in this endeavor by several unique circumstances. Most important was his immunity from direct central interference; all complaints regarding jitō had to be channeled through the bakufu. The eastern regime was thus thrust into the position of having to serve as policeman over its own men. Lawsuits, as we have seen, were numerous on both sides, but the absence of data on original precedents and Kamakura's growing reluctance to deal harshly with jitō inevitably benefited the latter. At the same time, jitō were now cast as the main antagonists of central owners: it was not long before the two sides were viewed as having equal claim to the land.

By the mid-thirteenth century, estate-owners themselves had accepted this new condition. They no longer entreated the bakufu for cancellations of jitō posts but sought instead to compromise with their rivals. This had two immediate effects. It signaled to jitō that stepped up pressure could create the conditions for compromise, and it marked a crucial retreat in Kamakura's control over justice. By countenancing direct accommodation between disputants, the bakufu substituted approval of settlements for their adjudication. It also made clear that precedents, as well as Kamakura's own laws, might be ignored in deference to a central–local compromise.

A final phase in this sequence did not come until the fourteenth century and can only be anticipated here. It involved the first signs of a move away from supralocal legitimacy. For an unknown though clearly small percentage of jitō, the obligations to higher authority—now meaning the bakufu—began to loom as the ultimate barrier. The result was an undermining of one of Japan's most sacred concepts—the subordination of local persons to some absentee interest. With jitō ignoring the financial demands of proprietors and rejecting the trial summonses of Kamakura, the country began to prepare for a new age.[100] Possession and proprietorship, once so far

100. For a jitō ignoring the consequences of repeated bakufu subpoenas, see

apart, now came to be bridged. In the end, this was to be the jitō's final legacy.

Myōkōji Monjo, 1314/8/27 Rokuhara gechijō, in Ichinomiya shishi hensan-shitsu, comp., *Ichinomiya shishi, shiryō hen 5* (Ichinomiya, 1963), doc. 10, p. 7. At the start of the Muromachi age, many jitō resurfaced as vassals of the new provincial hegemons called shugo. In this sense, the slide into localism was still in an early stage in 1300.

8 SHUGO AS REGIONAL OFFICERS

Success in the war against the Heishi had elevated the new government in Kamakura to the protector's role for the entire country. On the estate level this policing authority was parceled out, in the irregular fashion described in preceding chapters, to vassals who assumed the title of jitō. On the provincial level Yoritomo, after some initial hesitation, elected to deploy a network of officers called shugo. These shugo were conceived differently from the all-purpose provincial commanders of the war period. Unlike those earlier officers, the shugo of the post-1190 years were vassals charged under a legal prescription that carefully defined their duties. Later called *taihon sankajō* ("the three regulations for great crimes"), this prescription included shugo jurisdiction over incidences of murder and rebellion and responsibility for the mustering of provincial housemen for the *ōbanyaku*, an imperial guard service.[1] With minor adjustments, the taihon sankajō continued into Muromachi times as the legal definition for shugo functions.

This cardboard-like uniformity of shugo in law, however, does not really simplify our task of evaluation. Part of the problem lies in the relative scarcity of documents relating to shugo.[2] An even greater difficulty is the need to assess a figure who, if he truly approximated his legal definition, might not have been very important. The jitō's role in the institutional history of the early medieval period is

1. The name "taihon sankajō" first came into use about 1230. Its component parts were in existence from the 1190s, however. Note that only two crimes were involved despite the reference to three.
2. For several provinces (e.g., Shima, Awa, and Hida) not a single reference to a Kamakura shugo has ever been found. In others, the shugo-related documents number only two or three for a period of 150 years. Satō, *Zōtei-shugo seido*, p. 243.

unquestioned; the larger influence of the shugo is less certain and therefore needs to be proved.[3]

It was stated in chapter 4 that, traditional histories to the contrary, the year 1185 did not mark the birth of Kamakura's shugo network. If anything, the period 1185–90 saw a cutback in the deployment of provincial deputies using that title. At the same time there is confusion, as earlier, over the denomination sōtsuibushi. While some sources (especially *AK*) use the term "shugo" most often, other materials favor "sōtsuibushi." A case in point is that of Sasaki Sadatsuna, who is called "Ōmi shugo" in *AK* (1187) and "Ōmi sōtsuibushi" in *Gyokuyō* (1191).[4] To complicate matters further, *AK* refers to a debate within bakufu circles over whether to appoint sōtsuibushi to areas smaller than provinces. Yoritomo decided against this proposal on grounds that "disputes and lawsuits will be ceaseless" (*AK* 1186/3/7). On the other hand, what actions the Genji leader did take have clearly not survived. That his regime might have profited from a network of provincial deputies seems unquestioned. Two major problems of the period were containing local lawlessness and devising a means by which housemen could be kept in tow. Yet for unknown reasons Yoritomo did not launch his shugo system until the early 1190s. No contemporaneous references survive to shugo during the half decade beginning in 1186.[5]

How, then, are we to trace the beginnings of Kamakura's shugo program? Through hindsight we know that one of the main components of the taihon sankajō was shugo supervision of houseman performance of the ōbanyaku. During the period after 1185 we have seen that Yoritomo assumed jurisdiction over all warriors country-wide. Since guard duty in the capital was a traditional fighting-man function, it was natural that the Kamakura chieftain assume responsibility for it. Circumstantial evidence shows that this service

3. By definition, shugo and jitō have always stood as the archetypal institutional expressions of the Kamakura age. But this should not be taken to imply equality of importance between them.

4. *AK* 1187/2/9 and *Gyokuyō*, 1191/4/2, 3:674.

5. This lack of documentation can be seen in vol.1 of *KI* and in Satō, *Zōtei-shugo seido*. There are, however, one or two references to sōtsuibushi, e.g., *Tada-In Monjo*, 1186/11/25 Ōe Hiromoto hosho an, in *KI*, 1:116, doc. 195.

was supervised by the bakufu during the later 1180s.[6] However, it was not yet under shugo. The first connection between shugo and the imperial guard service did not come until 1192. This was the year in which bakufu efforts to register all housemen on provincial rolls began in earnest (p.152) and is the point at which we can posit a real beginning for the Kamakura shugo.[7]

During the sixth month of 1192 Yoritomo issued an edict to Kamakura vassals in the province of Mino. In it, he directed that all shōen-resident jitō in Mino obey the imperial guard recruitment orders of shugo Ōuchi Koreyoshi. Ōuchi was also called on to report the names of any nonhousemen who attempted to perform this service.[8] Several points stand out here. First, the bakufu was finally moving to decentralize its ōban supervisory authority by making the province the basic unit of organization and the shugo the local ōban commander.[9] Second, Kamakura was now taking steps to limit ōban duty (and hence its own jurisdiction) to bona fide housemen only. This had symbolic as well as practical meaning. The

6. The key source is *AK* 1187/9/13. See the discussion by Gomi Katsuo in "Kamakura bakufu no goke'nin taiseiK—yōto ōbanyaku no tōsei o chūshin ni," *Rekishi kyōiku* 11.7 (1963); 14–15. (Hereafter cited as Gomi, "Kyōto ōban-yaku.")

7. Legal-minded historians who have not been able to accept 1185 as marking the birth of shugo often cite 1190 instead, the year of Yoritomo's first trip to Kyoto. They reason that he must have been made shugo-in-chief for the entire country, for only then could he have begun to make provincial shugo appointments. There is no proof for this supposition, however, and anyway, we have little reason to suppose that Yoritomo would have waited for court permission to launch his shugo network. His earlier shugo were deployed quite independently of Kyoto.

8. *AK* 1192/6/20. Though the original of this edict has not survived, virtually all scholars accept its rendering in *AK* as authentic. The edict's reference to "shōen-resident jitō" is followed by an explicit exemption of housemen appointed to the public sector. Ishii Susumu has suggested that this was a gesture to the recently deceased In, who had been Mino's provincial proprietor. While a commemorative temple was under construction, Yoritomo authorized an ōban exemption. Ishii S., "Bunji shugo jitō," p. 29. Ōuchi Koreyoshi, who had been shugo of wartime Iga, was now given a peacetime assignment as shugo of neighboring Mino Province.

9. A Heian precedent existed for this. In earlier times, the ōban service was organized under provincial office (kokuga) direction. Gomi, "Kyōto ōbanyaku," pp. 12–13.

bakufu had acquired an elite warrior service and limited it to its own men; and it had devised an ingenious way to keep unesteemed western housemen in the west. By establishing a Kyoto guard service, rather than one based in Kamakura, the bakufu was spared the need to confront vassals with whom it was little concerned. Kamakura's provincial officers would discharge the responsibility of calling such housemen to service and periodically "renewing" their loyalty.[10]

Unfortunately, we know almost nothing of the actual mechanics of the ōban service during its early years. We can only surmise that as shugo came to be appointed—and as they completed their provincial registers of housemen—the bakufu formulated its guard schedule and began issuing directives. In 1196, for example, an edict similar to the one issued in Mino was addressed to the vassals of Izumi.[11] Considerable confusion probably attended this entire process. In much the same way that warriors had resisted Taira-dispatched governors in 1180–81, westerners may have reacted negatively to Minamoto-sent shugo.[12] In addition, the displeasure of central proprietors was almost certain. Shōen immunity was about to be breached by shugo agents delivering conscription orders. A collateral effect, as revealed in a document of 1195, was an attempt by housemen to shift ōban expenses to the peasantry. In this incident, involving Ōta Estate, Yoritomo assured the proprietor that such practices would be outlawed.[13]

Concerning the frequency and duration of ōban levies, all that is known is that the service period ranged from three to six months and fell on individual houses irregularly.[14] In Wakasa Province, for example, ōban contingents traveled to the capital in 1200 and 1220.

10. In the period before 1221 this effort ultimately failed to work to Kamakura's advantage. The result of bringing incompletely subordinated vassals to Kyoto was to impress upon them their greater ties with the traditional polity than with the bakufu. They were, after all, non-jitō residents of centrally owned estates. Hence the decision of many of these warriors to fight on the court side in 1221.

11. *Chikugo Wada Monjo*, 1196/11/17 saki no utaishō ke mandokoro kudashi-bumi an, in *KI*, 2:206, doc. 881.

12. E.g., the apparent difficulties of Tsutsumi Tadasue upon his arrival in Wakasa (000).

13. *Kōyasan Monjo*, 1195/6/5 Kantō gechijō, in *DNK, iewake 1*, 1:80, doc. 85.

14. For details, see Gomi Katsuo, "Kamakura goke'nin no banyaku kinshi ni tsuite," pt. 1, *Shigaku zasshi* 69.9 (1954): 29 ff.

But in Kazusa Province several decades later, housemen were obliged to mount guard after only nine years (1260 and 1269).[15] On another point, ōban recruitment was determined by a vassal's home region, not by the location of his jitō shiki. This was a matter of some importance to housemen from the Kantō: they would not have to serve guard alongside westerners. A clear illustration of this involves the Fukabori house of Kazusa. It traveled to Kyoto as a member of that province's contingent, even though its main jitō post was in Hizen, at the other end of Japan.[16]

Despite the sparsity of our data, it seems safe to conclude that recruitment for the imperial ōban service had become a regular shugo duty by the mid-1190s.[17] The joining of this responsibility with the other parts of the taihon sankajō, namely, the authority over "murderers and rebels," took place during the next several years and marked the final emergence of the Kamakura shugo. The clearest expression of this appears in an *AK* entry at the end of 1199. Koyama Tomomasa, a ranking eastern warrior, had just been appointed to the shugo post of Harima Province. The housemen there were directed to owe loyalty and obedience to Tomomasa and to discharge the Kyoto ōban under his command. It was further stipulated that the extent of Tomomasa's policing authority was for rebels and murderers; he was not to involve himself in general provincial governance (*kokumu*), and he was not to judge the complaints of the common people. Finally, he was not allowed to interfere with local persons of prominence (*jūnin*) (*AK* 1199/12/29).

The care with which Kamakura delineated its appointee's authority is the dominant note here. Clearly, the bakufu was intent on establishing proper spheres of activity for both the shugo and traditional representatives of the provincial office. Viewed broadly, each capital was to have its own network of deputies in the provinces.

15. For wakasa, see ibid., p. 33. For Kazusa, see *Fukabori Monjo*, 1260/8/7 Rokuhara tandai kyojō, and 1269/7/25 Rokuhara tandai kyojō, in *Saga ken shiryō shūsei*, 4:43 and 48, docs. 78 and 86.

16. *Fukabori Monjo*, docs. 78 and 86.

17. A Kamakura city ōban was instituted in the period after 1219, but shugo were little involved. This was because service performance was limited to vassals from the Kantō, most of whom were in direct touch with the bakufu. We see in this, of course, another illustration of Kamakura's antiwestern bias. The Kamakura ōban is treated in Gomi Katsuo, "Kamakura goke'nin," pt. 2, pp. 22 ff.

But why bother to evolve such a cumbersome system? Why, moreover, create a shugo definition that was in fact quite limited? Consistent with the bakufu's effort to revitalize traditional hierarchies, Kamakura must have determined that to sweep away the old governorships would be as disruptive as to invest jitō with carte blanche rights within shōen. Both courses held out the promise only of continued dislocation. In addition, to have released too much authority to a shugo might have involved some risk for Kamakura. A shugo who was also a governor and a great warrior could prove difficult to control. Finally, the taihon sankajō was, in fact, no more than a common denominator and could be expanded when conditions warranted. A case in point is the bakufu's 1197 instruction to Koremune Tadahisa, newly appointed shugo of Satsuma and Ōsumi.

In chapter 6 we saw that Tadahisa emerged after 1185 as the dominant figure in southern Kyushu. He was a man of unimpeachable loyalty in a part of Japan where central authority exercised little voice. Yoritomo could thus afford to be expansive. As was standard, he authorized Tadahisa to superintend the Kyoto ōban and to control incidences of murder (and implicitly, rebellion). But in addition, the Genji chief ordered his new shugo to enforce an imperial prohibition against the buying and selling of humans, and to take responsibility for abolishing local incursions against land (*rōzeki*). He was cautioned on only one point: while discharging these various functions, Tadahisa was not to bring false charges against guiltless persons.[18]

And so the respective shugo of Satsuma–Ōsumi and Harima were not, after all, the same. Massive Shimazu Estate had been designated "Heike-confiscated land," while Harima was a province near the capital. Koremune Tadahisa, possessor of a wide array of titles in southern Kyushu, was the acknowledged strongman in that region. By contrast, Koyama Tomomasa was merely the taihon sankajō officer of centrally located Harima.

Concerning the identities of the first shugo, it will come as no

18. *Shimazu Ke Monjo*, 1197/12/3 saki no utaishō ke mandokoro kudashibumi, in *DNK, iewake 16*, 1:8–9, doc. 11. Tadahisa is referred to in this document as "houseman supervisor" (*ke'nin bugyōnin*), though shortly he would be known by the regular title, shugo.

surprise that Yoritomo awarded these posts to low-ranking subordinates and to eastern warriors who had joined his movement early. The first shugo were thus *fudai* types, to borrow the well-known Tokugawa designation for "insider" vassal daimyo. Conversely, families who joined "later"—and this meant all houses not from the Kantō—were *tozama*, or "outsiders." No tozama family was ever granted a shugo title for the duration of the Kamakura period.[19] In this way, shugo posts were initiated and continued as an eastern warrior monopoly.[20] Their possession became a mark of power and influence within the bakufu.

As just mentioned, the first recipients were men who were either obscure or had shown special devotion to Yoritomo. The Shimazu, Mutō, and Ōtomo heads belong to the first group and divided as many as eight Kyushu shugo titles.[21] The Sasaki, originally from Ōmi but transplanted to Sagami after 1160, belong in the second category. They were one of the few families to identify with Yoritomo during the latter's period of exile (*AK* 1180/8/9). In return for this support, the sons of the original scion were assigned in the

19. Actually, the term "tozama" may have had its first usage near the end of the Kamakura period, and in a most interesting context. In the *Satamirenshō,* a kind of legal dictionary drawn up at the Hōjō's behest during 1319–23, the term is used to describe jitō and other Kamakura housemen owing loyalty to the shogun, i.e., old-line Kamakura vassals. The purpose of this usage is to distinguish such housemen from the private retainers of the Hōjō, the *miuchi*. Thus, families who had been insiders during Yoritomo's day, had become outsiders, i.e., tozama, under the Hōjō. See *Satamirenshō,* in *CHS,* 2:362. During the early Muromachi period "daimyo" came to be called "tozama" (*Buke myōmoku shō,* in *Shintei zōho kojitsu sōsho* [Tokyo, 1955], 13:243–47). The term "fudai" is much older and goes back at least to the Nara period. Ibid., pp. 247 ff.

20. Professor Kobayashi has argued that the Masuda of Iwami (see chap. 3) may have held their province's shugo post for an indeterminate period before and after the Jōkyū War. His conclusions, however, are entirely speculative (Kobayashi, "Iwami," pp. 144–46).

21. Before Yoritomo's death the Shimazu were appointed to Satsuma, Ōsumi, and Hyūga and the Mutō to Chikuzen, Buzen, and Hizen. Evidence for the Ōtomo is less certain: our earliest reference to the Ōtomo as shugo of Bungo is 1242 and of Chikugo, 1207. It is likely, however, that the Ōtomo's Bungo and Chikugo appointments came during Yoritomo's lifetime (Satō, *Zōtei-shugo seido*, pp. 211 ff.) The remaining shugo title in Kyushu, that for Higo Province, was apparently never associated with any of these three families.

1190s a major bloc of shugo titles.[22] There is a third group, conspicuous largely for its absence. As far as can be determined, the great
provincial officers—Chiba, Koyama, and Miura—received the
shugo posts only in their native provinces.[23] It is further evidence
of the Minamoto chieftain's reluctance to depend too heavily on
the greatest of his vassals.

The period 1199–1200 witnessed significant changes in bakufu
personnel, as several Yoritomo-appointed shugo were dismissed by
a new leadership. Gotō Motokiyo was the first to fall; he had been
shugo of Sanuki and in 1199/3 was accused simply of a "crime"
(*AK* 1199/3/5). A year later Sasaki Tsunetaka was dropped from his
Awaji, Awa, and Tosa shugo posts. This time the pretext was boister-
ous behavior in Kyoto (*AK* 1200/8/2), though obviously more than
that was involved. The bakufu was probably seeking to reduce the
Sasaki's overall shugo portfolio, while also clearing more of Shikoku
and central Japan of Yoritomo assignees. During this same period
and in the same region Yoritomo's most notorious confederate,
Kajiwara Kagetoki, was dismissed from the shugo posts of Mimasaka and Harima.[24] In short, a new administration was taking steps
to establish its control. Shugo, not jitō titles, were involved.

As noted above, the bakufu's replacement in Harima was Koyama Tomomasa (p.207). This was the first time a dominant Kantō
chieftain became shugo of a province in the west. But even the
exalted status of the Koyama was no guarantee of an ongoing tenure.
For reasons that have not survived, the Harima shugo post was
taken from Tomomasa around 1214 and given to the same Gotō
Motokiyo who fifteen years earlier had been dismissed from Sanuki.[25]
Gotō himself was replaced in 1221 for siding with the court in the
Jōkyū War. The new shugo of Harima was once again Koyama
Tomomasa.[26]

22. Information drawn from several different sources, some unreliable, suggests
a total of eighteen shugo posts distributed among the six sons (Fuzambō, *Kokushi
jiten*, 4:387–89). Corroboration, however, is impossible, and the tenure lengths,
anyway, must have been brief for most provinces.
    23. Satō, *Zōtei-shugo seido*, pp. 59–60, 69–71, 92–93.
    24. *AK* 1200/1/25, and Satō, *Zōtei-shugo seido*, p. 162.
    25. Satō, p. 154.
    26. Ibid., p. 155.

Another of Yoritomo's favorites, Koremune (Shimazu) Tadahisa, had his three Kyushu shugo titles taken from him in 1203 (*AK* 1203/ 9/4). The apparent reason was Tadahisa's implication in an anti-bakufu plot. But the loss in his case was not permanently damaging. While only one of the three posts (Satsuma) was returned, the house of Tadahisa drew most of its authority from titles held within Shimazu Estate, and these had not been affected.[27] With a somewhat different outcome, Tsutsumi (Wakasa) Tadasue, shugo of Wakasa Province, was implicated in the same conspiracy. In his case, not only the shugo post but a number of jitō rights were confiscated. Soon thereafter, however, a gradual return was begun, until his son was confirmed in the original portfolio in 1221. Tadasue himself had just been killed in the Jōkyū War. But the Tsutsumi revival proved only transitory. Toward the end of the 1220s, the son, Tadatoki, was accused of unnamed crimes and divested of most of his titles, including the shugo post. The direct beneficiary was the main line of the Hōjō, which seized the shugo authority and converted it into a hereditary possession.[28]

As the foregoing examples clearly reveal, then, the post-Yoritomo competition for power found much of its expression in the shuffling back and forth of shugo titles.[29] Much as the central elite continued to jockey for control of provincial proprietorships and the like, the warriors of the Kantō now joined in a competition for shugo posts. This parallel is extended when we note that shugo titles, like governorships, did not draw their holders out into the countryside.

27. A list of these titles and a discussion appears in Ishii S. "Kamakura 'shugoryō,' " p. 343.

28. Tanaka, "Wakasa," pp. 258–60. From this point, the Hōjō began to gather up shugo titles at an ever accelerating pace. By period's end they held a full thirty, nearly half the national total (Satō, *Zōtei-shugo seido*, pp. 245–46).

29. On a few occasions the bakufu was forced to make dismissals for shugo malfeasance or incompetence. Such was the case in 1204 when Yamauchi Tsune-toshi, shugo of Iga and Ise, ran from an attack staged by Heishi remnants. Here was a clear default on a taihon sankajō crime. His replacement, Hiraga Tomo-masa, was granted the two posts as recompense for distinguished service against the rebels. But then he too turned rebel, and a year later was executed. At this point the redoubtable Yamauchi petitioned the bakufu for return of his old titles. The request was denied (*AK* 1205/9/20). Also, in 1209, the bakufu complained generally of shugo lack of diligence in carrying out their duties (*AK* 1209/11/20).

Among all the known pre-1221 appointees, only the Mutō decided to seek fame and fortune away from the east. The rest made liberal use of deputies and limited themselves to irregular visits to their appointment provinces.[30]

Nevertheless shugo-holders sought eagerly to convert their titles into hereditary interests. While shugo offices "belonging" to no one were the norm before midcentury, there were some incumbents who began including these titles in testamentary documents. A prime example is that of Naganuma Munemasa, and in his case the presumption proved accurate: from 1221 until the end of the Kamakura period the Awaji shugo title was held continuously by the Naganuma of Shimotsuke.[31] But this unusual experience belied the ever-present threat of confiscation.[32] On the occasion, for example, of the family's 1283 inheritance, the new Naganuma head was made to wait sixteen years before receiving the bakufu's standard confirmatory document. It was a reminder, perhaps, that Kamakura and not the shugo possessed final authority over that post.[33]

The clearest illustration of this nonhereditary quality of the shugo office comes in a 1220s sequence relating to Echizen Province. The shugo post was originally assigned to Shimazu Tadahisa as a reward for service during the Jōkyū War. Six years later, Tadahisa willed it,

30. Even the several shugo who joined the court side in the Jōkyū War gave no indication that they were ready to abandon the east for their appointment areas. Their main objective, it would seem, was to destroy the Hōjō and reorganize the bakufu.

31. *Naganuma Monjo*, 1230/8/13 Naganuma Munemasa yuzurijō, in Aizu-Wakamatsu shi shuppan iinkai, comp., *Aizu-Wakamatsu shi, shiryō hen 1* (Aizu-Wakamatsu, 1967), p. 71.

32. There were only a handful of families who were able to retain shugo posts for the entire Kamakura period: the Hōjō (Izu and Suruga), Sasaki (Ōmi), Chiba (Shimōsa), Oda (Hitachi), and Mutō (Chikuzen). Several other cases are possible, e.g., Koyama (Shimotsuke), Ashikaga (Kazusa), Ōtomo (Bungo), and Sasaki (Oki). The Shimazu held the Satsuma post for all but a year or two during 1203–05 (Satō, *Zōtei-shugo seido*, p. 247).

33. *Onjōji Monjo*, 1299/12/6 shōgun ke mandokoro kudashibumi, in *Aizu-Wakamatsu shi, shiryō hen 1*, p. 76. The actual reason for the delay is unknown but was probably related to the Hōjō's efforts during these years to eliminate many old-line vassals, replacing them with private retainers. The standard treatment of this topic is Satō Shin'ichi, "Kamakura bakufu seiji no senseika ni tsuite," in Takeuchi Rizō, ed., *Nihon hōkensei seiritsu no kenkyū*, pp. 97–136.

along with numerous other holdings, to his son, Tadayoshi, and the bakufu immediately approved this transfer.[34] But Tadayoshi was not destined to be shugo for long. Within seven months of his accession, Gotō Mototsuna, son of the same Motokiyo who had defected in 1221, became the new choice for the Echizen title (*AK* 1228/5/16). Tadahisa's testament, as well as the bakufu's own confirmation, had been rendered invalid. The heritability of shugo posts, in contrast to jitō shiki, remained fragile.

In turning to the kendan portion (murder and rebellion jurisdiction) of the shugo's authority, our initial problem is to come to grips with the divergent arguments of the two dominant scholars in the field, Ishii Ryōsuke and Satō Shin'ichi. The major question for them bears on the inclusiveness of the shugo's kendan privilege, in particular the matter of entrance into immune estates. In a word, Ishii has asserted that shugo could enter such domains, while Satō has denied it. For the one scholar pursuit and capture were the essence of the shugo's kendan right, while for the other it was receipt and punishment of arrested criminals. The two men are able to agree only on the ancillary question of whether this kendan applied to Kamakura vassals, nonvassals, or both. Their conclusion is that the shugo enjoyed no independent authority over housemen, though the bakufu could, when conditions warranted, entrust to shugo any portion of its own disciplinary power over vassals.[35]

A search for uniformity on the entrance question is the source of all the difficulty. This is made clear by Kamakura's own statements about the shugo. What crimes were to be handled, not how, was the only matter ever taken up by bakufu lawmakers. In 1202, for instance, an edict prohibited shugo from becoming involved in provincial administration, adding that violators would be dismissed (*AK* 1202/int.10/15). Twenty years later, Kamakura decreed that

34. *Shimazu Ke Monjo*, 1221/7/12 Kantō gechijō, in *DNK, iewake 16*, 1:13, doc. 16, and 1227/10/10 shōgun ke ando kudashibumi, doc. 27, pp. 18–19.

35. The classic expressions of these positions are Ishii Ryōsuke, "Taihon sankajō—Kamakura jidai no shugo no kengen no kenkyū," *Hōgaku kyōkai zasshi* 69.1 (1951): 1–16, and Satō, *Soshō seido*, pp. 129–65. Only in Kyushu are shugo alleged to have exercised some level of independent jurisdiction (see pp. 221–23).

except for jurisdiction over the ōban recruitment, rebels, and capital criminals, shugo were to take no part in provincial business. Specifically, they were denied any competence over thieves, arsonists, and kidnappers.[36] In 1231, there was a general reiteration of this: aside from the three regular duties, there was to be no involvement in "small matters" (*saisei no zōji*).[37] Finally, in 1232, article three of the Jōei Formulary provided a definitive statement. While inflating the sankajō to include several additional crimes, the statement was carefully restrictive elsewhere. The shugo was not to appoint agents into public units, assess labor services in the domains of either sector, pursue land profits, or use nonhousemen for the ōban.[38] In short, shugo were to adhere closely to the taihon sankajō.

What is significant is that from beginning to end no formula on the entrance question was ever announced—or even contemplated. Actual procedure was simply intended to vary on a case-by-case basis. A definition of shugo duties that begged the entrance question would be the least disruptive. The result was multiformity, as we see in the following examples.

An incident of 1209 involving Usa Shrine lands in Bungo Province shows one kind of procedure. After receiving the matter for adjudication, the bakufu ruled that the full kendan was to lie with the shrine, save only for murder and rebellion cases. In that eventuality, the shugo was to receive the wrongdoers at his office.[39] Here, then, was a shugo kendan authority that began with a criminal's jailing. The shugo's right was one of extradition rather than pursuit, entrance, and arrest.

In other instances, the shugo was allowed to cross an estate's boundaries. This was so, for example, in Iga Province's Nagata Domain. What complicated matters here was the presence of a jitō. Eventually a dispute broke out between this figure and the shugo over the latter's right to enter; each side was clearly seeking an un-

---

36. *Shimpen Tsuika*, nos. 1–3, 1222/4/26, in *CHS*, 1:61.

37. Ibid., no. 31, 1231/5/13, p. 76. Also *AK*, same date.

38. *Goseibai Shikimoku*, art 3, in *CHS*, 1:4–5, 37–38. The crimes added were night attack, robbery, mountain brigandage, and coastal piracy. Whether the court was consulted concerning this infringement of governor powers is not known.

39. *Itōzu Monjo*, 1209/12/6 Kantō migyōsho, in *Ōita ken shiryō*, 1:81, doc. 32.

encumbered kendan privilege. In its 1223 resolution, the bakufu elected to divide this authority along taihon sankajō lines. To the shugo went the right to enter for ōban recruitment and for murder and rebellion cases; to the jito went the remainder.[40] Typically, however, the logic of this settlement was not applied consistently. In a parallel dispute in Aki Province's Miri Estate, the shugo was denied entrance outright; major criminals were to be delivered to him by the jitō.[41]

The examples cited thus far all refer to precedents established from the 1190s on. This suggests something very important. Since the shugo was an entirely new addition to the provincial landscape, it was apparently left to the bakufu to set (or legitimize) all precedents affecting shugo entrance rights. This could lead in virtually any direction, indeed even to authorizations for a competence over non-sankajō crimes. A case in point concerns Nabari Gun in Iga Province, a Tōdaiji holding. Despite the bakufu's own prohibition of 1222 against shugo jurisdiction for kidnappers (note 36), only three years later it authorized the Iga shugo to receive all murderers and kidnappers arrested by Tōdaiji officials. Thus the Iga shugo was denied entrance in pursuit of a sankajō criminal, but granted a post-arrest competence for a non-sankajō lawbreaker. We see in this the meaning of Kamakura's freedom to interpret the scope of any shugo's kendan authority.[42]

It should also be noted that the Iga incumbent, who was here refused the right of entrance into Tōdaiji lands, was the same man who had received such authorization for a different estate just two years earlier (note 40). Clearly, the taihon sankajō was to be variously applied even in neighboring domains. But local custom was not the only determinant of shugo authority. In Harima, for ex-

40. *Shimazu Ke Monjo*, 1223/8/6 Kantō gechijō, in *DNK, iewake 16*, 1:16, doc. 23.

41. *Kumagai Ke Monjo*, 1231/2/13 Kantō gechijō, in *Kumagai ke monjo*, doc. 10, p. 30. The jitō had argued that earlier shugo had been refused entrance.

42. *Tōdaiji Monjo*, 1225/5/3 Kantō migyōsho, in *DNS 5*, 2:630. In another case, murderers and arsonists (the latter also prohibited in 1222) were to be remanded to the shugo of Izumo Province. *Kitajima Monjo*, 1215/7 Izumo shugo gechijō, in *Izumo Kokuzō ke monjo*, doc. 8, p. 8. This directive, however, came from the shugo himself.

ample, the shape of the provincial kendan, the passage of time, and the identity of the shugo-holder were all important considerations.

In 1199, as we recall, Koyama Tomomasa was granted the shugo title along with strict instructions not to abuse his authority. An incident of several years later showed that Kamakura stood ready to back up its regulations: in 1203, it condemned an illegal entrance by shugo agents into a Tōdaiji estate.[43] Other cases of a similar nature followed.[44] But this commitment by the bakufu to a moderate shugo authority was not to continue indefinitely. A sequence of events occurring after the Jōkyū War paved the way for a massive enlargement of that competence. In 1222, the traditional kendan agent for the Harima governorship, a houseman named Nakahara Nyoimaru, received a confirmatory decree from the bakufu concerning his police authority. In the words of this decree, "Is it not a precedent that the punishment responsibility (*hangai sata*) be exercised [by the Nakahara] without public–private (*shōkō*) distinction?"[45] The significance of this must be understood retrospectively. According to a record from the next century, the 1222 confirmation had the desired effect of ending the civil governor's right to interfere with the Nakahara kendan. But having accomplished that, it also allowed for a transfer of these privileges to a shugo. As described in 1324, the original kendan holders (the Nakahara) exercised that authority only during the brief periods between shugo incumbencies.[46]

The true import of this is revealed when we note that it was the Hōjō who eventually became shugo of Harima. For the bakufu's leading family, it involved no great difficulty to compromise the traditional interests of a western province vassal.[47] The result was a Hōjō kendan right entirely free from the shugo's regular limitations;

43. *Zatsu Komonjo*, 1203/5/17 shōgun ke mandokoro kudashibumi, in Kobayashi Takeshi, ed., *Shunjōbō Chōgen shiryō shūsei* (Tokyo, 1965), p. 455.

44. E.g., bakufu rebukes of 1214 and 1216 (Satō, *Zōtei-shugo seido*, p. 154).

45. *Mibu Monjo*, 1222/2/8 Rokuhara gechijō, in *DNS* 5, 1:486. The immediate inducement was interference in the kendan by newly appointed post-Jōkyū jitō.

46. *Hiromine Jinja Monjo*, 1324/12/21 Kantō gechijō, in *KBSS*, 1:375–76, doc. 302.

47. When this shift in favor of the shugo took place is not known. Nor is it clear exactly when the Hōjō became shugo. Satō suggests the 1270s (*Zōtei-shugo seido*, pp. 155–56).

the taihon sankajō had been rendered obsolete. In practice, this permitted incidents such as the following. In 1286, the shugo office was ordered to suppress warrior outrages taking place in a certain local temple's lands.[48] No sankajō crime was involved, and the question of entrance does not seem to have come up. With the regular governorship no longer involved in provincial enforcement, the shugo simply assumed total jurisdiction.[49]

The example of Harima has suggested a gradual coalescence under the bakufu of the pre-Kamakura kendan authority of the Nakahara and the post-1190s taihon sankajō. The drift was thus clearly in the direction of an expanding range of activities ascribed to the shugo. In other instances, something quite different occurred. In Izumi near the capital, for example, there is evidence of a shugo authority that had been broken down and divided between the In (the kendan portion) and the untitled son of a deceased shugo (the ōban authority). The case is interesting, and is worth looking at. After the death of Sahara Yoshimura in 1203, his shugo posts over Izumi and Kii provinces were not granted anew. Instead, the normal sankajō (kendan) profits were awarded to the imperial house to meet pilgrimage costs to Kumano Shrine, while the ōban recruitment duty for Izumi was assigned to Morimura, the former shugo's son. For the time being Izumi and Kii had no shugo.[50]

The expendability of the shugo's kendan privilege is what immediately strikes us. There is no satisfying explanation. Both Izumi and Kii had high concentrations of shōen, and the former province, with its central locale, was probably reasonably well governed. Kii, on the other hand, was a region of frequent instability; its selection can only be due to Kumano Shrine's location there. When we turn to Morimura's special ōban assignment, entirely different problems were involved. Unlike the kendan, the guard duty could not readily

48. *Taizanji Monjo*, 1286/int.12/25 Rokuhara migyōsho, in Uchiyama Jōshin, comp., *Taizanji monjo* (Hyōgo, 1935), doc. 8, p. 8.

49. This does not mean that the shugo was now free to enter all domains. Shōen immunity still mattered, though presumably the question of delivery of criminals had come to include more than "murderers and rebels." Only in unencumbered areas (e.g., "public land") would the shugo's kendan authority have been close to complete. In the event of a jitō's presence, special accommodations were probably required.

50. Satō, *Zōtei-shugo seido*, p. 8.

be eliminated: its performance served as Kamakura's major control over western province vassals. Thus, in 1207, when it fell to Izumi to provide the ōban contingent, Morimura was given an emergency commission. He was not, however, appointed shugo since at that time in Izumi Kamakura held no constabulary powers. Not until the bakufu had retrieved the kendan in 1221 would Izumi and Kii again have a shugo.[51]

In another central province, Yamato, the formal kendan authority remained from first to last with the great Kōfukuji Temple of Nara. Consequently, there was no shugo.[52] This did not mean, however, that Kamakura's influence was entirely unfelt in Yamato. In fact, rather numerous bakufu-issued documents relate to that province. In a directive of 1225, for instance, the bakufu ordered its Rokuhara office to investigate on reports of outrages committed against lands belonging to Kasuga Shrine.[53] As we shall note shortly, gathering information in advance of a Kamakura judicial settlement was a common shugo responsibility. It seems clear, therefore, that in the absence of a Yamato Province shugo, Rokuhara itself performed this task. While Kōfukuji may have held the formal authority and received most of the kendan-related profits, it was the bakufu that exercised at least a portion of the actual kendan responsibility.

In the provinces of eastern Japan, Kamakura's easy access to the

51. This raises the question of whether non-shugo served as ōban commanders in other provinces. The answer is probably yes, since shugo were not appointed on a consistent basis everywhere. In Settsu, for example, no reference to a pre-1221 shugo has ever been found (ibid., p. 19). Nevertheless, seven years earlier a Settsu Province houseman appealed to Kamakura for an ōban exemption. This suggests that Settsu did send an ōban contingent, presumably under a special assignee. *Tōji Monjo*, 1214/11/4 Kantō migyōsho an, in Toyonaka shishi hensan iinkai, comp., *Toyonaka shishi, shiryō hen 1*, (Toyonaka, 1960), doc. 26, p. 17.

52. In an undated fourteenth-century document we see the statement: "In the province of Yamato there is no shugo. In imitation of a shugo, priest officials exercise the kendan. . . ." *Saidaiji Monjo*, Saidaiji so sōjō, in *Yamato komonjo juei*, doc. 101, p. 93, 11. 6-7. Also, Satō, *Zōtei-shugo seido*, p. 11. In a document of 1298, however, there is a reference to "shugo deputies" and jitō committing outrages against Saidaiji and the latter's branch temples. Unfortunately, it is not made clear whether Yamato Province itself is meant here. *Saidaiji Monjo*, 1298/9/9 Rokuhara gechijō an, in *Yamato komonjo juei*, doc. 93, p. 83.

53. *Kasuga Jinja Monjo*, 1225/5/2 Kantō migyōsho, in *Kasuga Jinja monjo*, 1:380–81, doc. 338.

total kendan authority tended to reduce the institutional importance of the different shugo there. This was especially true for shugo whose kendan-related activities pre-dated the bakufu's formation. For this group the grant of a shugo title was little more than a confirmation of a much larger public governance; the sankajō-defined kendan right was entirely superfluous. The ōban recruitment duty was extraneous also, though for a different reason. In most provinces of the east, vassal families were in direct communication with the bakufu and performed the ōban service at its immediate behest. The shugo may have led the contingent to Kyoto, but that was all.[54] A major result of this minimal importance for eastern shugo was the post's dispensability. Musashi never had a shugo, and Sagami had its shugo office permanently abolished after 1247.[55]

In most of the Kantō, then, shugo based their kendan authorities less on the taihon sankajō than on a unitary command over the provincial office. Only in Hitachi was the pattern substantially different. In that province there was a shugo in possession of the normal sankajō complement, and a traditional kendan shiki-holder who was also a Kamakura houseman. This reminds us of Harima, although in the present instance conditions remained unchanged for the duration of the Kamakura period. Thus the shugo executed rebels, suppressed outlaw bands (*akutō*), and enforced gambling prohibitions,[56] while the kendan-holder continued to exercise his regular authority. As late as 1331 we find a Hitachi governor decree confirming Saisho Ienari in his family's hereditary post.[57] Other documents reveal that the agency issuing this edict, the provincial office, was entirely controlled by the bakufu.[58] Its continued involvement in provincial

54. A case in point is the bakufu's direct order to the Fukabori of Kazusa to follow the Ashikaga shugo house to the capital. See n. 15.

55. In Musashi the regular provincial governor, who was always a Hōjō, exercised full authority throughout; while in Sagami, the bakufu's ouster of the Miura house was followed by a subsuming of the shugo competence under an organ of the bakufu itself (Satō, *Zōtei-shugo seido*, pp. 59–65).

56. *AK* 1203/5/25, 1248/4/30, and 1250/11/28. The latter two were made regular shugo duties in the mid-thirteenth century.

57. *Saisho Monjo*, 1331/3 chōsen an, in *Ibaragi ken komonjo shūsei, 2, Saisho monjo*, doc. 10, p. 39. A document of 1302, referring to Saisho performance of both the Kyoto and Kamakura ōban services, confirms the family's status as bakufu housemen. Ibid., 1302/6/13 wayojō, doc. 6, pp. 35–36.

58. E.g., ibid., 1239/3 rusudokoro kudashibumi, doc. 2, pp. 24–25.

affairs was doubtless due to its reliability as an instrument of Kamakura policy.

The shugo, in his capacity as agent of the bakufu's judicial authority, held an important responsibility entirely separate from his own kendan jurisdiction. As we will see, shugo were consistently involved in investigating allegations of lawlessness and collecting local depositions. On occasion they also issued "lower court" judgment decrees.

As with so much else concerning the shugo, the extent of judicial involvement was a function of the bakufu's wish on any particular matter. In a case of 1225, for instance, the bakufu ordered the shugo office in Tosa to summon both sides in a dispute and to forward the interrogation results and all relevant documents. The dispute itself concerned a vassal's claim that a nonhouseman had violated a local kumon post, presumably in some relation to the plaintiff.[59] We see no hint in this of the shugo's regular sankajō authority. Instead, the Tosa shugo headquarters was performing as a kind of bakufu detached office: facts would be gathered in advance of Kamakura's actual hearing of the case.

An incident of 1205 shows the Izumo Province shugo engaged at another stage in the judicial process. In this complex episode, the Izumo Grand Shrine had brought charges against a jitō deputy, whereupon the bakufu had questioned his superior, who was a Kantō resident. The jitō's defense had considerable weight behind it, leaving the bakufu uncertain as to how it should dispose of the matter. At this point Kamakura called on the Izumo shugo to investigate all local particulars and prohibit outrages.[60] The bakufu had thus transferred jurisdiction to the shugo, but had not given him much leeway. Within the framework of the status quo he was to order the cessation of violence. What remains unclear is whether the shugo now possessed a right of enforcement. This might have involved him in forcibly suppressing non-sankajō crimes.

The Tosa and Izumo examples show shugo in pre- and post-judgment phases of bakufu adjudication. In still other cases, a shugo was

59. *Maeda Ke Shozō Monjo*, 1225/12/15 Kantō migyōsho, in *DNS* 5, 2:917.
60. *Kitajima Monjo*, 1205/4/22 Kantō migyōsho, in *Shinshū Shimane kenshi, shiryō hen 1*, p. 252.

involved at several stages, sometimes from beginning to end. An instance of this occurred in Shinano Province in 1229. The matter itself was not of great consequence—the theft of hawks from a mountainside—but the difficulties encountered in settling the case raise interesting questions. At the start the bakufu had asked the shugo to resolve the matter, but the latter's deputy had been unsuccessful in forcing one of the disputants, a houseman, to produce the leader of the thieves. Arguments were presented at the shugo's headquarters, but without this key witness the deputy was unable to reach a judgment. Through the actual shugo, he appealed that Kamakura reassume jurisdiction.[61] At this point, the bakufu turned the matter back to the shugo, who for his part ordered the deputy to resolve the dispute once and for all. He directed that the thieves be immediately summoned and that their lawless acts be abolished.[62] Events had traveled full circle with the incident still unsettled.[63]

A logical next question is whether there were any shugo who exercised an independent judicial right over housemen. A standard theory has long maintained that the shugo of Kyushu (not elsewhere) did enjoy such an authority. But we must be very careful here: the few extant shugo judgment decrees suggest a power that was both irregular and derivative of the bakufu. A clear view of this emerges in a 1229 Hizen shugo settlement of a Kamakura vassal's inheritance dispute. Our attention is drawn to a postscript, which can be summarized as follows: while aware that the bakufu held jurisdiction in the matter, the shugo had been forced by events to intervene. Should there be any dissatisfaction, however, the disputants might take their case directly to Kamakura.[64] The fortuitous presence in Kyushu of the Mutō shugo himself undoubtedly facilitated this development. Even at that, the shugo's responsibility was merely one of a lower court.

61. *Ichikawa Monjo*, 1229/11/28 Saemon no jō Kanemasa shojō, in *Shinano shiryō*, 4:25–26.

62. Ibid., 1229/12/13 shugo Hōjō Shigetoki migyōsho, pp. 27/28.

63. There is a reference in the 11/28 document to the interrogation's being held in the "administrative office" (mandokoro) of the local shugo headquarters. This suggests a considerable degree of organization, though to obviously little effect.

64. *Isshi Monjo*, 1229/12/23 Hizen shugosho gechijō, in *Hirado Matsuura ke shiryō*, pp. 146–48.

An Ōsumi Province shugo decree of several decades later appears to make the leap to full judicial independence. Unlike the Mutō example above, there is no reference to a right of appeal. However, in this case the shugo's decision was no more than a confirmation of a compromise agreement worked out between the disputants. Any continuation of trouble would almost certainly have found its way into a bakufu courtroom.[65] But our strongest proof of the incidental quality of shugo judicial rights derives from the statistical record. The Ōsumi shugo post was held in heredity by the Hōjō, yet for the remainder of the period we find only one additional settlement decree issuing from that office.[66] This compares with more than 400 bakufu judgment edicts relating to Kyushu as a whole.[67]

At least two cases can be cited of shugo deputies (*shugodai*) affixing their names to judicial settlement decrees. In Izumi Province in central Japan a shugodai resolved a dispute centering on allegations of peasant encroachment on a certain houseman's lands.[68] In Kyushu's Satsuma Province, the dispute involved conflicting claims by two housemen.[69] But here also it is difficult to argue for judicial independence. The number of cases is too few, and shugodai anyway were not immune from direct bakufu influence. Not only did Kamakura regularly address edicts to shugodai,[70] but there is even some indication of bakufu rewards to these deputies.[71] On the other hand, the use of deputies, as with jitō, clearly led to abuses and probably reduced the overall effectiveness of the shugo program. In some instances, the shugo himself spent so little time in his

65. *Nejime Monjo*, 1258/10/18 Ōsumi shugo Nagoe (Hōjō) Tokiaki gechijō, in Kawazoe Shōji, comp., *Nejime monjo* (Fukuoka, 1955), 1:48–49, doc. 62.

66. Ibid., 1305/12/3 Ōsumi shugo Hōjō Tokinao gechijō, doc. 138, p. 102.

67. *KBSS*, vols. 1 and 2. A convenient listing of all known Kyushu-related Kamakura period documents is Seno Seiichirō, ed., *Kyūshū chihō chūsei hennen monjo mokuroku* (Fukuoka, 1966).

68. *Matsuodera Monjo*, 1276/6/20 Izumi shugodai gechijō in *Izumi Matsuodera monjo*, doc. 5, p. 11. The shugo of Izumi at this time was a Hōjō (Satō, *Zōtei-shugo seido*, p. 18).

69. *Hishijima Monjo*, 1312/9/10 Satsuma shugodai gechijō, in *Sappan*, 8:94–95, doc. 774.

70. E.g., *Tōdaiji Monjo*, 1225/5/3 Kantō migyōsho, in *DNS* 5, 2:630. This was an order to the Iga Province shugodai regarding an investigation of alleged criminal acts.

71. E.g., *AK* 1246/3/18, in which the Sanuki shugodai is rewarded for capturing coastal pirates.

province that the deputy was regarded locally as the actual shugo.[72] In other cases, a shugodai guilty of some crime proved difficult to dislodge.[73]

We can approach the problem of shugo justice in one final way— by briefly noting the fragile nature of shugo competence over murderers and rebels. The bakufu could, and often did, compromise even this minimal definition of shugo authority. Generally, this resulted from proprietors taking their appeals in sankajō cases directly to Kamakura. Since the shugo's decisions promised little finality, they were commonly bypassed. We see this in incidents of 1221 and 1247. In the former, a murder case in Higo was accepted for adjudication without the shugo's name ever being mentioned.[74] In the latter, even the investigation of a slashing incident was not entrusted to this officer. A special bakufu agent (*monchū bugyōnin*) was sent to distant Satsuma to inquire into the matter.[75]

Aside from implementation of the periodic ōban responsibility, the thirteenth-century shugo enjoyed a number of other opportunities for contact with Kamakura housemen. On the few occasions when military forces had to be raised, shugo (especially those in the west) were expected to serve as commanders.[76] Also, as we have just

72. And hence scholars today cannot always determine which of two figures was the shugo and which only the deputy. E.g., Satō, *Zōtei-shugo seido*, pp. 145–46.

73. This is what happened in Ōmi where repeated subpoenas to the shugodai of Asai District went unheeded. See *Chikubujima Monjo*, 1285/2/24 Rokuhara migyōsho, in Higashi Asai kyōikukai, comp., *Higashi Asai gunshi,* (1927), 4:195. Dismissals, however, would probably have had to go through the shugo.

74. *Asō Monjo*, 1221/1/18 Kibara Sanezumi keijōan, in *DNS* 5, 1:416. For another Kyushu murder case tried in Kamakura see *Ibusuki Monjo*, 1235/8/28 Kantō gechijō, in *Sappan*, 2:206–07, doc. 232.

75. *Nitta Jinja Monjo*, 1247/10/25 Kantō gechijō, in Kagoshima kenritsu toshokan, comp., *Satsuma no kuni Nitta Jinja monjo* (Kagoshima, 1960), doc. 71, pp. 23–25.

76. Actually, very little is known about the military organization of Japan's first warrior government. This is partly the result of the infrequency of war during the Kamakura period. But it is also due to the bakufu's apparent utilization of a variety of organizational techniques. In the east, the pride of individual vassal houses had to be taken into account; service as extended family units under a loose regional, as opposed to shugo, command may have been common (Satō, *Zōtei-shugo seido*, pp. 255 ff.).

seen, when information had to be gathered prior to bakufu settlement of a lawsuit, vassal litigants might be summoned to answer questions before the shugo. On still other occasions, the shugo, at bakufu behest, might actually have cause to issue documents confirming the personal status and/or shiki holdings of a houseman. An episode of 1221 clearly suggests the agential quality of this act. In the wake of the Jōkyū War, a certain Kamakura vassal of Mino Province appealed to the bakufu for a decree that would establish his gesu post in heredity.[77] The bakufu's leading figure, Hōjō Yoshitoki, passed this request on to the Mino shugo, commenting that the appellant had served loyally in the recent fighting and should have his petition granted, if justified. The shugo examined the relevant documents and issued the confirmatory decree.[78] Victory in the Jōkyū War had burdened the bakufu with a vast number of similar appeals. Lacking reliable information on persons presenting their claims, it was natural that Kamakura should have turned part of this task over to shugo.

Such involvement in the fate of a bakufu vassal takes on a somewhat different expression in a Tosa Province case of 1226. In response to an inquiry from Kamakura, the shugo, Miura Yoshimura, had his agent seek out a man who was challenging a jitō on some point. Through the shugo's efforts the challenger eventually issued a statement explaining his position. Thereupon, Yoshimura issued an endorsement of the jitō, as the latter took his appeal to Rokuhara.[79] The intermediary role of the shugo is once again revealed.

While the Mino and Tosa investigations ended happily for the bakufu housemen involved, this was not always the case. The truth is that few shugo were able to line up consistently with local housemen in an effort to create a provincial band. All too often they were called on to engage in disagreeable tasks, such as taking charge of an inquiry antecedent to the dispossession of Kamakura vassals. A case in point involved the newly assigned shugo of Izumi in 1222.

77. As we saw in chap. 5, gesu posts normally remained under a central owner's discretionary authority. But we also noted that the traditional jitō–gesu cleavage was upset by the Jōkyū upheaval.
78. *Chōzenji Monjo*, 1221/7 Mino shugo kudashibumi, in *Gifu kenshi, shiryō hen, kodai-chūsei* 1:767
79. *Kasokabe Ke Den Shōmon*, 1226/9/22 Miura Yoshimura shojō, in Maeda Kazuo, ed., *Kasokabe shiryō* (Kōchi, 1964), doc. 8, p. 146.

The investigation he conducted proved that lands recently receiving a cluster of post-Jōkyū jitō were traditionally exempt areas. The appointments were overturned.[80]

Perhaps the most frequent shugo activity in this middleman capacity was his issuance of so-called "enforcement decrees" (*shigyōjō*). Such documents would be drawn up and served by a shugo following the bakufu's appointment (or confirmation) of a jitō shiki. For example, one month after a Shinano Province jitō award, the shugo issued his shigyōjō.[81] This practice was even carried at times to the level of shugo deputies. On 1265/8/22 the bakufu issued a standard confirmatory edict after a jitō's inheritance in Izumo Province. Two weeks later, the Izumo shugo followed with a shigyōjō. In the spring of the next year the two shugodai added their own "approvals."[82]

It is important to note that the issuance of these documents never became an essential part of the jitō system. Suits, for example, might be won or lost depending on possession of the appropriate bakufu, central owner, testamentary—or even peasant—records; one searches in vain for shugo shigyōjō. By making such documents essentially extraneous to the legalization of jitō shiki, shugo were denied thereby a potential form of leverage. Edicts from Kamakura shugo were only reflections of decrees (or directives) handed down by the bakufu itself.[83]

Until recently all scholars were in agreement that land perquisites did not accompany shugo titles. A statement by Satō Shin'ichi is representative:

80. *Kumeidadera Monjo*, 1248/12/5 Kantō gechijō, in *Izumi Kumeidadera monjo*, doc. 2, p. 12.
81. *Moriya Monjo*, 1246/11/7 shōgun ke kudashibumi, and 1246/12/19 Shinano shugo shigyōjō, in *Shinano shiryō*, 4:125–26.
82. *Kitajima Monjo*, 1265/8/22 Kantō gechijō, 1265/9/6 Izumo shugo shigyōjō, 1266/5/24 Izumo shugodai jungyōjō, in *Izumo Kokuzō ke monjo*, docs. 22–24, pp. 72–73.
83. It is in this sense that Paul Varley has spoken of the bureaucratic nature of the Kamakura shugo. H. Paul Varley, *The Onin War* (New York, 1967), pp. 10–11. During the Mongol War crisis, shugo commonly issued documents (*fukkanjō*) acknowledging the services of housemen and nonhousemen alike. But these records were readily dismissed in Kamakura court proceedings, e.g., *Nitta Jinja Monjo*, 1289/4/7 Kantō gechijō, in *Satsuma no kuni Nitta Jinja monjo*, p. 10.

The so-called shugo lands [*ryō*] were not landholdings that had been included from the outset under a shugo shiki. It may be thought that these were lands that the shugo had confiscated by exercise of his kendan authority, or lands granted afterward by the bakufu.[84]

Ishii Susumu has questioned this standard view in an essay of 1968. Not only did shugo lands exist in great quantity, he argues, but these were often legitimate "office lands" whose administration and profits remanded to new shugo as part of their appointment packages.[85] The position adopted here is closer to the more conservative line: while admitting that shugo commonly held jitō and other shiki, a serious question arises as to whether these titles and their income were identified with the shugo post itself.

The strongest support for the Ishii argument comes from a bakufu record of 1235. This document did two things: it assigned the Aki shugo post along with other titles to a new incumbent, and ordered that the precedents of a pre-1221 shugo-holder—the Sō—be obeyed.[86] To understand the significance of this we must sketch in some of the background. We will recall from chapter 4 that the Heishi had exercised a dominant authority in Aki through the instrumentality of their chief vassal, Saeki Kagehiro. This meant that when the Taira were defeated, the bakufu claimed all Saeki interests as "Heike-confiscated lands." The resulting portfolio was divided in the 1190s between the Sō family as shugo and another vassal house, the Nakahara. Finally, in 1235, the Nakahara heir himself became shugo and assumed title to the entire package.

It is obvious from the foregoing that many of the perquisites cited by Ishii as "*shugoryō*" were in fact shiki held by the Nakahara before acceding to the shugo title. The reverse phenomenon could also occur: a family might continue to hold various titles after leaving a shugo post. Wakasa Tadatoki, for example, did not surrender his entire land portfolio after ceasing to be shugo.[87] This raises an important question. To the extent that such shiki were not "shugo

---

84. Satō, *Zōtei-shugo seido*, p. 248.

85. Ishii S., "Kamakura 'shugoryō,' " pp. 309 ff.

86. *Itsukushima Jinja Monjo*, 1235/6/5 Kantō gechijō, first quoted in Ishii S., "Aki," p. 2.

87. Tanaka, "Wakasa," p. 258.

lands" either before or after a shugo incumbency, how accurate is it to call them so even during the incumbency? Because of the arbitrary way the bakufu could package a shugo assignment, is it fair to say that regular income components actually attended the shugo office?

A comparison with the jitō on this point will be instructive. Once the precedents of a jitō shiki had been settled on, no changes were permitted in either function or income level. Thus, in the event of a jitō dismissal, the new appointee was expected to continue the income and duty practices of his predecessor. The condition of the shugo was very different: he began his tenure enjoying perquisites that could expand or contract without affecting the nature of his post. Shugo lands in this sense were extrinsic; the office was not a shiki. It is for this reason that shugo appointment decrees are evidently so scarce. Since the awarding of this title only rarely involved the direct assignment of land rights, documentation, the sine qua non of shiki holding, would not normally have been required.[88] A related observation concerns the shugo's absence from a context so common for jitō: shugo did not go into court to complain of insufficient salary lands or office perquisites. The shugo may have been plaintiff at times in legal actions, but the objects of his efforts were jitō shiki, not shugoryō.[89]

A final perspective on the shugo emerges when we compare him to an equivalent figure outside Japen. The obvious choice is the

---

88. Thus, the very few shugo appointment decrees we do find all include appointments to one or more jitō shiki. Documentation was in behalf of the latter, not the former. E.g., *Minagawa Monjo*, 1221/6/25 Kantō gechijō, in *Toyonaka shishi, shiryō hen 1*, doc. 30, p. 18.

89. And hence the extreme rarity of any designation implying "shugo lands." In fact, I have found only three such references, all in provinces (Ise and Nagato) where the Hōjō possessed a hereditary shugo post: (1) *Kanazawa Bunko Komonjo*, 1278/12/25 Rokuhara gechijō, in Seki Yasushi, comp., *Kanazawa bunko komonjo* (Yokohama, 1937), 1:7, doc. 6 (a worm-eaten fragment in which a certain Kunikage was granted "shugoryō"); (2) ibid., 1314/8/27 Rokuhara gechijō, doc. 30, p. 34 (refers to a jitō deputy in shugoryō); and (3) *Iminomiya Jinja Monjo*, 1326/3/20 Kantō migyōsho, in Nishioka Toranosuke. *Shōen shi shiryō* (Tokyo, n.d.), p. 36 (refers to a shugo land share [*shugo no bunryō*] within a shōen). I have seen no references at all to shugo *tokubun*, the regular term for "income."

ninth-century European count.[90] Within the framework of a developing feudalism, shugo and count played roughly similar roles: each was the highest provincial officer under his regime, and each was linked to his chief through the bond of vassalage. However, the count enjoyed better prospects. Not only were dispossessions by the king less easily managed than in post-Yoritomo Japan, but the Carolingian government showed none of the bakufu's steadfastness in refusing to appoint native officers. Counts were often local lords in their own right, while shugo tended to be absentee figures highly dependent on Kamakura's patronage. The major result is that counts tended toward independence at a pace and scale far exceeding that of shugo. The political system fragmented faster in Europe because its officers found it easier to convert themselves into territorial magnates. By contrast, in Japan the accumulation of shugo posts by the Hōjō after 1250 indicates that the slow movement toward disintegration took place on a level other than that of the shugo and the province.[91]

In conclusion, there were two conditions above all that kept the Kamakura shugo in check. First was the less advanced state of provincial government decay in Japan as opposed to Europe. While counts in the ninth century (often as natives in their appointment areas) were not obliged to share authority with some still-viable officer of the old empire, central and western province shugo remained limited police captains and Kamakura surrogates for more than a hundred years. The shugo emerged as a key figure in the court–bakufu dual polity. The second circumstance relates to the institutional mechanisms for controlling shugo. The bakufu was never in competition with these officers and was able to sustain the taihon sankajō as a working definition for autonomous shugo duties. At the same time, Kamakura kept alive its threat of dispossession and refused for 150 years to appoint non-Kantō shugo. The final bakufu control was a refusal to identify the post with landholding. Shugo incumbents were denied the right to parcel out anything more than deputyships.

90. Material on the count is drawn from two studies: Heinrich Fichtenau, *The Carolingian Empire* (New York, 1964); and F. L. Ganshof, *Frankish Institutions under Charlemagne* (New York, 1970).
91. Too little is known of what the Hōjō did with their growing shugo monopoly. This distortion of the original shugo concept requires separate treatment.

It has been said of the ninth century in Europe that "the office of count worked badly from the king's point of view."[92] Perhaps the clearest measure of the Kamakura shugo is that he seems to have held an office of precisely the opposite character. Far from hastening the collapse into feudal anarchy, the thirteenth-century shugo was one of the major props for the bakufu in the latter's continuing effort to hold Japanese society together.

92. Fichtenau, *The Carolingian Empire*, p. 107.

GLOSSARY

akutō 悪党
an 案
ando 安堵
atsujō 圧状
azukari dokoro 預所
bakufu 幕府
benzaishi 弁済使
bettō 別当
buninjō 補任状
bushi 武士
bushidan 武士団
chigyō 知行
chigyōkoku 知行国
chigyōkokushu 知行国主
Chinzei bugyō 鎮西奉行
chishi 地子
chō 牒
chō 町
chōfu 徴符
chōsen 庁宣
chūnagon 中納言
chūshinjō 注進状
dainagon 大納言
dajōdaijin 太政大臣
dajōkan 太政官
dazaifu 太宰府
denpata 田畑
fudai 譜代
fugen 浮言
fukkanjō 覆勘状
gechijō 下知状
gedai 外題

gejō 下状
geppō 月俸
gesu 下司
gō 郷
goke'nin 御家人
gōmu 郷務
gon 権
gonjōjō 言上状
gōshi 郷司
gumpei 軍兵
gun 郡
gunji 郡司
haibunjō 配分状
heishi 兵士
ho 保
hompo jitō 本補地頭
honjo 本所
honke 本家
honryō ando 本領安堵
hontaku ando 本宅安堵
hōō 法皇
hoshi 保使
hōsho 奉書
hyakushō 百姓
hyōranmai 兵乱米
hyōrōmai 兵粮米
ichinomiya 一宮
In 院
In-no-chō 院庁
inzen 院宣
jikkenshi 実検使
jinushi 地主

231

jitō 地頭
jitōdai 地頭代
jitōnin 地頭人
jitō ni nozomu 地頭に臨む
jitōsho 地頭所
jungyōjō 遵行状
jūnin 住人
junkenshi 巡見使
kachōmai 加徴米
kaihotsu ryōshu 開発領主
kajishi 加地子
kami 守
kammon 貫文
kampei 官平
kan 貫
kannōshi 勧農使
kannushi 神主
kebiishi 検非違使
keijō 契状
kemmon seika 権門勢家
kenchū mokuroku 検注目録
kendan 検断
kengen 権限
ke'nin 家人
ke'nin bugyōnin 家人奉行人
kenzan 見参
kirokujo 記録所
kishinjō 寄進状
kishōmon 起請文
koku 石
kokuga 国衙
kokugaryō 国衙領
kokumu 国務
kokushi 国司
kokuyaku 国役
kondei 健児
kōri 郡
kudashibumi 下文
kuge 公家
kugen 公験
kugyō 公卿

kuji 公事
kumon 公文
kumonjo 公文所
kuni 国
kyō 卿
kyūdenpata 給田畑
kyūhata 給畑
mandokoro 政所
migyōsho 御教書
mikuriya 御厨
miuchi 御内
mokkanryo 没官領
mokudai 目代
monchū bugyōnin 問注奉行人
monchūjo 問注所
mōshijō 申状
muhon 謀叛
myō 名
myōshu 名主
nengu 年貢
ōbanyaku 大番役
okibumi 置文
ōryōshi 押領使
Ōshū sōbugyō 奥州惣奉行
otsukai 御使
ranso 濫訴
rensho 連署
rimu 吏務
rinji 綸旨
rōjū 郎従
Rokuhara tandai 六波羅探題
rōnin 浪人
rōtō 郎等
rōzeki 狼藉
rusudokoro 留守所
rusu shiki 留守職
ryō 領
ryōji 令旨
ryōke 領家
ryōshu 領主
saisho 税所

samurai dokoro 侍所
sangi 参議
saribumi 避文
sata 沙汰
seibaijō 成敗状
sei i tai shōgun 征夷大将軍
sesshō 摂政
shigyōjō 施行状
shiki 職
shimpo jitō 新補地頭
shin'on 新恩
shinshi 進止
shintai ryōshō 進退領掌
shiryō 私領
shitaji chūbun 下地中分
shitsuji 執事
shobunjō 処分状
shōen 荘園
shōji 荘司
shōjitō 小地頭
shōkan 荘官
shōkō 庄公
shoryō 所領
shoshiki 諸職
shotō 所当
shugo 守護
shugodai 守護代
shugonin 守護人
shugoryō 守護領
shugosho 守護所
sōbugyō 総奉行
sōgesu 総下司
sōhei 僧兵
sōjitō 総地頭

sojō 訴状
sōkan 惣管
sōryō 惣領
sōtsuibushi 総追捕使
suke 介
tadokoro 田所
taihon sankajō 大犯三箇条
tan 段
to 斗
tō 党
tōgoku 東国
tokubun 得分
tozama 外様
tsuibushi 追捕使
tsuitōshi 追討使
tsukuda 佃
ukebumi 請文
ukesho 請所
ureijō 愁状
watashijō 渡状
wayo 和与
wayojō 和与状
yashiki 屋敷
yose-gōri 寄郡
yōto 用途
yūshi 勇士
yuzurijō 譲状
zaichō 在庁
zaichōkanjin 在庁官人
zaike 在家
zasshō 雑掌
zokuto 賊徒
zōshiki 雑色
zuryō 受領

BIBLIOGRAPHY

Documents, Chronicles, and Diaries

Aizu-Wakamatsu shi, shiryō hen 1 会津若松史, 史料篇. Compiled by Aizu-Wakamatsu shi shuppan iinkai 会津若松史出版委員会. Aizu-Wakamatsu, 1967.

Aokata monjo 青方文書. Compiled by Seno Seiichirō 瀬野精一郎. Kyūshū shiryō sōsho, 10 九州史料叢書. 2 vols. Fukuoka, 1957.

Azuma kagami 吾妻鏡. Shintei zōho kokushi taikei 新訂増補国史大系. 4 vols. Tokyo, 1968.

Azuma kagami Edited by Ryō Susumu 竜粛. Iwanami bunko series 岩波文庫. 5 vols. Tokyo, 1939–44.

Azuma kagami hyōchū 吾妻鏡標註. Edited by Hotta Shōzō 掘田璋左右. 2 vols. Tokyo, 1943.

Buke myōmoku shō 武家名目抄. Shintei zōho kojitsu sōsho, 13 新訂増補故実叢書. Tokyo, 1955.

Chiba ken shiryō, chūsei hen, Katori monjo 千葉県史料, 中世篇, 香取文書. Compiled by Chiba ken 千葉県. Chiba, 1968.

Chūsei hōsei shiryōshū 中世法制史料集. Compiled by Satō Shin'ichi 佐藤進一 and Ikeuchi Yoshisuke 池内義資. 3 vols. Tokyo, 1969.

Dai Nihon komonjo, iewake 1, Kōyasan monjo 大日本古文書, 家わけ 1, 高野山文書. Compiled by Tōkyō daigaku shiryō hensanjo 東京大学史料編纂所. 8 vols. Tokyo, 1968.

————, *iewake 4, Iwashimizu monjo* 石清水文書. 6 vols. Tokyo, 1968.

————, *iewake 5, Sagara ke monjo* 相良家文書. 2 vols. Tokyo, 1970.

————, *iewake 7, Kongōji monjo* 金剛寺文書. 1 vol. Tokyo, 1970.

————, *iewake 11, Kobayagawa ke monjo* 小早川家文書. 2 vols. Tokyo, 1971.

————, *iewake 16, Shimazu ke monjo* 島津家文書. 3 vols. Tokyo, 1971.

————, *iewake 19, Daigoji monjo* 醍醐寺文書. 6 vols. Tokyo, 1972.

Dai Nihon shiryō, series 4 and 5 大日本史料. Compiled by Tōkyō daigaku shiryō hensanjo. 17 and 23 vols. Tokyo, 1968–.

Dazaifu-Dazaifu Tenmangū shiryō 大宰府-大宰府天満宮史料. Compiled

by Takeuchi Rizō 竹内理三. 8 vols. Dazaifu, 1964–.

Documents of Iriki. Compiled by Asakawa Kan'ichi. Tokyo, 1955.

Ehime ken hennen shi 愛媛県編年史. Compiled by Ehime kenshi hensan iinkai 愛媛県史編纂委員会. 6 vols. Matsuyama, 1963–69.

Etchū shiryō 越中史料. Compiled by Toyama ken 富山県. 4 vols. Toyama, 1909.

Fukushima kenshi, kodai-chūsei shiryō 福島県史, 古代中世資料. Compiled by Fukushima ken. Fukushima, 1966.

Gakuenji monjo no kenkyū 鰐淵寺文書の研究. Compiled by Gakuenji monjo kankōkai 鰐淵寺文書刊行会. Hirata, 1963.

Gifu kenshi, shiryō hen, kodai-chūsei 岐阜県史, 史料篇, 古代一中世. Compiled by Gifu ken. 3 vols. Gifu, 1969–71.

Gukanshō 愚管抄. Fujiwara Jien 藤原慈圓. Kokushi taikei, 14. Tokyo, 1901.

Gyokuyō 玉葉. Fujiwara Kanezane 藤原兼実. 3 vols. Tokyo, 1966.

Heian ibun 平安遺文. Compiled by Takeuchi Rizō. 13 vols. Tokyo, 1963–68.

Hennen Ōtomo shiryō 編年大友史料. Compiled by Takita Manabu 田北学. 2 vols. Kyoto, 1942–46.

Higashi Asai gunshi, monjo hen 東浅井郡史, 文書篇. Compiled by Higashi Asai kyōikukai 東浅井教育会. 1927.

Hirado Matsuura ke shiryō 平戸松浦家資料. Compiled by Kyōto daigaku bungaku-bu kenkyūshitsu 京都大学文学部研究室. Kyoto, 1951.

Hizen no kuni Kanzaki-no-shō shiryō 肥前国神崎荘史料. Compiled by Seno Seiichirō 瀬野精一郎. Kyushu shōen shiryō sōsho 九州荘園史料叢書. Fukuoka, 1963.

Hōryaku kanki 保暦間記. Gunsho ruijū, zatsu bu, 16 群書類従雑部. Tokyo, 1908.

Hyakurenshō 百錬抄. Kokushi taikei, 14. Tokyo, 1901.

Ibaragi ken shiryō, chūsei hen 1 茨城県史料, 中世篇. Compiled by Ibaragi kenshi hensan chūsei shi bukai 茨城県史編纂中世史部会. Mito, 1970.

Ichinomiya shishi, shiryō hen 5 一宮市史資料編. Compiled by Ichinomiya shishi hensan-shitsu 一宮市史編纂室. Ichinomiya, 1963.

Iwate ken chūsei monjo 岩手県中世文書. Compiled by Iwate ken kyōiku iinkai 岩手県教育委員会. 3 vols. 1960–68.

Izumi Kumeidadera monjo 和泉久米田寺文書. Compiled by Ōsaka fu kyōiku iinkai 大阪府教育委員会. Osaka, 1959.

Izumi Matsuodera monjo 和泉松尾寺文書. Compiled by Ōsaka fu kyōiku iinkai. Osaka, 1957.

Izumo Kokuzō ke monjo 出雲国造家文書. Compiled by Kitajima Hidetaka. Osaka, 1968.

"Kaburaya Ise hōki" (Ichiki monjo) 鏑矢伊勢方記 (櫟木文書). Compiled by Nishigaki Seiji 西垣晴次. Tokyo gakugeidai fuzoku kō 東京学芸大付属高. *Kenkyū kiyō* 4 and 5 研究記要. (1966–67): 15–46, 15–37.

Kajika chūsei shiryō 何鹿中世史料. Compiled by Ayabe shidankai, 綾部史談会. Kyoto, 1951.

Kamakura bakufu saikyojō shū 鎌倉幕府裁許状集. Compiled by Seno Seiichirō. 2 vols. Tokyo, 1970–71.

Kamakura ibun 鎌倉遺文. Compiled by Takeuchi Rizō. 5 vols. Tokyo, 1971–.

Kamakura shishi, shiryō hen 鎌倉市史. Compiled by Kamakura shishi hensan iinkai 鎌倉市史編纂委員会. 3 vols. Kamakura, 1956–58.

Kanagawa kenshi, shiryō hen 1, kodai-chūsei 1 神奈川県史, 資料篇 I, 古代-中世 I. Compiled by Kanagawa ken. Yokohama, 1971.

Kanazawa bunko komonjo 金沢文庫古文書. Compiled by Seki Yasushi 関靖. 2 vols. Yokohama, 1937–43.

Kano komonjo 加能古文書. Compiled by Kanazawa bunka kyōkai 金沢文化協会. Kanazawa, 1944.

Kashima Jingū monjo 鹿島神宮文書. Compiled by Kashima Jingū shamusho 鹿島神宮社務所. Kashima, 1942.

Kasokabe shiryō 香宗我部史料. Compiled by Maeda Kazuo 前田和男. Kōchi, 1964.

Kasuga Jinja monjo 春日神社文書. Compiled by Kasuga Jinja shamusho 春日神宮社務所. Nara, 1928–42.

Katsuodera monjo 勝尾寺文書. Compiled by Ōsaka fu shiseki meishō tennen kinenbutsu chōsakai 大阪府史蹟名勝天然記念物調査会. Osaka, 1931.

Kokushi shiryōshū 国史資料集. Compiled by Kokumin seishin bunka kenkyūjo 国民精神文化研究所. 4 vols. Tokyo, 1940–43.

Kōyasan monjo 高野山文書. Compiled by Kōyasan shi hensanjo 高野山史編纂所. 7 vols. Kyoto, 1936–41.

Kugyō bunin 公卿補任. Kokushi taikei, 9. Tokyo, 1899.

Kujō ke monjo 九条家文書. Compiled by Kunaichō shoryōbu 宮内庁書陵部. 3 vols. Tokyo, 1972–.

Kumagai ke monjo 熊谷家文書. Compiled by Saitama kenritsu toshokan 埼玉県立図書館. Urawa, 1970.

Kumamoto ken shiryō, chūsei hen 熊本県史料, 中世編. Compiled by Teramoto Hirosaku 寺本広作. 5 vols. Kumamoto, 1961–67.

Kutsuna ke monjo 忽那家文書. Compiled by Kageura Tsutomu 景浦勉. Iyo shiryō shūsei 1 伊予史料集成. Matsuyama, 1964.

Masaki komonjo 正木古文書. Compiled by Kōzuke kyōdoshi kenkyūkai 上毛郷土史研究会. Maebara, 1938.

Masu kagami 増鏡. Edited by Wada Hidematsu 和田英松. Iwanami bunko. Tokyo, 1931.

Mibu shinsha komonjo 壬生新写古文書. Compiled by Kunaishō toshoryō 宮内省図書陵. Tokyo, 1930.

Minase Jingū monjo 水無瀬神宮文書. Compiled by Ōsaka fu shiseki meishō tennen kinenbutsu chōsakai 大阪府名勝天然記念物調査会. Osaka, 1939.

Miyagi kenshi, shiryōshū 1 宮城県史, 史料集. Compiled by Miyagi kenshi hensan iinkai 宮城県史編纂委員会. Sendai, 1965.

Munakata gunshi, chū 宗像郡誌. Compiled by Itō Shirō 伊東四郎. Fukuoka, 1932.

Nejime monjo 禰寝文書. Compiled by Kawazoe Shōji 川添昭二. Kyushu shiryō sōsho, 14 九州史料叢書. 3 vols. Fukuoka, 1955–58.

"Ninnaji monjo shūi" 仁和寺文書拾遺. Compiled by Tanaka Minoru 田中稔. *Shigaku zasshi* 68.9 (1959): 74–86.

Ōita ken shiryō 大分県史料. Compiled by Ōita ken shiryō kankōkai 大分県史料刊行会. 25 vols. Ōita, 1960–64.

Okayama ken komonjo shū 岡山県古文書集. Compiled by Fujii Shun 藤井駿 and Mizuno Kyōichirō 水野恭一郎. 3 vols. Okayama, 1953–56.

Okuyama-no-shō shiryōshū 奥山庄史料集. Compiled by Niigata ken kyōiku iinkai 新潟県教育委員会. Niigata, 1965.

Ōshū Fujiwara shiryō 奥州藤原史料. Compiled by Tōhoku daigaku Tōhoku bunka kenkyūkai 東北大学東北文化研究会. Tokyo, 1969.

Ōshū Hiraizumi monjo 奥州平泉文書. Compiled by Iwate ken kyōiku iinkai 岩手県教育委員会. Morioka, 1958.

Sado Honma ibun Sakurai ke monjo 佐渡本間遺文桜井家文書. Compiled by Shimoide Sekiyo 下出積与. Kanazawa, 1966.

Saga ken shiryō shūsei 佐賀県史料集成. Compiled by Saga kenritsu toshokan 佐賀県立図書館. 12 vols. Saga, 1955–.

Saisho monjo 税所文書. Compiled by Miyata Toshihiko 宮田俊彦. Ibaragi ken komonjo shūsei, 2 茨城県古文書集成. Mito, 1962.

Sappan kyūki zatsuroku, zempen 薩藩旧記雑録. Compiled by Kyūshū shiryō kankōkai 九州史料刊行会. Kyūshū shiryō sōsho 九州史料叢書. 10 vols. Fukuoka, 1955–65.

Satamirensho 沙汰末練書. Edited by Satō Shin'ichi and Ikeuchi Yoshisuke. Chūsei hōsei shiryōshū, 2. Tokyo, 1969.

Satsuma no kuni Nitta Jinja monjo 薩摩国新田神社文書. Compiled by Kagoshima kenritsu toshokan 鹿児島県立国書館. Kagoshima, 1960.

Shinano shiryō 信濃史料. Compiled by Shinano shiryō kankōkai 信濃史料刊行会. 28 vols. Nagano, 1956–67.

Shinshū Shimane kenshi, shiryō hen 1, kodai-chūsei 新修島根県史, 史料篇 I, 古代-中世. Compiled by Shimane ken. Hirata, 1966.

Shizuoka ken shiryō 静岡県史料. Compiled by Shizuoka ken. 5 vols. Shizuoka, 1932–41.

Shōen shiryō 荘園志料. Compiled by Shimizu Masatake 清水正健. 2 vols. Tokyo, 1933.

Shōen shi shiryō 荘園史資料. Compiled by Nishioka Toranosuke 西岡虎之助 Tokyo, n.d.

Shunjōbō Chōgen shiryō shūsei 俊乗房重源史料集成. Compiled by Kobayashi Takashi 小林剛. Tokyo, 1965.

Suwa komonjo shū 諏訪古文書集. Compiled by Suwa shiryō sōsho kankōkai 諏訪史料叢書刊行会. Suwa shiryōshū, 15 and 16 諏訪史料集. Nagano, 1931.

Taizanji monjo 太山寺文書. Compiled by Uchiyama Jōshin 内山定真. Hyōgo, 1935.

Tōdaiji monjo 東大寺文書. Compiled by Nakamura Naokatsu 中村直勝. Osaka, 1945.

Tōdaiji yōroku 東大寺要録. Zoku zoku gunsho ruijū, shūkyō bu, 11 続続群書類従宗教部. Tokyo, 1908.

Tosa monjo kaisetsu 土佐文書解説. Compiled by Kimura Tokue 木村徳衛. Tokyo, 1935.

Toyonaka shishi, shiryō hen 1 豊中市史, 史料篇 I. Compiled by Toyonaka shishi hensan iinkai 豊中市史編纂委員会. Toyonaka, 1960.

Wakasa gyoson shiryō 若狭漁村史料. Compiled by Fukui kenritsu toshokan 福井県立図書館. Fukui, 1963.

Wakasa no kuni shugo shiki shidai 若狭国守護職次第. Shinkō gunsho ruijū, 3 新校群書類従. Tokyo, 1930.

Yamato komonjo juei 大和古文書聚英. Compiled by Nagashima Fukutarō 永島福太郎. Nara, 1943.

Yasaka Jinja monjo 八坂神社文書. Compiled by Yasaka Jinja shamusho 八坂神社社務所. 2 vols. Kyoto, 1939–40.

Yoshitsune, A Fifteenth Century Chronicle. Translated by Helen Craig McCullough. New York, 1966.

Unpublished Works

Hori Kyotsu. "The Mongol Invasions and the Kamakura Bakufu." Ph.D. dissertation, Columbia University, 1967.

Hurst, G. Cameron. "Insei: Abdicated Sovereigns in the Politics of Late Heian Japan." Ph.D. dissertation, Columbia University, 1972.

Kiley, Cornelius Joseph. "Property and Political Authority in Early

Medieval Japan." Ph. D. dissertation, Harvard University, 1970.

Mass, Jeffrey P. "The Early Development of the Kamakura Bakufu: A Study of the Shugo and Jitō." Ph. D. dissertation, Yale University 1971.

———. "The Jōkyū War—Origins and Aftermath." Mimeographed. Yale University, 1971.

Published Works

Asakawa Kan'ichi. "The Founding of the Shogunate by Minamoto-no-Yoritomo." Reprinted in Asakawa, *Land and Society in Medieval Japan*, pp. 269–89. Tokyo, 1965.

———. *Land and Society in Medieval Japan*. Tokyo, 1965.

Bloch, Marc. *Feudal Society*. 2 vols. Chicago, 1964.

Carr, Edward Hallet. *What is History?* New York, 1965.

Egashira Tsuneharu 江頭恒治. *Kōyasan ryō shōen no kenkyū* 高野山領荘園の研究. Tokyo, 1938.

Fichtenau, Heinrich. *The Carolingian Empire: The Age of Charlemagne*. New York, 1964.

Fukuda Toyohiko 福田豊彦. "Dainiji hōken kankei no keisei katei—Bungo no kuni Ōtomo shi no shujūsei o chūshin to shite" 第二次封建関係の形成過程—豊後国における大友氏の主従制を中心として—. In *Shoki hōkensei no kenkyū* 初期封建制の研究, edited by Yasuda Genkyū, pp. 1–64. Tokyo, 1964.

———. "Yoritomo no zōshiki ni tsuite" 頼朝の雑色について. *Shigaku zasshi* 史学雑誌 78.3 (1969): 1–21.

Fujiki Kunihiko 藤木邦彦. *Nihon zenshi, 3, kodai 2* 日本全史 3, 古代 2. Tokyo, 1959.

Fuzambō, comp. 富山房. *Kokushi jiten* 国史辞典. 4 vols. Tokyo, 1940.

Ganshof, F. L. *Frankish Institutions under Charlemagne*. New York, 1970.

Gomi Katsuo 五味克夫. "Kamakura bakufu no goke'nin taisei—Kyōto ōbanyaku no tōsei o chūshin ni" 鎌倉幕府の御家人体制—京都大番役の統制を中心に *Rekishi kyōiku* 歴史教育 11.7 (1963): 12–19.

———. "Kamakura goke'nin no banyaku kinshi ni tsuite" 鎌倉御家人の番役勤仕について. *Shigaku zasshi* 63.9–10 (1954): 28–45, 22–33.

Hall, John W. *Government and Local Power in Japan, 500–1700*. Princeton, 1966.

——— and Mass, Jeffrey P., eds. *Medieval Japan: Essays in Institutional History*. New Haven, 1974.

Hattori Kentarō 服部謙太郎. *Hōken shakai seiritsu shiron* 封建社会成立史論. Tokyo, 1958.

Hayashiya Tatsusaburō 林屋辰三郎. "Chūsei shi gaisetsu" 中世史概説.

Iwanami kōza, Nihon rekishi, 5, chūsei 1 岩波講座, pp. 1–56. Tokyo, 1962.

Hurst, G. Cameron. "The Structure of the Heian Court: Some Thoughts on the Nature of 'Familial Authority' in Heian Japan." In *Medieval Japan: Essays in Institutional History*, edited by Hall and Mass. New Haven, 1974.

Iida Hisao 飯田久雄. "Heishi to Kyūshū" 平氏と九州. In *Shōensei to buke shakai* 荘園制と武家社会, compiled by Takeuchi Rizō hakushi kanreki kinenkai 竹内理三博士還暦記念会編, pp. 31–68. Tokyo, 1969.

———. "Kamakura jidai ni okeru chōbaku kankei" 鎌倉時代における朝幕関係. *Rekishi kyōiku* 11.6 (1963): 33–44.

Inoue Mitsusada 井上光貞. "Ritsuryō taisei no seiritsu" 律令体制の成立. *Iwanami koza, Nihon rekishi, 3, kodai 3*, pp. 1–31.

Ishii Ryōsuke 石井良助. "Kamakura bakufu no seiritsu" 鎌倉幕府の成立. *Rekishi kyōiku* 8.7 (1960): 1–8.

———. "Taihon sankajō—Kamakura jidai no shugo no kengen no kenkyū" 大犯三箇条一鎌倉時代の守護の権限の研究. *Hōgaku kyōkai zasshi* 法学協会雑誌 69.1 (1951): 1–29.

Ishii Susumu 石井進. "Bunji shugo jitō shiki ron" 文治守護地頭職論. *Shigaku zasshi* 77.3 (1968): 1–37.

———. "Dazaifu kikō no henshitsu to Chinzei bugyō no seiritsu" 大宰府機構の変質と鎮西奉行の成立. *Shigaku zasshi* 68.1 (1959): 1–37.

———. "Heishi-Kamakura ryōseiken ka no Aki kokuga" 平氏-鎌倉両権下の安芸国衙. *Rekishigaku kenkyū* 歴史学研究 257 (1961): 1–12.

———. "Kamakura bakufu ron" 鎌倉幕府論. *Iwanami kōza, 5, chūsei 1*, pp. 87–134.

———. "Kamakura jidai 'shugoryō' kenkyū josetsu" 鎌倉時代「守護領」研究序説. In *Nihon shakai keizai shi kenkyū, kodai-chūsei hen* 日本社会経済史研究, 古代-中世篇, compiled by Hōgetsu Keigo sensei kanreki kinenkai 宝月圭吾先生還暦記念会編, pp. 309–53. Tokyo, 1968.

Ishimoda Shō 石母田正. "Heishi seiken ni tsuite" 平氏政権について. In *Kodai makki seiji shi josetsu* 古代末期政治史序説, pp. 470-87. Tokyo, 1968.

———. "Heishi seiken no sō-kan shiki setchi" 平氏政権の総官職設置. *Rekishi hyōron* 歴史評論 107 (1959): 7–14.

———. "Heishi seiken to sono botsuraku" 平氏政権とその没落. In *Kodai makki seiji shi josetsu*, pp. 384–402.

———. "Kamakura bakufu ikkoku jitō shiki no seiritsu" 鎌倉幕府一国地頭職の成立. In *Chūsei no hō to kokka* 中世の法と国家, edited by Ishimoda Shō and Satō Shin'ichi, pp. 1–134. Tokyo, 1965.

———. "Kamakura seiken no seiritsu katei ni tsuite" 鎌倉政権の成立

過程について. *Rekishigaku kenkyū*, 200 (1956): 2–16.

Kamei Hideo 亀井日出男. "Kennin sannen Kamakura seihen o meguru ni san no mondai" 建仁三年鎌倉政変をめぐる二・三の問題. *Seiji keizai shigaku* 政治経済史学 11 (1963): 30–35.

Kanai Madoka 金井圓. "Kamakura jidai no Bizen no kokugaryō ni tsuite" 鎌倉時代の備前国衙領について. *Nihon rekishi* 日本歴史 150 (1960): 36–54.

Kano Kayoko 鹿野賀代子. "Shikken ki ni okeru Kamakura bakufu no seikaku" 執権期における鎌倉幕府の性格. *Nihon rekishi* 239 (1968): 56–75.

Kawai Masaharu 河合正治. "Kamakura bakufu no seiritsu to saigoku no dōkō" 鎌倉幕府の成立と西国の動向. *Rekishi kyōiku* 8.7 (1960): 30–36.

Kawanishi Sachiko 河西佐知子. "Bunji gonen Ōshū seibatsu ni tsuite no ichi shōsatsu" 文治五年奥州征伐に就いての一省察. *Seiji keizai shigaku* 11 (1963): 21–30.

———. "Ōshū heiran to tōgoku bushidan" 奥州兵乱と東国武士団. *Rekishi kyōiku* 16. 12 (1968): 27–40.

Kikuchi Takeo 菊池武雄. "Heishi zuryō hyō" 平氏受領表. *Sekai rekishi jiten* 22 世界歴史辞典. Tokyo, 1956, pp. 159–62.

Kiley, C. J. "Estate and Property in the Late Heian Period." In *Medieval Japan: Essays in Institutional History*, edited by Hall and Mass. New Haven, 1974.

Kobayashi Hiroshi 小林宏. "Iwami no kuni Masuda shi no ryōshusei ni tsuite" 石見国益田氏の領主制について. In *Shoki hōkensei no kenkyū*, edited by Yasuda Genkyū, pp. 119–80.

Kōchi ken, comp. 高知県. *Kōchi kenshi, kodai-chūsei hen* 高知県史, 古代-中世篇. Kōchi, 1971.

Koizumi Senyū 小泉宣右. "Jitō uke ni kan suru ichi kōsatsu" 地頭請に関する一考察. *Nihon rekishi* 298 (1973): 13–34.

Kuroda Toshio 黒田俊雄 "Wakasa no kuni Tara-no-shō" 若狭国太良庄. In *Shōen sonraku no kōzō* 庄園村落の構造, edited by Shibata Minoru 柴田実, pp. 197–307. Osaka, 1955.

Lopez, Robert. *The Birth of Europe*. New York, 1967.

Maitland, F. W. *The Constitutional History of England*. London, 1963.

Mass, Jeffrey P. "The Emergence of the Kamakura Bakufu." In *Medieval Japan: Essays in Institutional History*, edited by Hall and Mass. New Haven, 1974.

———. "Jitō Land Possession in the Thirteenth Century: The Case of Shitaji Chūbun." In *Medieval Japan: Essays in Institutional History*, edited by Hall and Mass. New Haven, 1974.

Matsumoto Shimpachirō 松本新八郎. "Rokuhara jidai" 六波羅時代. In *Chūsei shakai no kenkyū* 中世社会の研究, pp. 231–50. Tokyo, 1967.

Munakata Jinja fukkō kiseikai, comp. 宗像神社復興期成会. *Munakata Jinja shi* 宗像神社史. 2 vols. Tokyo, 1966.

Nakada Kaoru 中田薫. *Shōen no kenkyū* 庄園の研究. Tokyo, 1948.

Nishioka Toranosuke 西岡虎之助. *Shōen shi no kenkyū* 荘園史の研究. 3 vols. Tokyo, 1957–66.

Ōae Ryo 大饗亮. "Jitō shiki o meguru shomondai" 地頭職をめぐる諸問題. *Hōkei gakkai zasshi* 法経学会雑誌 13.4 (1964): 387–436.

Okutomi Takayuki 奥富敬之. "Kamakura bakufu kuni goke'ninsei no kenkyū" 鎌倉幕府国御家人制の研究. *Mejiro gakuen joshi tanki daigaku kenkyū kiyō* 目白学園女子短期大学研究紀要 5 (1968): 17–26.

Ōtsuka Tokurō 大塚徳郎 "Kamakura bakufu no seiritsu to Ōshū Fujiwara shi no dōkō 鎌倉幕府の成立と奥州藤原氏の動向. *Rekishi kyōiku* 8.7 (1960): 23–29.

Ōyama Kyōhei 大山喬平. "Kokugaryō jitō no ichi keitai" 国衙領地頭の一形態. *Nihon rekishi* 158 (1961): 58–66.

Ryō Susumu 竜粛. "Rokujō-In ryō to Taira Masamori" 六条院領と平正盛. Ryō Susumu. *Heian jidai* 平安時代, pp. 117–35. Tokyo, 1962.

Saga kenshi hensan iinkai, comp. 佐賀県史編纂委員会. *Saga kenshi*, 1 佐賀県史. Saga, 1968.

Satō Shin'ichi 佐藤進一. "Kamakura bakufu seiji no senseika ni tsuite" 鎌倉幕府政治の専制化について. In *Nihon hōkensei seiritsu no kenkyū* 日本封建制成立の研究, edited by Takeuchi Rizō, pp. 97–136. Tokyo, 1955.

———. "Shoki hōken shakai no keisei" 初期封建社会の形成. In *Shin Nihon shi taikei, 3, chūsei shakai* 新日本史大系中世社会, edited by Toyoda Takeshi 豊田武, pp. 1–80. Tokyo, 1954.

———. *Kamakura bakufu soshō seido no kenkyū* 鎌倉幕府訴訟制度の研究. Tokyo, 1943.

———. *Zōtei-Kamakura bakufu shugo seido no kenkyū* 増訂-鎌倉幕府守護制度の研究. Tokyo, 1971.

Schlessinger, Walter. "Lord and Follower in Germanic Institutional History." In *Lordship and Community in Medieval Europe*, edited by Frederic L. Cheyette, pp. 64–99. New York, 1968.

Seno Seiichirō 瀬野精一郎. "Chinzei bugyō kō" 鎮西奉行考. *Kyūshū bunka shi kenkyūjo nijū shūnen kinen rombun shū* 九州文化史研究所二十周年記念論文集, pp. 37–42.

———. "Chinzei ni okeru tō—Matsuura tō no baai" 鎮西における党—松浦党の場合. *Rekishi kyōiku*, 7.8 (1959): 66–72.

———. "Chinzei ni okeru tōgoku goke'nin" 鎮西における東国御家人.

Nihon rekishi, 167–68 (1962): 16–26, 32–42.

———. "Hizen no kuni ni okeru Kamakura goke'nin" 肥前国における
鎌倉御家人. *Nihon rekishi*, 117 (1958): 30–40.

———. "Kamakura bakufu no seiritsu to Kyūshū chihō no dōkō"
鎌倉幕府の成立と九州地方の動向. *Rekishi kyōiku* 8.7 (1960): 37–44.

———. *Kyūshū chihō chūsei hennen monjo mokuroku* 九州地方中世
編年文書目録. Fukuoka, 1966.

———. "Nakahara Chikayoshi to Chinzei to no kankei" 中原親能と
鎮西との関係. *Kyūshū shigaku* 九州史学 37–39 (1967): 29–40.

Shimada Jirō 島田次郎 "Zaichi ryōshusei no tenkai to Kamakura bakufu
hō" 在地領主制の展開と鎌倉幕府法. In *Chūsei no shakai to keizai*
中世の社会と経済, Inagaki Yasuhiko 稲垣泰彦 and Nagahara Keiji
永原慶二, eds. pp. 215–304. Tokyo, 1962.

Shinoda Minoru. *The Founding of the Kamakura Shogunate, 1180–1185.*
New York, 1960.

Southern, R. W. *The Making of the Middle Ages.* London, 1959

Takeuchi Rizō 竹内理三 "Chinzei bugyō ni tsuite no ichi ni no kōsatsu"
鎮西奉行についての一, 二の考察. In *Kokushigaku ronsō* 国史学論叢,
compiled by Uozumi Sensei koki kinenkai, 魚澄先生古稀記念会,
pp. 414–27.

———. "Heishi seiken ron" 平氏政権論. *Nihon rekishi* 200 (1965): 41–48.

———. "Heishi seiken seiritsu no shojōken" 平氏政権成立の諸条件.
Nihon rekishi 163 (1962): 2–12.

———. "Heishi seiken to insei" 平氏政権と院政. *Iwanami kōza, Nihon
rekishi 5, chūsei 1.* pp. 57–85.

———. *Nihon no rekishi, bushi no tōjō* 日本の歴史, 武士の登場. Tokyo,
1965.

———. "Zaichōkanjin no bushika" 在庁官人の武士化. In *Nihon hōkensei
seiritsu no kenkyū*, edited by Takeuchi Rizo, pp. 1–42.

Tanaka Minoru 田中稔. "Jōkyū kyō-gata bushi no ichi kōsatsu—rango
no shin jitō bunin chi o chūshin to shite" 承久京方武士の一考察—乱後
の新地頭補任地を中心として-. *Shigaku zasshi* 65.4 (1956): 21–48;
79.12 (1970): 38–53.

———. "Kamakura bakufu goke'nin seido no ichi kōsatsu—Wakasa no
kuni no jitō gokenin o chūshin to shite" 鎌倉幕府御家人制度の一考察
—若狭国地頭御家人を中心として. In *Chūsei no hō to kokka*, edited by
Ishimoda and Satō, pp. 223–93.

———. "Kamakura dono otsukai kō" 鎌倉殿御使考. *Shirin* 史林 45.6
(1962): 1–23.

———. "Kamakura jidai ni okeru Iyo no kuni no jitō goke'nin ni tsuite"
鎌倉時代における伊予国の地頭御家人について. In *Shōensei to buke*

shakai, compiled by Takeuchi Rizō hakushi kanreki kinenkai, pp. 245–92.

——. "Kamakura shoki no seiji katei—Kenkyū nenkan o chūshin ni shite" 鎌倉初期の政治過程—建久年間を中心にして. *Rekishi kyōiku*, 11.6 (1963): 19–26.

——. "Sanuki no kuni jitō goke'nin ni tsuite" 讃岐国地頭御家人について. In *Nihon shakai keizai shi kenkyū, kodai-chūsei hen*, compiled by Hōgetsu Keigo Sensei kanreki kinenkai, pp. 355–82. Tokyo, 1968.

Tomoda Kichinosuke 友田吉之助 "Bunji gannen shugo jitō setchi ni tsuite no saikentō" 文治元年守護地頭設置についての再検討. *Nihon rekishi* 133 (1959): 11–29.

Toyoda Takeshi 豊田武. *Bushidan to sonraku* 武士団と村落. Tokyo, 1963.

—— et al. *Dokushi sōran* 読史総覧. Tokyo, 1966.

Uchida Minoru 内田実. "Heian makki ryōshusei kenkyū no isshiten—shiryōshu to shōen ryōshu to no kankei" 平安末期領主制研究の一視点—私領主と荘園領主との関係 *Rekishigaku kenkyū* 233 (1959): 46–49.

——. "Jitō ryōshusei to Kamakura bakufu" 地頭領主制と鎌倉幕府. *Rekishi kyōiku* 8.7 (1960): 15–22.

Uwayokote Masataka 上横手雅敬. "Jitō genryū kō" 地頭源流考. *Shisō* 史窓 12 (1957): 19–33.

——. "Jōkyū no ran no rekishiteki hyōka" 承久の乱の歴史的評価. *Shirin*, 39.1 (1956): 22–44.

——. "Juei ninen jūgatsu senshi to Heike mokkanryō" 寿永二年十月宣旨と平家没官領. *Nihon rekishi* 228 (1967): 17–25.

——. "Kamakura seiken seiritsu ki o meguru kingyō" 鎌倉政権成立期をめぐる近業. *Hōseishi kenkyu* 法制史研究 11: (1960): 175–81.

Varley, H. Paul. *The Onin War*. New York, 1967.

Watanabe Tamotsu 渡辺保. *Genji to Heishi* 源氏と平氏. Tokyo, 1967.

Yamakuma Korezane 山隈惟実. "Sōjitō ni tsuite" 惣地頭について. *Nihon rekishi*, 170 (1962): 56–62.

Yasuda Genkyū (Motohisa) 安田元久. *Bushidan* 武士団. Tokyo, 1964.

——. "Heike mokkanryō ni tsuite" 平家没官領について. In *Nihon hōkensei no kenkyū*, edited by Yasuda Genkyū, pp. 311–51.

——. *Jitō oyobi jitō ryōshusei no kenkyū* 地頭及び地頭領主制の研究 Tokyo 1961.

——. "Kodai makki ni okeru Kantō bushidan" 古代末期における関東武士団. In *Nihon hōkensei seiritsu no shozentei* 日本封建制成立の諸前提, edited by Yasuda Genkyū, pp. 1–111. Tokyo, 1960.

——. *Minamoto Yoshiie* 源義家. Tokyo, 1966.

——. *Nihon shōen shi gaisetsu* 日本荘園史概説. Tokyo, 1966.

———. *Nihon zenshi, chūsei 1* 日本全史, 中世 1. Tokyo, 1958.

———. *Shugo to jitō* 守護と地頭. Tokyo, 1964.

Yawata Yoshinobu 八幡義信. Kamakura bakusei ni okeru Hōjō Tokimasa no shiteki hyōka" 鎌倉幕政における北条時政の史的評価. *Rekishi kyōiku* 11.6 (1963): 27–32.

Yoshimura Shigeki 吉村茂樹. *Kokushi seido hōkai ni kan suru kenkyū* 国司制度崩壊に関する研究. Tokyo, 1957.

INDEX

Ōsumi Province, 152, 153, 208, 209n, 222
Ōta Estate (Bingo), 22, 131–32, 141, 155–56; and jitō, 174n, 181, 191n; and ōban expenses, 206
Ōtomo family, 159–60, 183, 184n, 209, 212n; Yoshinao, 160
Ōuchi Koreyoshi, 94n, 96, 99–100, 205
Owari Province, 42n, 104, 148; Tomita Estate, 191n, 194, 195–96
Ōya Estate (Noto), 178, 181

Patron. See Honke
Peasants. See Farmers
Police authority. See Kendan
Prime minister. See Dajōdaijin
Proprietors, 4, 5, 22, 71, 77, 126, 175; and warrior development in eastern Japan, 37n, 46, 54; and jitō, 116, 126, 128–32, 138, 174–75, 180–81, 196–201
Provinces, 1–7, 32, 34–35, 82, 89; proprietary, 4, 25, 26, 28. See also Shugo; and by individual name of province
Public land. See Kokugaryō
Public officer families. See Zaichōkanjin

Religious institutions, 1, 4, 27n, 71, 76, 78, 132, 142. See also by name
Rice, 28, 165, 173, 191, 193. See also Taxes
Rokuhara, 140, 199, 200, 218, 224; tandai, 135n
Rokujō-In, 16
Rōtō (civil or military retainer), 25
Rusu (proxy governor), 151
Rusu family, 151
Rusudokoro, (absentee provincial headquarters), 3, 99
Ryōke. See Proprietors
Ryōshu (local lord), 46, 47, 51, 103

Sadamori, 36n
Sado Province, 28, 149, 180
Saeki family, 153n; Kagehiro, 23, 24, 108–11; Tamehiro, 153n
Sagami Province, 39–41, 64, 67, 69, 159, 219
Sahara Morimura, 217–18
Sahara Yoshimura, 217
Saidaiji Temple (Yamato), 126, 218n
Saisho (provincial tax office), 155
Saisho family, 219n
Samurai dokoro (vassal control bureau), 69
Sangi (adviser), 18
Sanuki Province, 81, 88, 135n, 210, 222n
Sanyōdō, 97
Sasakibe Estate (Tamba), 132, 187, 193n, 198
Sasaki family, 209, 210, 212n; Sadatsuna, 171n, 204; Tsunetaka, 210
Satake family, 42, 66
Satamirenshō, 209n
Sata shiki, 63
Satō Shin'ichi, 25n, 75n, 213, 216n, 225–26
Satsuma District, 106n
Satsuma Province, 105n, 149, 152, 180, 181; shugo post in, 208, 209n, 211, 212n, 222, 223
Schlessinger, Walter, 54n
Sei i tai shōgun, 74, 133n
Seiwa Genji, 35, 37n, 39, 43, 49
Seno Seiichirō, 83n, 158n, 159n, 166n
Sesshō (imperial regent), 19
Settsu Province, 26, 27, 77, 78n, 80n; jitō in, 124n, 137n, 185; shugo in, 218n
Shida family, 42, 66, 161
Shigehira, 22
Shigemori, 20
Shigyōjō (enforcement decrees), 225
Shiki system, 4, 6, 95. See also by title
Shikoku, 62, 80n, 81, 84, 118, 210
Shima Province, 130, 203n